THE FAMILY TRACK

THE FAMILY TRACK

Keeping Your Faculties while You Mentor, Nurture, Teach, and Serve

Edited by

Constance Coiner and Diana Hume George

UNIVERSITY OF ILLINOIS PRESS

URBANA AND CHICAGO

This book is printed on acid-free paper.

Library of Congress Cataloging-in-Publication Data
The family track : keeping your faculties while you mentor, nurture, teach, and serve /
edited by Constance Coiner and Diana Hume George.
p. cm.
Includes bibliographical references (p.).
ISBN 0-252-02291-2 (cloth). — ISBN 0-252-06694-4 (pbk.)
1. College teachers—United States—Family relationships.
2. Women college teachers—United States—Family relationships.
3. Work and family—United States.
I. Coiner, Constance.
II. George, Diana Hume, 1948–   .
LB1778.2.F358 1998
378.1'2—dc21 97-33786
CIP

This book is dedicated to a family:

Ana Duarte-Coiner
Constance Coiner
and
Steve Duarte

CONTENTS

ACKNOWLEDGMENTS

Diana Hume George

Support for *The Family Track* was provided by grants from Pennsylvania State University at Erie, the Behrend College, and the University of Binghamton English Department. At Penn State, special thanks to Bob Light, John Lilley, and Roberta Salper. Norma Hartner has worked on all my books, and at this point my debt to her is incalculable. For other kinds of help, I thank Janet Zandy, Valerie Begley, Alan Gross, and Liz Rosenberg; for encouragement from the sidelines, Ann Fitzgerald and Lillian Robinson; for being present at this book's creation at a Modern Language Association conference several years ago, Naomi Miller, Sarah Webster Goodwin, and Naomi Yavneh. To Elaine Hedges, who died as this book was going to press, I am grateful for inspiration throughout years of preparation. Constance and I met as a result of Elaine, Shelley Fisher Fishkin, and Tillie Olsen, to all of whom I give thanks.

For believing in this book when few others did, I thank Martha Evans of the Modern Language Association. Conversations in the early stages with Paul Lauter and Linda Wagner-Martin were important to Constance and me. For extraordinary patience and unflagging dedication, I thank Annette Kolodny. For providing work space in the early stages as well as for later assistance, I thank David Bartine. Several of Constance's graduate students offered help at various points; except for Marjorie Feld, your names have escaped me, but not your faces, and your efforts are represented in the results. You know who you are. Thank you. Deborah Rosenfelt and Lillian Schlissel were also among Constance's inspirations through many years. I know there are a dozen other people Constance would want me to remember here, and I ask that you realize how much she appreciated every conversation, e-mail message, note, and phone message, every moment of encouragement you gave her. You must pardon me for not knowing who all of you are. Billy Smith is among you, as are many people involved in the Radical Caucus of the Modern Language Association and the Subcommittee on Family Care of the MLA Committee on the Status of Women in the Profession, the editorial board of *Radical Teacher*, and Constance's colleagues in the American Studies Association. Both Constance and I were gratified by the dozens of women who told us their stories at the Berkshire Women's History Conference in the early 1990s.

Deborah Calloway gave me her own money for postage and phone calls when I ran out; what heart she has. I thank Michael Richardson for patience during the middle phases when Constance and I talked on his phone all the time and John Edwards for giving me personal support in the later phases, including making phone calls on the book when I ran out of time. Joe Firment was called off the bench at the end and did whatever I needed, as did Terry Hintson.

As always, Ann Lowry and Becky Standard have my gratitude for being wonderful, tough, fine, patient editors. Detailed readings by Judith Kegan Gardiner and Tey Diana Rebolledo made this a far better book. I am more grateful than I can say to many contributors who do not appear in this book but who stayed with the project for years while it changed shape—and in the process was necessarily cut to half of its original length.

Most of all, I thank members of my immediate family for making this book our family project. Mary Ellen Sullivan-George served as research assistant for two years. When I was out of town she kept the project running smoothly and knew more about what was going on than I did. Literally, I could not have completed this book without her. Bernie George entered the project when Constance died, offering both emotional support and expertise on the Internet. I thank my grandchildren, Sequoia, Storm, and Ayron, for doing without my attention as this project drew to an end, and my mother, Janice Ruth Hume, for abiding interest and love. Love is finally what this book is about, and I also extend my affectionate thanks to members of Constance Coiner's family, especially and always Steve Duarte and Virginia Coiner Classick.

Diana Hume George

For Constance Coiner, 1948–96

Dare you see a soul at the White Heat?
Then crouch within the door—
Red—is the Fire's common tint
But when the vivid Ore
Has vanquished Flame's conditions
It quivers from the Forge
Without a color, but the Light
Of unanointed Blaze.
    —Emily Dickinson, Poem 365

Constance Coiner and Ana Duarte-Coiner, her daughter, died on TWA Flight 800 on July 17, 1996, as this book was nearing completion. Their deaths are so horrifying that no words are adequate to express how I and hundreds of others around the country feel. So what I want to say here is not about Constance's death, but rather her life, and in particular her labor on this book.

Constance's work was at the core of her identity. As a lifelong activist, she devoted herself professionally and personally to witness and engagement. *Solidarity Forever,* she declared of both work and play, echoing the cooperative convictions she grew up sharing with her sisters. Clean conviction drove her belief in what a world fueled by activism for peace and justice could realize. Her insistence on possibility was not easy or blind; she understood the genesis of the power and greed that run the world but refused cynicism or despair and renewed herself for struggle every day.

Diana Hume George is a professor of English and women's studies at Pennsylvania State University at Erie, the Behrend College.

Constance and Steve Duarte, her life partner, remind me of an earlier generation of socialist idealists wholly dedicated to mediating transformation in individuals and institutions, to binding the wounds of an ill society, a struggling planet. They have worked quietly and clearly, without fanfare, to change many lives. Hers was a scholarship of challenge and counterpoise, a fluent heteroglossia in which she often represented the voices of the silenced. Constance also researched the works of other women who have tried to change the world—Tillie Olsen, Meridel Le Sueur, Carolyn Forché. In her writing, in her activist classroom she was their sister and their peer. Ana Duarte-Coiner was the child of her parents in every respect. Her enthusiasm, wit, and knowledge already radiated the possibility of synthesizing their goals.

Constance's light was Dickinson's unanointed blaze. Her soul was more often at white heat than any I've known, capable of both impassioned joy and prophetic wrath. She was as heartfelt in personal connection as any friend could be. And she gave of her heart to her students as well as her friends. For many of them, Constance embodied what they most admire, who they hope to become. *Constance:* steadfastness of mind under duress, fortitude, fidelity, loyalty, fixed value. *Constance* means unchanging, standing firm, consistent, resolved. No one ever meant her name more than Constance Coiner.

I can no longer remember whether this book was Constance's idea or mine. Probably it was the child of our synergy, because no one could energize me or fire me up like Constance could. Fixing me with her stop-traffic gaze when I wondered if we should attempt it at all, she said, We're going to do this, we're going to make it happen. And we did. When we began, however, we had no idea what we were getting into.

We worked both independently and together on this book, talking on the phone daily during intense phases and leaving messages of such length on each other's answering machines that we used up the tapes. In our regular marathon editing sessions, I loaded up my van, drove six hours to Binghamton, and stayed with Constance, Ana, and Steve for up to five days. We assembled at her dining room table amidst our sacred preparatory objects. By the end of the first day we spilled over into the living room, with Steve and Ana patiently ignoring the mess. By day two we virtually took over the house. By day three we always made desperate calls to hire on-site grad student help. We stared each other down across that table when we disagreed, our voices strained with conviction, so clean with each other that many friendships would have had trouble surviving what we said. Ours thrived on this dynamic. We generated mutual electricity, excitement, a synchronous hum and buzz for sixteen, eighteen, twenty hours a day. It's this atmosphere that's gone, this palpable feel in the air that no one but Constance could create.

Out of these sessions also came plenty of fun. When I went to her home for our first work-fest, Ana was about eight years old. Constance grabbed her hand and they stood on the sidewalk dancing together. When I left days later, the same small ceremony. She was always ready to dance—and to work and to speak out and to challenge and to confront and to make peace. Near the end of one long work night, in bleary discussion of this book's endlessly revised contents, I accidentally called her Contents. From then on, half her notes, half her calls, were with love from Contents, which, her sister Virginia tells me, was a family nickname. I have since discovered that it was also her friend Lillian Robinson's name for her. And her dedication to work did make her a walking table of contents—learned, intellectual, with an easy authority.

I talked with Carolyn Forché, on whom Constance was writing a book when she died, just after Constance's death and just before Carolyn herself was about to embark on a flight to Paris with her child. Constance will always, she said, be flying with Ana to Paris. I think of Constance and Ana, elated, holding hands at takeoff. There they will always be, her choice to be with her daughter clear against the backdrop of loved work put finally aside.

How we both decided, the summer of 1996, to put work aside is a story in itself, one that Constance would want me to tell. My third grandchild, to whose birth I'd been invited, decided to arrive early. But Constance and I were to meet to work on the book. In more than three hours of phone talk—a long conversation even for us—Constance declared that this was nuts, that my priorities were skewed, that this was a perfect example of the dilemma described by our book, and were we ourselves once again going to embody the contradictions, represent the imbalances, in ways that damaged us and our families?

Impassioned, Constance said, No, I won't allow it, we're both going to be sane this time. We explored in that conversation the issues of this book in our own lives at great length. She told me we were both right to choose family, that it wouldn't make any ultimate difference to the book. If you come here to work on the book, she argued, and you miss that baby's birth, you will regret it for the rest of your life. But a year from now, it will make no difference at all if we postpone our work for a few more weeks.

In normal circumstances she would have been right about that. Instead, she and I never finished our joint introduction, which I know would have borne more of her mark than of mine. And she never got to edit her essay, to make her own choices about how she is represented in this book. On the day of the crash, Constance sent me three packages, all with letters and notes, all meticulously organized and labeled. She made lists all the way to the George Washington Bridge, for this and other projects. Then she put all work away, ready, as she wrote to her old friend Billy Smith, for "full-on fun" with Ana. The packages I received after her death included a detailed itinerary of our upcoming tasks as well as notes on the then-current version of the manuscript.

When I decided to be with my children and grandchildren, and she to go to Paris with Ana, it was with the sense of a joyous pact made to choose life and play and family. I was present at the birth of my grandson Storm Creek George and then I took my granddaughters away to my cottage on Lake Erie—no phone calls, no radio, no TV. I knew nothing, not even that there had been a plane crash, until my son, Bernie, came to find me. He informed me as lovingly as he could of this tragedy that has changed my life, and the lives of many others, inalterably.

In a piece of editing-meets-life that Constance loved, my daughter-in-law, Mary Ellen Sullivan-George, had become my research assistant, and while we awaited the baby's birth, she worked nonstop with me, composing page counts and charts and checklists and traveling back and forth to my office with photocopies and mailings. She even took the book with her into the birthing room, where her labor eventually became literal. The last letter Constance wrote me ends with "I wish I could hold Storm George." My son's elegy to Constance and Ana ends with his assurance to the spirit of Constance: "You have held Storm." Finishing this book about family, love, and work became for us a family affair. Constance, who valued family above all else, would like knowing that a whole family finished her book.

Most people who lose someone they love like this have no concrete way to be with their sadness. But Constance left work for me and for others to finish and I know that the legacy of one's labor is the kind of immortality she believed in. In a 1992 letter, Constance wrote to me about her sense of our book's focus: "We're trying to share, to organize, to bring people together around a crucial quality-of-life and human rights issue, and make change—collectively—for the betterment of parents, our profession, and higher education in this country." I have the honor to help keep her alive by finishing this project for her. But all of us who knew her can keep her work going by challenging our own complicities, being of use, speaking out for the dispossessed—and for children who are literally the future's hope. So it is for Ana, too, that I try to stay clear, be vigilant, break the silence.

During the year of editing following Constance's death, I have often felt as if she were here with me, working into dawn, helping me decide what to do. She was made of eloquent vigilance, and her heart beating in me will make me more honest every moment of the life I have left. Like Dickinson's, her unanointed Blaze, her human soul at White Heat, is with me still, and she still burns me. Solidarity forever, Constance.

WHEN THEY SLEEP ALL THE TIME

Liz Rosenberg

I don't remember it that way,
and even when he slept, it was
like sitting beside a dozing volcano,
trying not to move or breathe,
to will the silence of the telephone;
learning how to eat left-handed,
the cooling food two feet away.
But it wasn't that, and not the tea-kettle shriek
at hours of the night I never knew existed,
no, God, it was fanatical love for this quivering
air-swimmer, his tiny hand pushing
at the nights, the dawns,
and the long slow explosion of our days.

Liz Rosenberg teaches English and Creative Writing at the State University of New York at Binghamton.

Constance Coiner and
Diana Hume George

This project originated in a 1988
Modern Language Association session commemorating the tenth anniversary of the publication of Tillie Olsen's *Silences.* Crossing gender,
race, and class boundaries, Olsen's groundbreaking work examines the
circumstances that promote—or that impede or silence—creative and
intellectual production. We did not know each other at that time, but
we each responded to the call for papers and both of us were included in *Listening to Silences: New Essays in Feminist Criticism,* a compi-
lation of session papers edited by Shelley Fisher Fishkin and Elaine
Hedges. Coiner's contribution concerned the invisibility of literal
parenting in the academy; George's addressed the unrecognized, un-
rewarded emotional labor of mentoring (or metaphorical parenting),
work disproportionately carried out by women academics. These related concerns brought us together.

While our focus is on academe, we are gratified to note that in the
years during which this book has been in progress, the term "family-
friendly" has been transformed from a rarefied special-interest, spe-
cial-pleading "women's issue" into a buzz term employed by progressive corporations and businesses to accommodate the needs of all
workers, male and female, in the American marketplace. A mere three
years ago, one of our administrators, confronted with the term, wondered what it might mean. Possibly increased programs for parents of

---

Before her death, Constance Coiner was an associate professor of English at the
State University of New York at Binghamton. Diana Hume George is a professor of
English and women's studies at Pennsylvania State University at Erie, the Behrend
College.

students visiting the campus? Now he says that he's up on it and is interested in how he might be of help, if it is not too costly.

Aided by the visibility of books such as Terri Apter's *Working Women Don't Have Wives*, Sylvia Ann Hewlett's *A Lesser Life*, and Arlie Hochschild's *The Second Shift*, administrators may soon regard family-friendly ideas as old news. But more recent cover stories in publications such as *Business Week* indicate that these issues are still foremost in the minds of progressive management. Similarly, the American Management Association's 1996 Conference for Working Women indicates growing rather than receding concern, as does the Women's Bureau of the United States Department of Labor, which identifies the "difficulty of balancing work and family obligations" as the problem female workers feel should be number one on the president's list of priorities. Can academe be far behind?

Well, yes. Articles such as "Scheduling Motherhood" in the *Chronicle of Higher Education* appeared in 1995 and studies ranking colleges and universities by their family-friendly quotients have received wide press. In 1996 the *Chronicle of Higher Education* reported the results of the College and University Work-Family Association's study of 375 four-year institutions. Twenty-nine campuses scored high in the study, and 65 others are cited as "leadership campuses," but the survey-based study found that "the majority of institutions are doing very little to help their employees" (Clark). According to a study by Phyllis Hutton Raabe in *Academic Couples: Problems and Promises*, higher education institutions are indeed "strikingly advanced in providing on-site child-care centers"—but corporate America is more likely than higher education employers to provide financial assistance for child care, allow job sharing, and provide eldercare programs (Raabe 219). Underlying these comparisons, however, is the generally low level of availability of most work-family policies in both education and business in America. In other words, we're doing better than the private sector in some ways, worse in others, but the extent, availability, caliber, and utilization rates of such policies is low overall. Paid child-care leave for mothers is very common, but other kinds of support are less common, and women still have to deal with invisible discriminatory behavior on the job.

In "(EN)Gender(ING) Socialization," a chapter in *Promotion and Tenure: Community and Socialization in Academe*, William G. Tierney and Estela Mara Bensimon identify in exceptionally balanced and equitable terms the problem: "We wish to dispel the widely held belief that gender blindness—the claim that the professor's sex is invisible—

constitutes equal treatment for female and male academics. To the contrary, we maintain that the eradication of overt and covert discrimination against women requires critical and gender-based appraisals of academic structures, practices, and policies" (76). What we call metaphorical mothering is called "Mom work" by Tierney and Bensimon, who also designate "smile work" as a female academic task (85–90). The "structured absence" of the personal and the "communal unconscious" of departmental cultures in academe creates disadvantages for women with children (92–96). And, increasingly, we would add, for men interested in living fully human lives.

The academy assumes a freedom from primary responsibility for maintaining a home, a family, and other human relationships that simply does not exist for many academic women and many of our male colleagues. This problem can be particularly acute for faculty in the lower ranks because tenure and biological clocks often tick in unison. Eldercare is also an issue; some academics find themselves on the mommy track and the daughter track, or the daddy and son tracks, at the same time.

Granted, academics have it easier than many. Our positions are not as physically demanding as manual labor performed around the world, at which children, women, and men are disabled or killed at alarming rates. Our jobs are not as time-consuming as those of nurses or truck drivers. Ours are not as inflexible as those of workers forced to punch time clocks—or of many of our own staff members. Most of us do not have to work two or three or four jobs to support ourselves and our families. But we also are not the leisured elite that conservatives paint us to be, teaching a few hours a week—and not at all in the summer—but otherwise free to think deep thoughts. Academe has entered a period of speed-up in which we must teach larger classes and more hours per week to accomplish the minimum amount of work deemed acceptable. To earn tenure at many colleges and universities, we must devote more and more time to research as well as to teaching, advising, and service. The profession is becoming an ever more demanding arbiter and shaper of our lives.

Issues such as productivity, job security, and job-related stress are pertinent to professions and workplaces outside the academy, of course, and so this book implicitly places our profession in a broader social context. The United States has historically resisted government-subsidized child care, and attempts to reform our profession must be accompanied by parallel efforts to promote further government-funded pro-family policies, such as those enacted by President Clinton in the Family and Medical Leave Act of 1993. Other time-intensive professions also need to be restructured to accommodate family needs, and our book thus joins the national conversation about family-friendly policies in the workplace.

The academy is in a period of retrenchment, vulnerability, and legitimation crisis. We know that decreasing budgets, faculties, and institutional flexibility—as well as increasing demands from state governments and taxpayers for faculty "accountability"—will surely affect reform efforts. Therefore, while envisioning significant changes in our working conditions and professional ethos, we also identify cost-effective and administratively uncomplicated ways to accomplish immediate and necessarily partial goals. We know that grander visions of a family-friendly profession won't be realized in a time of educational cutbacks. But we can implement those policies that cost little; we can work toward half- and quarter-measures; we can maneuver creatively within constraints; and we can raise consciousness about family-care issues.

To increase awareness of such concerns requires women and men to tell the truth about the quality of their lives. The contributors here express honestly the difficulties and benefits of combining a full professional life with caring for children, partners, and aging parents. The essays address the following questions, among others: How do the demands of caring for others deter, benefit, or redefine research and teaching? What have our universities done, or neglected to do, to help parents, commuting couples, and domestic partners? What specific pro-family policies should we expect despite educational budget crises? That men and women share equitably the responsibility of caring for children remains a distant rather than an achieved goal in many academic families. As contributor Naomi Miller points out, the majority of full professors in the academy are still male, and the majority of these men are also fathers; among senior women, the majority are childless. We must take seriously the implications of this statistical tendency.

Moreover, as an increasing number of academics enter "the sandwich generation," in which eldercare overlaps with child care, yet another problem of gender inequality arises. The federal government estimates that by the end of the first quarter of the twenty-first century, Americans over sixty-five will make up 40 percent of the dependent care population. Women are overwhelmingly responsible for aging parents, including their partners'. And women in their prime earning years are more likely to have both kinds of dependents. Several of our contributors address these issues.

Others probe metaphoric parenting in the academic workplace. Professors frequently become maternal and paternal figures for students, who often expect of us some subtly transmogrified form of parenting. While most students expect from their male professors relatively little in the way of personal and emotional presence, they often unconsciously take for granted that female teachers will be available and empathic. Female professors who want to subvert the academy's emphasis on autonomy do so at the price of increasing their maternal burden. And the problem of metaphoric parenting only increases at the associate professor stage, when women who can no longer protect some of their time because of preparation for tenure can become targets for requests from departments, university administrators, younger professors, and graduate students.

Prominent senior scholars whose children are now grown, the first generation of women to enter our traditionally male profession in significant numbers, tell their stories here. Theirs is a living history of difference whose moment we want to record for their own and younger academic generations. We also present those in the apprenticeship years, including graduate students and pretenure faculty, who express their hopes and fears. Some acknowledge that they have lowered their career aspirations partly because they see that their role models are overwhelmed. Although our emphasis remains on full-time academics, several of our narratives are from those who made nontraditional choices, including a few who have left academia altogether.

This book also raises the question of how those of us in the profession should advise pretenure faculty and graduate students as well as promising undergraduates considering Ph.D. programs. More particularly, *The Family Track* confronts the difficulty of advising students who have insufficient resources to pay for the infrastructure necessary to combine parenting with achieving tenure—an infrastructure one cannot afford, in this period of economic decline, on an assistant professor's salary. Will gender inequality in the academy, we ask, continue to be countered partly by an unacknowledged reliance on class privilege?

We view "the maintenance of life" (Tillie Olsen's term for domestic labor, child care, and cultivating human relationships) as a feminist issue, and not exclusively a "women's issue." Because we are determined to include the stories of male colleagues we have assiduously sought contributions from male feminists and fathers. Genuine change will not occur unless increasing numbers of such men emerge. Our project is driven by the conviction that women should not be forced to choose mothering over professional achievement and that men should not be coerced into emphasizing professional achievement at the expense of involvement in the lives of their children.

This book will contribute valuably to the historiography/autobiography of the academic profession, especially that of faculty and graduate students. *The Family Track* records and makes available for discussion the frank testimonies of those who number among the first two generations of women to enter academia in significant numbers. We envision what former dean Annette Kolodny calls that rare place where neither love of learning nor love of family needs to be sacrificed. This volume is part of a long view of our profession, one that resists the siege mentality (while respecting the serious economic factors that contribute to people's developing such a mentality) and considers the long-term consequences of decisions made today—including, to cite just one example, how to attract people of color to the academic profession at a time when our nation's demographics are shifting radically and rapidly.

On a more immediate front, *The Family Track* makes practical, implementable suggestions, including refinements of already existing policies. To borrow again from Annette Kolodny, a "failure of imagination" need not accompany our "paucity of financial resources." The book also comprises a partial reply to the bombardment of attacks by the media and political pundits characterizing professors as underworked and overpaid. Although we did not compile this anthology as a response to such attacks, our contributors document the multiple demands on professors' time, informing the American public that many in our profession are devoted to teaching and to the welfare of their students.

By design, our format differs from the usual academic anthology. We include various genres—standard academic essays that theorize or historicize family-care issues; brief, informal personal narratives; poetry; and edited transcriptions of interviews. We have striven for other kinds of balance and diversity, in terms of race, class, ethnicity, sexuality, (dis)ability, family configuration, age, geography, institutional affiliation, and professional rank. Most of our contributors come from the fields we know best—literature, creative writing, cultural studies, American studies—but they represent several other disciplines as well, including communication, history, sociology, anthropology, law, public health, and psychiatry.

One large audience for this volume will likely be academic women who have "been there, done that" and who may feel, with a rush of relief, that their own struggles and painful choices have finally been recognized. But another audience is graduate students, who are now required to be aware of professional expectations and options increasingly early. Some graduate programs have instituted formal seminars and informal workshops on professional issues, in which we hope this book might serve as a core text. For entry-level assistant professors, this book should function as a survival manual.

We hope our readers will also include department chairs, directors of graduate programs, deans, and other administrators who may not have had the experiences of our contributors or as yet heard their voices. Many higher-level administrators, male and female alike, have been insulated from primary responsibility for a family, but they must, increasingly, oversee—and understand—faculty who have not. Because a polite code of silence about certain topics persists, especially among junior faculty who fear jeopardizing tenure by making demands or appearing unable to cope with their myriad responsibilities, chairs and administrators might well be enlightened by candid writing about the quality of academics' lives. We intend this book to persuade those with the power to enact pro-family policies within the academy to do so.

WORKS CITED

American Management Association. "Conference for Working Women." New York, Oct. 23, 1996.

Apter, Terri. *Working Women Don't Have Wives: Professional Success in the 1990s.* New York: St. Martin's Press, 1993.

"Balancing Work and Family." *Business Week* Sept. 16, 1996: 74–80.

Clark, Robin. "A Report Praises Twenty-Nine Colleges for 'Family Friendly' Policies." *Chronicle of Higher Education* Oct. 11, 1996: A13–A14.

Hedges, Elaine, and Shelley Fisher Fishkin, eds. *Listening to Silences: New Essays in Feminist Criticism.* New York: Oxford University Press, 1994.

Hewlett, Sylvia Ann. *A Lesser Life: The Myth of Women's Liberation in America.* New York: Morrow, 1986.

Hochschild, Arlie. *The Second Shift: Working Parents and the Revolution at Home.* New York: Viking-Penguin, 1989.

Raabe, Phyllis Hutton. "Work-Family Policies for Faculty: How 'Career- and Family-Friendly' Is Academe?" *Academic Couples: Problems and Promises.* Ed. Marianne A. Ferber and Jane W. Loeb. Urbana: University of Illinois Press, 1997. 208–25.

"Scheduling Motherhood." *Chronicle of Higher Education* Mar. 10, 1995: A14.

Tierney, William G., and Estela Mara Bensimon. "(EN)Gender(ING) Socialization." *Promotion and Tenure: Community and Socialization in Academe.* Albany: State University of New York Press, 1996. 75–102.

Women's Bureau of the United States Department of Labor. *Working Women Count: A Report to the Nation.* Washington, D.C.: U.S. Department of Labor, 1996.

YOUR FIRST TWO STEPS

Alan Michael Parker

On the morning of your first two steps
the day before my birthday,

the cold outside was cold enough
to stay inside and write a poem.
I did. We did. Yours was everywhere,

a little elegy for one emotion or another,
or the convergence of the twain—

the terrible confusion of your smile
with its collapse. Dak!
you called your poem:

Dak, dak, dak, dak, dak, dak, dak!
Me? I called my poem

but it would not come.
I whistled in a frequency so high
it stung the angels' ears.

No luck, no dice, no poem.
And by the waters of your bath

I sat down and wept,
and then I named my poem
"Your First Two Steps."

Alan Michael Parker is an assistant professor of English at Pennsylvania State University at Erie, the Behrend College.

PART ONE

How It Has Been: Personal Histories

The Maternal Mind

Alicia Ostriker

My life as a teacher, poet, and critic dates from the late neolithic. In 1965, when I took my first job as an assistant professor, our universities were dominated by Neanderthal Man, Homo Erectus, the Thinking Reeds of high humanism. History at that time was white men's history. Literature was white men's literature. The token women in the canon—Emily Dickinson and Marianne Moore, Jane Austen and George Eliot—were, not coincidentally, unmarried and childless. For it was a truth universally acknowledged that a woman might produce books or babies, but not both, just as she might organize her life around marriage or a career, but not both. Certainly nothing in my professional training suggested otherwise. I had indeed studied with female teachers in graduate school: the eminent medievalist Helen White and the eminent Renaissance scholar Madeline Doran. Both were unmarried, both childless. My new colleagues at Rutgers University included one other female assistant professor, also unmarried and childless.

As a beginning assistant professor I had two sections of freshman composition and an eighteenth-century literature course to teach. At home I had a scientist husband just beginning to climb the academic ladder himself and two daughters in diapers. The two year old with the naturally sunny disposition had temporarily turned into a prematurely old and cynical person at the advent of her little sister; the six-month-old colicky little sister had not yet slept through the night. I nursed the first child until I got pregnant with the second; I nursed the

Alicia Ostriker is a professor of English at Rutgers University.

second until the week I started work. This, by the way, was a mistake, but again not an accidental one. According to the ideologies of 1965, one either breastfed or bottle-fed. And I believed that dogma, undogmatic though I considered myself to be. Not until my son's birth five years later did it occur to me that I could combine nursing when I was at home with formula when I was at work.

What was I doing as a young mother and teacher? Mostly going crazy. Mostly feeling discouraged, despairing, exhausted, a failure. No day possessed enough hours. My children were infinitely demanding. So were my students. Whatever time I spent on one was being guiltily stolen from the other, and I could never be adequate, never catch up, never be good enough. Our au pairs worked half days. The rest of the time, Mom was in charge. I am a person who needs freedom, as I need air; I had absolutely none.

Yet I was clearly living the life I had chosen and was proud of choosing. I wanted to teach literature, which I loved; I wanted children, whom I loved. Having children was for me like having sex: heartache comes with the territory, but would I have liked to go to my grave a virgin? Not at all, and going childless would have seemed to me another sort of virginity. But to be the self-sacrificing twenty-four-hour-a-day mother my mother had been was unthinkable. I was proud to be defying convention, breaking boundaries, rejecting the either/or categories the world wished to impose on me. I consider the nuclear family of mommy daddy baby one of the stupidest inventions ever to roll down the turnpike of inherently dysfunctional social institutions. An extended family was what I tried to reproduce, in the implausible setting of an academic suburb, by treating au pair girls like real family, sharing mommying with neighbor mommies, and holding classes in our apartment so that my students would see my children and vice versa. It seemed important to me, and to my husband, that my daughters should perceive their mother as a person with a working life not totally devoted to them, and at the same time that I could offer my students the image of a woman breaking the mold. I was an intellectual and a mother. Perhaps my boy students could marry one like me. Perhaps my girl students would see my option as possible for them.

And there was not only pride, I must admit. There was joy too. Children are ecstasy as well as agony. The sheer delight of their beauty, their energy, the spectacle of their growth, the privilege of their lives enfolded in ours is like nothing else on earth. And it was a joy when I could squeeze time out for poetry, to shape the raw material of motherhood's agonies and ecstasies into art.

I loved my kids, my undergraduates, and the wonderful graduate students in our department, with whom I could talk without hesitation. But my colleagues? Those gentlemen professors, witty, brilliant, who behaved as if they had never in their lives seen a baby's behind? As if the world contained no babies? Among them I was in the closet. I had been hired as an eighteenth-century scholar, not a mom. Not a poet either, but that is another story. I spoke not a mumbling word, in my professional camouflage, about my life, my family, my husband, my children, my feelings, my beliefs.

No form of institutional support was available. I did my job, I published, and therefore I did not perish. But I was crazy all the time. And horribly lonely. And only dimly aware of what became dazzlingly clear years later, when I read De Beauvoir's *The Second Sex,* Dorothy Dinnerstein's *The Mermaid and the Minotaur,* Adrienne Rich's *Of Woman Born,* Nancy Chodorow's *The Reproduction of Mothering.* What these great women writers and thinkers told me, that I should have seen for myself, is that the world of the mind, as it has constituted itself in the West and is reconstructed every generation in the institutions of higher learning, is not only androcentric and misogynist in general but intensely antimaternal. Mothers are powerless not only vis-à-vis the authority of fathers, doctors, teachers, psychoanalysts, welfare workers, judges in courts of law, and the Selective Service. It is not simply that the domestic sphere of nurturance and the public sphere of political and economic policy-making are supposed never to overlap. No, if you are a mother who aspires also to be an intellectual, or vice versa, your double bind is a more radical one. For the maternal is what the life of the mind exists to escape—to ignore, most of the time, and the rest of the time to sentimentalize or demonize. To read canonical philosophy and literature, from Plato to James Joyce, is to discover that moms are brain-dead.

Now look at Sarah Ruddick's *Maternal Thinking,* a meditation on the complex, contradictory, often conflicting claims mothering makes on our intelligence. Ruddick considers how maternal work, far from being instinctive or intuitive, requires discipline, flexibility, resourcefulness, idealism, realism, and sustained acts of attention not divided from but infused by passionate caring. Perhaps this is what any mother knows, but we have been divided from our knowledge by the propaganda of patriarchy. The maternal style of teaching I and many other women (and some men) deliberately practice is of tremendous value to our students, as it presumes a caring for the whole individual; we do not make the mistake of supposing that a mind develops independently of the rest of a student's personality and life. We who are maternal teachers even go to the great length of keeping the appointments we make with students and listening to them when they speak. We do this with students as with our children, because we have the habit of responsibility.

Grace Paley's prose-poem "A Midrash on Happiness" describes maternal labor like this:

> By work to do she included the important work of raising children righteously up. By righteously she meant that along with being useful and speaking truth to the community, they must do no harm. By harm she meant not only personal injury to the friend the lover the coworker the parent (the city the nation) but also the stranger; she meant particularly the stranger in all his or her difference, who, because we were strangers in Egypt, deserves special goodness for life or at least until the end of strangeness. (8)

Do these values of child rearing sound as if they might be embodied in our teaching? For many of us they already are. Maternal minds can handle multiculturalism better than nonmaternal minds. And maternal minds as applied to our disciplines would mean more linking of theory to praxis, more questioning of androcentric categories and priorities, more truly original research in the humanities and social sciences—and maybe even in the sciences. If we had the courage to use our maternal minds in our research, we could no longer be obedient daughters of those talking heads, the intellectual fathers. We would invent. We would think for ourselves. Because mothers, face it, have to be ingenious. We have to be smart. Why hide that smartness under a bushel of matrophobic theory? Why confine it to "the domestic sphere," while permitting that sphere to be controlled by everyone and everything outside it? Why not let our little light shine?

My point is a simple one. Maternity, even when it drives us personally crazy, far from being a professional defect, is a resource. It is an advantage, not a disadvantage; a source of wisdom, invention, and potential political change. We who are academic mothers are not some whining special interest group. We should regard ourselves with respect and should struggle to make our institutions respect us, not because we can transcend our motherhood, but because we can funnel it into our work and the work of creating a better civilization.

WORKS CITED

Paley, Grace. "A Midrash on Happiness." *Long Walks and Intimate Talks.* New York: Feminist Press, 1991. 6, 8–9.

Nine-Syllable Riddle

Katherine Callen King

I'm a riddle in nine syllables. . . .
Boarded the train there's no getting off.
—*Sylvia Plath, "Metaphors"*

It is November 1961, and I am in my sophomore year at Vassar College. A white dress hangs in my closet to be worn under academic dress at compulsory convocations. Only virgins are allowed to study at Vassar. No married women and certainly no pregnant ones. It goes without saying that if the college learns I am pregnant I will be expelled. Unlike my fiancé, who tells all his friends at Columbia and celebrates his impending parenthood with whoops and champagne, I tell only my roommate, Muriel. Talking tense and low in our room, we plan how to get me through the semester with no one noticing my morning (and evening) sickness or my bulging waistline.

We work out this routine: in the morning I pretend to be not quite ready so that Muriel can get our floor mates on the way to the dining hall before I dash to the bathroom to wash out the coffee can in which I have thrown up upon waking. After breakfast she distracts them while I rush into the bathroom and throw up again. As we rise from dinner she distracts them once again while I flee to the bathroom. At lunch, I eat as much as I can so that my weight doesn't drop too far while my waistline expands. This goes on for six weeks. Muriel nearly

Katherine Callen King is chair of the Program in Comparative Literature and associate professor of classics at UCLA.

has a nervous breakdown, but she is too kind to tell me this for many years.

I am too focused on academic survival to notice what this necessary subterfuge is doing to Muriel. I manage to win grudging permission from the administration to return to the dorms for the ten-day post-Christmas examination period with a wedding ring (an obvious sign of sexual activity) on my finger. I write acceptable papers and struggle to learn enough art history, American history, psychology, and Shakespeare so that I can leave Vassar not only with minimal honor but with credit for three full semesters (in addition to the baby) under my belt.

How much easier it would have been if I could have broken my silence and worked *with* my pregnancy rather than against it. I do not, at this date, blame Vassar, for I know that parietal rules at women's colleges were established to guard intellectual women against almost automatic charges of sexual immorality. I do, however, blame the academic powers that ruled the male institutions (and therefore the female ones), because the deeper reason for insisting upon female virginity was, I have come to believe, the desire to deny the feminine a real presence in academe.

The academy from Plato onward has focused on ideas that transcend mortality, while women, the birthers of bodies and layers-out of corpses, have consistently been seen as mired in it. Given that the "immortal" intellect and the mortal body do not easily mix in the oppositional European culture that Greece spawned, it behooves students to be as far removed from "female" as possible. The academy has come to be structured, therefore, around the rhythms of the aristocratic male body, which can be seen as a birther (and burier) of *ideas,* rather than around the working "female" body. Women who are sexless are clearly regarded as less female, less corporeal, while those who are pregnant are as obviously female, as obviously corporeal, as they can be.

I hope that my story will show how this denial of the feminine is effected through the everyday gendering of academic life, with specific reference to the requirement that higher education be pursued full-time, and I hope to persuade my readers to work to transform such denial into an encouraging acceptance that will at the same time transform academe into a truly liberatory and democratic institution. The pleasure I got from combining part-time school with parenting is essential to this goal, and I hope this positive part of my experience is not overwhelmed by the negative.

Eric was born at the end of May, and by July I was back in the class-room, filling my new hunger for intellectual work by auditing a sum-mer school course in English literature at Columbia. This was the tran-sition to part-time school in the fall, taking one course at a time in the late afternoon or evening at City College (CCNY). Although I had ap-plied to and was admitted to the day (or "regular") session, I was forced to take night courses (which had no admission requirements) because the day session turned out to be reserved for full-time stu-dents. This was my first lesson in class politics: those who needed to work a full-time job were given what was clearly considered an inferior education and degree.

I had not been a particularly good student at Vassar, but I became an excellent student now, engrossed in reading assignments, devoting serious hours when my son was asleep to writing the papers that I had always left until the last possible moment when I was a childless full-time student. When I took off one semester the next year to be a full-time parent, I discovered that what applied to my academic life also applied to my personal life: just as I had been a mediocre full-time student, I was an unhappy (and therefore mediocre) full-time parent. But when I combined the two, my energy for parenting and scholar-ship increased tenfold.

Eric benefited from my being a happier parent, but he benefited socially from my studies as well. That first summer school course had been made possible by one of my husband's classmates, who prac-ticed his belief in education by staying with my two-month-old infant for the two hours daily I needed to be gone. But aside from this single brave young man, my enablers were other women with children, wives of Columbia students, some of whom were part-time students like me. My husband, like theirs, could not help out because he was working more than half-time while attending school full-time. So we women exchanged child care while we were in class and the library, feeling secure that our babies were not only in good hands but were being socialized by other babies to boot.

Although combining school and parenting became more difficult when I left this support network to return to Vassar in 1964, it still worked well. My husband had a job that kept him traveling the roads of New York State from Sunday afternoon to Friday night, so Poughkeepsie seemed as central a place as any for us to live. Inez Nelbach, a wonderful new dean of studies at Vassar who was committed to the education of *all* women, not just virgins, had begun recommending the experimental admission of a few "returning" students. She encouraged my reapplication, aided me through the process, and arranged for me to pay partial tuition for half-time study. I took out a student loan to cover tuition and for the first year contracted for child care four hours a day, three days a week in a local woman's home while I attended classes.

Everything was fine as long as the car did not break down. But of course it did—just as I was trying to finish a difficult paper on *King Lear*. No car meant no babysitter. No babysitter meant that I had only the night hours to worry *Lear* into submission, for although Eric did not mind playing by himself while I did housework, when I would try to study he would object strenuously, sensing my total absorption in something other than him. I imposed on kindly neighbors to watch Eric and lend me their car so I could race to a not-to-be-missed Greek class for an hour. I borrowed a car again to turn in my paper. When my husband returned on Friday night, I fainted for the first time in my life. It turned out I had a bleeding ulcer that would require a week's hospitalization and four pints of blood to repair.

The following year Eric was old enough to enter the Vassar Nursery School, which made my life immeasurably easier. If the antiquated Morris Minor broke down, Eric and I could get a ride to our joint destination with community parents and students we had made friends with at the school; sometimes other parents could look after Eric on campus for a short time if I knew I would be detained. Eric got wonderful attention at this laboratory school five mornings a week, he and I spent the afternoons companionably doing errands and household tasks, and I continued to take five courses a year for two years until I moved on to graduate study in classics at Columbia.

Having denied me a fellowship reportedly because a woman with a child could not be serious about graduate study, the professors who manned the Classics Department found their worst fears confirmed when I arrived for pre-registration counseling eight months pregnant. The eminent Gilbert Highet was only the first of several faculty who resolutely kept their eyes from straying below my chin. None of them, perfect gentleman all, ever mentioned my pregnancy in my presence; I, ladylike in return, never mentioned it either. Since it could not be spoken, no one could suggest I might start classes in January rather than September. So I started with everyone else, made sure my seminar reports would come before the critical period, took two weeks off to have my baby—as if I had the flu—and returned flat-bellied and full-breasted never to miss another class, racing home to nurse and cuddle after each.

My economic and domestic situation had dramatically improved. My husband, now an acquisitions editor for Random House, was home at least two weeks out of every month, we lived in a building that housed many women with young children, our income was high enough to enable me to hire a neighbor to babysit a couple of hours a day in addition to whatever child care we might exchange, and my sister Diana, who lived only twenty minutes away, could help with child care. Despite this improved situation, I am amazed—and somewhat horrified—to see on my transcript that I took a full-time load my first semester, my only concession to motherhood being an incomplete in my Plato seminar necessitated by surgery nine-weeks-old Ethan had for pyloric stenosis. The only thing I remember about that last dreadful week of the semester is racing from class to subway to Columbia Presbyterian Hospital to spend as much time as possible cuddling tiny emaciated IV-tubed Ethan until I needed to go home to feed and comfort five-year-old Eric.

Luckily for my and my children's sanity, by the second semester I had learned how to manipulate the system. Columbia allowed one to register for two types of credit, examination or registration. R-credit courses required no papers or examinations, merely class participation, but they counted toward full-time status. So when the time came to register for the spring semester I took two courses for E-credit, and two for R-credit. This schedule, approximately three-fifths time, was manageable if not ideal. The following year, when I was studying for my master's examinations, I took almost *all* R-credit courses and was delighted when, clearly now a de facto part-time student, I passed my oral examination with distinction and was admitted into the Ph.D. program. I hoped that my professors would learn a lesson about part-time students being as "good" as full-time students, but if they did they do not seem to have passed it on.

I did not continue at Columbia, for I decided to focus on comparative literature instead of classics. Because my marriage, which began to break up in May 1970, was irrevocably over by October 1971, I entered Princeton University as a single parent in 1972, and my first three years there are almost too painful to write about. The university was in two ways very supportive: it gave me a very inexpensive apartment in married student housing and, unlike Columbia, awarded me a full-tuition, partial-stipend fellowship. The hitch was that this support was predicated upon full-time study.

I placed Ethan, now in kindergarten, with a warm and competent woman for afternoon day care and enrolled ten-year-old Eric in an after-school program at the YMCA, which was about one and a half miles from his school. There was no public transportation, so he had to ride his bike, rain or shine. When really bad weather came, I had to let him stay home after school unsupervised, something that made me very uneasy. When afternoon seminars ran past 5:00, as they often did, I would get terribly nervous, wondering what Eric was doing, whether Ethan's babysitter would quit if I was late one more time. Evening events were impossible to attend and I could do no library work at night until Eric was thirteen and marginally old enough to babysit.

There was no money for fun, but then, I was too tense to have fun anyway. When I wasn't worried about seminar reports and papers, I anguished over the possibility that my sons would become permanent enemies during their struggles for my always inadequate attention. I was too busy studying and taking care of the kids to have time to make friends, and since there was no one like me around, there was no one to commiserate with. I am sure I was the only single parent enrolled in the university, and I may have been the only mother. It was three years of hell until the dissertation stage, when I won a Kent Fellowship that allowed me to stretch the normal two years of writing to three, thus effectively allowing me to go back to part-time study.

Eric, who cheerfully shared the cooking if not the cleaning and babysitting chores, never complained about my being less attentive than the mothers of his friends, but I will never forget a conversation we had one day in the car. Then about thirteen, he said to me out of the blue, "I am not going to get married until I'm through graduate school." Sensible child, thought I in my exhaustion, but when I asked him why, he replied, "because it's so hard on the kids." All I could reply was a choked "Yes." His words still give me pain, not only because of personal regret but because I hate the thought that other parents and children are needlessly going through what we did. I am very lucky that we all survived those terrible Princeton years, me to join a profession that I love, my sons to become such wonderful young men that I need feel no guilt—only regret that part of it had to be so unnecessarily painful. Others might not be so fortunate.

It is time for the academy, which has been shaped around the relatively unconstrained male body, to change. If the keepers of culture did not consider the achievement and well-being of its citizen body merely ancillary to a main focus on keeping the middle- and upper-class male in power, they would support those women who choose to accomplish *both* childbearing and professional academic training at their simultaneously optimal times. They would destigmatize part-time study, award proportionate financial support for part-time study, and make campuses family friendly by building playgrounds outside the libraries and establishing flexible child-care centers. They would solve the mind-body riddle that need never have been posed in the first place.

Harvard in the Sixties: (Un)Speakable Memories

Ellen Cantarow

One day in 1965, early in my progress toward a Ph.D. in comparative literature at Harvard, I was asked to serve tea at a department function. I'd just returned after two years of "real-world" jobs. I'd served time as a secretary at Harper and Row where "manuscript-reader," an editorial apprenticeship, was a position given only to men; as a file clerk at the *Providence Journal* where all first-time reporters were male. Surely at Harvard I would be an intellect; surely at Harvard people wouldn't automatically regard me as a housewife.

I remember my shock when I was asked to do that little thing: pour the tea. I hadn't yet grasped that being an angry young woman amounted to insubordination, since I still held the touching belief that academia was above gender prejudice. So I refused, saying something acid about women's always being asked to do "that sort of thing." I don't recall that I made any decorous ("I'll be out of town") excuse, and I must have showed my anger, because the graduate student deputized to ask me made his irritation very plain. Into the breach leaped my graduate colleague Roger: HE would pour the tea. Roger was effusively commended for his humility, good will, and generosity. And it was made very clear that I was being unreasonable, mean-spirited, and ungracious.

I begin with the tea-pouring incident because it's one of those "trivial" moments when wake-up bells sound: You're a woman, and don't you forget it. The sexism inherent in it—mute, potent—was more

Ellen Cantarow is senior editor of the *Women's Review of Books*.

common than that of my undergraduate French professor who hissed one day, when too many of us flubbed an answer, "But why am I teaching all of you anyway? You're all nice young ladies who are only going to meet nice young men and have babies." But I ran into enough of both sorts of prejudice to have acquired, some years before the women's movement began, a gut understanding of the implications of my womanhood in academia; how much of my sexuality was at once inferred and curtailed.

Harvard did not tolerate mothers—unless they were those ancillary persons, faculty wives. By 1965 I'd already met the man I would marry. Twelve years older than I, he already had tenure. Of his colleagues' wives, one was a concert pianist; none of the others was a professional. Two of the younger women already had children. There was a deep divide between the wives and mothers on one side and the men and a few childless women academics and grad students on the other.

My mother was a faculty wife with (unusual in her day) a master's degree in psychology. When I was born she left full-time work for good. It's telling that although I don't know precisely how many days a week she worked while I was growing up, I heard from my mother, my parents' families, and all their friends about my father's work. My mother supported him energetically and with self-effacement. Her own rearing by a beautiful, spoiled, self-involved mother had ravaged her self-confidence. In later life she suffered from severe depressions. These no doubt owed to biology and upbringing, but "the feminine mystique" of the postwar period certainly didn't help. In my mother I saw the latter-day experiences of the heroine of Charlotte Perkins Gilman's *The Yellow Wallpaper.*

The sixties were still boom years in the United States. Upper-middle-class young women entering the professions didn't confront the issues of economic survival their daughters would in the eighties and nineties. We had time and leisure to drop out of school as I did between 1963 and 1965. We could become part-time or volunteer workers like our mothers and raise families, or we could be what our parents and their friends called "career women." Or we could marry AND have children, AND carry on careers if we had the courage and stamina. We had a Hobson's choice.

There were no older role models either at Wellesley or at Harvard to help me fight clear of my schizoid notions about gender and sexuality. There may have been women faculty members who had children, but we never heard about their lives outside the classroom. There was no such thing as women's studies: senior faculty members like Alice

Rossi and Florence Howe and junior faculty and grad students like Lillian Robinson and me invented the courses that launched that discipline.

At Harvard I became an activist. In the antiwar and women's movements I gained self-confidence as an intellectual and began to get encouragement for my writing. It was a new life, one I feared compromising, especially for that permanent obligation, a child. Perhaps, I thought, I wouldn't have children at all. At the very least I'd wait until I'd established my career.

A few women graduate students at Harvard—very few—took the path I rejected. One married an academic scientist. She continued her graduate studies in French and her motherhood and her wifehood. She was central in activism at Harvard, agitating for a teaching fellows' union and against the university's involvement in the Vietnam war.

At some point she told the dean of the Graduate School that she was pregnant. "I was a teaching fellow," she told me recently, "and in some way or other part of those funds provided for some of my health care. He said in a very hostile way that he wouldn't let my teaching funds pay for a private or even semi-private room. He would let them go only for a room of the sort used by people on welfare. And what I remember was that after I gave birth I came back to a room where there were ten other women who had all given birth a few days earlier. They all wanted to play cards and eat pizza and I was exhausted and just wanted to sleep." When it came to coping with classes and motherhood, she recalls only adversity: "There was no child care anywhere. The only thing Harvard provided was married students' housing." Harvard punished women students who, in my friend's words, "had the nerve" to be mothers.

So I fought for mothers instead of becoming one. In 1969 the New University Conference charged Lillian Robinson, then an assistant professor at MIT, and me with writing feminist resolutions to bring to the MLA business meeting. These resolutions supported on-campus day care, paid maternity leave, paid parental leave for men and women, the overturning of antinepotism rules, equal employee benefits for women, space in MLA publications for professional women's concerns, women's studies courses, birth control, and preference to women in hiring. Even thirty years later, most higher educational institutions have not met these goals.

In the early seventies I was writing my dissertation and job hunting in a market just beginning its descent into recession. The struggles to find an academic job, assert myself in marriage to a much-respected professor, and keep both personal and professional life afloat were hard enough without bringing a child into the picture. As for my husband, he was avoiding parenthood for reasons of his own. Instead of becoming parents ourselves, we moved in 1970 into a house with two academic couples who had infants. In the intimacy of communal living we saw firsthand the toll child rearing, despite everyone's best intentions, took on the mothers. Still, one summer I burst out, "Oh, why DON'T we have a kid?" "Wait till the winter," rejoined my husband, "when you're studying full-time. If you still want to do it, we can talk." Notice the hermetic nature of this conversation: it was him versus me versus the future baby. He might have said, "Your college's day-care center or mine? And, by the way, are we ready for this?" No: in sink-or-swim-by-yourself America it was "an individual decision"—one from which he exempted himself.

To do him justice, my then-husband, known for both his loyalty and his sense of responsibility, would have become a full-time father if he'd had to. I was preoccupied in studies and political pursuits as men were supposed to be but women weren't; I showed only a patchy interest in other people's children. The bottom line was that I—as I put it to myself—"just didn't want children enough to insist." Nor did I feel it right, given that I didn't want to run the multiple-lives marathon, to make someone else do it.

While I was making (or not making) up my mind, Rosalie, a friend living alone in Paris after getting a graduate degree from MIT, had a baby. She was in her midthirties and writing her second dissertation for a doctorate at the Sorbonne. There were major differences between Rosalie and me. She was hell-bent on having a child; I wasn't. She was far braver than I; I would never have had a child as a single woman. But she also lived in France, whose national health care system included options that far outreached those for U.S. mothers and still do. I believe she got three months off before the birth and between six and nine months after. She received her full salary; no one penalized her for her absence when she returned to work. Her health care and that of her child were and still are guaranteed by the state. In France the law takes account of the whole scope of a woman's life; the state does not view pregnancy, childbirth, and child rearing as irresponsible self-indulgences.

Had there been a similar atmosphere in the United States in the sixties and early seventies, I might have felt more comfortable having a child. Had I been a dutiful daughter rather than an isolated rebel in my department, I'd have undoubtedly gotten a full-time job in the region, if not the city, gotten my career "in place," and felt more at leisure to have a baby. Had I been born eight to fifteen years later, with the benefit of older role models and a curriculum friendlier to women, I'd have felt a surer right to both children and career. I might have been certain in my desire when I made my impulsive suggestion to my husband that summer. And in turn he might have said, "Yes, let's."

Plus Ça Change...?

Regina Morantz-Sanchez

In November 1970, when I proofread my dissertation in the hospital during contractions, I knew only that balancing work and family life was my private problem and that resourcefulness, energy, and economical approaches to time management were my great personal strengths. I would like to think that over the years I have learned a great deal more than that, but I'm not sure such a claim would be accurate. When graduate students drop by my office to ask how I have done what I have—a creditable academic career, two marriages, and the typically eventful rearing of three children—I don't know how to answer them. My solutions were always personal and piecemeal. I didn't know in 1970 that the burdens I carried should not have been mine alone, that in a society in which women had equal opportunity, support networks for families with working parents would exist. I know that now, however, as viscerally as I know that such changes have not yet come about, and in many ways my graduate students are struggling with the same problems that plagued me. Why have we had such difficulty bringing about change in the organization of work and family life?

Perhaps Jean Baker Miller's observations about the "female psyche" can help us grope toward an answer. "Women's great desire for affiliation," she reminds us, "is both a fundamental strength, essential for social advance and at the same time the inevitable source of many of women's current problems. That is, while women have reached for and already found a psychic basis for a more advanced social existence,

Regina Morantz-Sanchez is a professor of history at the University of Michigan.

they are not able to act fully and directly. . . in a way that would allow it to flourish" (86). Miller goes on to identify one of the central dilemmas of women's lives in our society. "How," she asks, can we "create a way of life that includes serving others without being subservient?" (72). I don't think our problem has been subservience as much as work schedules and work structures. I would ask Miller's question a different way: How can we serve others and have time left over to serve ourselves? Or, can we adequately serve ourselves and still find time to serve others?

Our problem is particularly acute because our current society is notorious among industrial nations (with the exception of Japan) for its long and speeded up work hours for those of all classes. For example, only ten years ago, the average number of annual billed hours expected of a young Wall Street lawyer was approximately 1,700 per year. Now, a new associate is typically expected to bill 2,300–2,600 hours per year (Williams). Parallel examples exist for industrial and service workers. Moreover, women, whose hours spent in housework have not been significantly reduced even when they labor full-time, struggle with a work culture that not only makes little allowance for the rhythms of their daily responsibilities but also is vastly more demanding than it was only a decade ago. These dilemmas are collective and cultural; they have nothing to do with the stamina, efficiency, organizational ability, or insight of particular individuals. We academic women partake in the predicaments of working parenthood with American women of all races, ethnic groups, and classes. More recently, we have begun to share these problems with increasing numbers of young fathers (see Schor).

How can we women, and the men who are choosing to live their lives more like us, accomplish all that is expected and all that we expect of ourselves in a society so inimical to our goals? I have not yet answered this question for my own life; indeed, I have only fitfully and unsatisfactorily learned how to serve others and still serve myself. Indeed, this has been the central problem of my existence for the past twenty years.

I have been married twice. I have a daughter in graduate school and another who just gave birth to her second child. I also have a twelve-year-old son. I have experienced a bad marriage, a better marriage but one that still cast me in a caretaking role that severely truncated my ability to do my own work, divorces, single motherhood, reconstituting a stepfamily—indeed, the broad array of personally disruptive events of modern life. But through all of these states and stages, some themes recur, one set personal, the other structural.

The Personal versus the Professional

I have particularly despaired of learning how to make adequate time for my professional life without disconnecting from the relationships that have sustained me on an emotional level. This was true of my life with an unsupportive husband as well as with a kinder one. It has been the same whether there were one, two, or three children in the house. From the moment my first child was born until the present, I have felt continuously that I was doing my professional and intellectual work on the run, always with one hand tied behind my back. I remember only brief periods in the span of my career—periods that lasted at most only a couple of months—that I have felt free of the psychological and temporal intrusions of managing a household, free of the demanding and intricate emotional and physical connections to husband and children. This has meant that I have not been able to focus completely on ideas and on my own creative abilities in the same intense way that I was able to do so in college and early graduate school. I have had to learn to think about my work while moving in and out of the trivia of daily life, switching gears at will. Of course adulthood demands these skills, and there are times when this balancing act has worked better than others. But I have always felt more emotionally and intellectually constrained than my male colleagues seem, whose wives care for their children, or my female peers who do not have families. The responsibilities of engaged parenting—especially when only one partner in a marriage is required to attend to them— are overwhelming only occasionally, but they are most definitely constant, and they work in myriad ways to pull one away from serving the demands of the academy.

I think it only fair to point out that I have been deeply complicit in this situation. Those who think that my difficulties might have been alleviated by good help and a caring partner do not understand the complexity of the problem. As rare and as necessary as those two things are, they are not enough. And it is here that Jean Baker Miller's insight is helpful: Our desire for affiliation is both a fundamental strength and the inevitable source of our predicament. For my part, I have not yet learned—even after twenty years in this business—how to put my work first, to privilege my time over and against that of a husband's, a child's, or even a graduate student's. This has been the source of deep emotional fulfillment as well as a professional Achilles' heel. I have consistently allowed my work needs and my intellectual concerns to move to the back burner. This has never been intentional but is an unanticipated outcome of my delicate balancing act. Though a chronic source of frustration and pain, it was not something I have ever been willing to admit or to discuss with colleagues. Even the larger women's community within academia has not always been congenial to the choices I have made; many would probably disapprove of the way these priorities have affected my scholarly output.

The Structures of Impartiality: Our Workplaces

When Miller says that "women have reached for and already found a psychic basis for a more advanced social existence [but] they are not able to act fully and directly," I think of the structural constraints of academia. Here, too, it seems, I have been complicit in a system that has ultimately hampered my ability to make time for research and writing. From 1988 to 1993 I taught at a university that overworks and underrewards those professors who take seriously teaching, mentoring, and creating affiliation and community. These tasks, to which I gave a great deal of my time, are persistently ignored. Such criteria were, not surprisingly, applied to me, but also to others in my department—more gifted teachers than I—many young, and some of them male. And, indeed, it takes more ingenuity to evaluate contributions toward the building of an intellectual community, or the mentoring of students or younger faculty, than it does to evaluate a piece of written work.

So caring individuals get unfairly exploited, not necessarily out of meanness, but because academic culture mirrors our larger culture's values. We are powerless to change the university as long as Americans hold productive output to be a measure of worth. I have spent a portion of my time as a senior faculty member thinking about and trying to bring about change. Not only have I failed, but I have not even been able to describe what is wrong in a manner that most of my colleagues can understand. I have not learned to speak the language of affiliation and community without appearing to threaten individualism, meritocracy, orderly hierarchy, and free competition.

Over the last few years, academic women have identified difficulties, sought answers, and suggested some practical solutions. Most suggestions are nuts and bolts life-cycle strategies—like stopping the tenure clock or helping to provide affordable day care—that require some sensitivity to the problems parents or those caring for elderly family members face.

Although I support these gradualist changes, gradualism is by definition slow and that makes me pessimistic about our immediate future. I am skeptical as well because I believe a radical restructuring of our entire society's work culture is really needed. The economist Juliet Schor has suggested that we Americans enjoy a high standard of living at the cost of leisure time and a more moderate work pace. She claims that these choices were made for us by the structure of a uniquely American capitalist enterprise.

Thus, only sweeping social changes can put women and men who are also active caregivers and women and men without children on a more equal footing with respect to "choices" about work. One doubts whether our society is prepared to tolerate—or even collectively desires—such changes. They will be costly and will challenge some of our most deeply held values of individualism, equal opportunity, and freedom of choice. Changes are especially difficult to bring about when feminists disagree about what kinds of family and support systems are needed to nurture healthy children.

Thus, while women are increasingly visible in the academy than they were when I received my Ph.D. in 1971, we have, alas, accomplished little in changing our constraining work structures and habits of personal interaction. For this reason, my advice to graduate students is to practice how to endure. Balancing personal and professional demands is difficult. There is no formula for success. One must learn how to commit to self and others without any maps for accomplishing such a goal; one's solutions will be constantly renegotiated. One must be prepared to transcend a work environment that is not likely to be supportive; one must know how to cope with being alone and lonely. Frustration is an inevitable consequence of aspiration. I do believe that there are rewards, but they come at a price. Knowing about that price beforehand may give us the strength to continue to push for change. And push for change we must.

WORKS CITED

Miller, Jean Baker. *Toward a New Psychology of Women*. 2d ed. Boston: Beacon Press, 1986.

Schor, Juliet B. *The Overworked American: The Unexpected Decline of Leisure*. New York: Basic Books, 1992.

Williams, Joan. "Sameness Feminism and the Work/Family Conflict." *New York Law School Law Review* 35.2 (1990): 347–60.

Around 1971

Linda Wagner-Martin

The vomit hit the wallpapered wall opposite the stairway as my five year old came crying down into the lower level. As I sat there at the kitchen table, holding the four month old as she took her customary middle-of-the-night bottle, I wondered how I could face that hostile graduate seminar at 9:00 A.M. But that was the least of my worries: with the seven year old long in bed with a 102° fever, and the baby acting as if something were wrong with her usually hearty appetite, and now the middle child sick with the same damned flu, and their father gone on a two-week business trip, my own queasy stomach demanded attention. Putting the fragile baby down on the floor of the kitchen despite her look of surprise, I rushed for the nearby bathroom and barfed. My five year old moved over to me and looked somewhat horrified as his pillar of strength succumbed just as he had. We laughed together and then barfed again at intervals as the baby cried forlornly in the next room.

At the end of that graduate class, the only woman in it, herself a mother, came to my office to tell me—privately—that she had understood my distractions. The dozen or so men in the course, if they had anything to say at all, commented that they had never had a woman for a teacher—as if sex explained why they couldn't quite figure out my approach to Hemingway, Faulkner, and Dos Passos. It was my worst class ever (but as Tillie Olsen would say, we learn from those experiences, and maybe the horror of it helped me change teaching styles).

Linda Wagner-Martin is Hanes Professor of English at the University of North Carolina at Chapel Hill.

It was the only class I taught so soon after a child's birth—undoubtedly the key was there.

It was an earlier time, 1970 to be exact. The workplace was not unsympathetic to the problems of young women professionals—it simply didn't recognize that women had problems that differed from anyone else's. To use your family's needs to have a schedule changed or to avoid a committee assignment was simply unheard of. Three or four of those early years were darkened considerably because one of my department colleagues was a member of the local school board and single-handedly fought instituting a school lunch program. He insisted that every child have eighty minutes for a noon break so that he or she could have lunch at home (his wife was a full-time homemaker). The nightmare of having to hire a sitter every day that I was on campus so that the kids didn't come home to an empty kitchen seemed interminable. Not only did I pay at least twice as much as the going rate for that eighty minutes but the difficulty of finding someone who would interrupt her day to do kitchen duty for my three kids was real. Once the community saw that being the only town in Michigan without a school lunch program was not a mark of pride, it offered a paid lunchroom service, where the children who "had to stay" with their sack lunches from home were treated like pariahs. All three of mine stayed. Life was becoming less of a nightmare.

My memories of the 1970s were nightmares, however, simply—and almost totally—because of our child-care situation. No matter how much I was willing to pay, very few people that I would have hired answered my carefully written ads. "Child care only—no cleaning or laundry. The children's experience is the most important thing in this position." Out of sixty calls, perhaps three women would have done—but luck was with me in each instance. My children had the most wonderful sitters in the world, the last a brilliant older soul who could no longer stand being at home herself because her husband was retired. She arrived three mornings a week at 8:30 in a better car than I drove and was truly the angel in the house. I missed her so terribly the summer that the three children went through the chicken pox (she had had lung cancer and could not be exposed to any such illness) that I realized that she was my support as much as theirs.

After coming from the struggle that finding good child care was, rising out of the cauldron that the responsibility for children became, women of my generation—like those of Tillie Olsen's—understand that in many ways the child-care problem has grown worse. Its visibility has made the lives of professional women even more subject to public scrutiny: Who have you chosen to take care of your valuable children? Where do you take them, bundled in rushed outfits and breakfastless at 8:00 A.M.? Does the guilt you feel as you leave your infant disappear once you are on campus? While none of these answers is anyone else's business, the worst torture comes from within. It is hard to convince yourself that children are resilient. Children like change. Children know you love them even if you leave them to go to work. What kind of guilt trip is this, that society keeps hammering away at us, when all we are trying to do is earn a living, do our work, have it all? What had ever been wrong with having it all?

I have just returned from my oldest child's wedding some twelve hundred miles away. He is twenty-nine and none the worse for the parade of baby-sitters he grew up with. Neither is my other son, a graduate student with his own business on the side; or my daughter, also a graduate student. I mention the three of them not only because I am so proud of them but also so you can take heart from the obvious fact that children do mature, they do become the kinds of people you hoped they would be, whether you took care of them every hour of every day or someone else did. In fact, they may turn out better because of the latter. What this means for today's inflexible, taciturn, and prudish workplace attitudes—as people give you that cold eye and say, "I could never leave my children that way," or whatever the current locution—is that we *can* vanquish them, our self-righteous and envious colleagues who believe our place is in the home as well as our own self-divided conscience. But damn, it takes years of anguish.

Single Parent Manuevers in Academia

Susan O'Malley

"And are you pregnant?" asked the woman as I sat in the draft board with my husband in New Orleans. It was August 1966. I was twenty-three years old and preparing to take my doctoral exams at Tulane University. Suddenly there was a wrench in my plans: my husband was to be sent to Vietnam. Being a somewhat self-possessed Northerner in the deep South, I replied, "No, but give me ten minutes." (At that time paternity kept a man from being drafted.) I'll never forget the shocked look on her face. Ten months later on June 22 my first child, Catherine Ragan O'Malley, was born.

Fortunately being pregnant didn't hinder my performance on my doctoral exams. A fine undergraduate education at Smith College and two years at Tulane taking courses filled in whatever gaps I had in English and American literature. Pregnancy caused me to sleep a lot while preparing for my comprehensives. Although my supervisor worried that I would give birth during my class, I assured him that I had everything under control. Mine was to be a June baby, and I would get my Ph.D. in three and a half years. I felt so confident that I accepted a position at Tulane for the fall, the first woman to teach full-time in the English department.

The summer after my daughter was born was painful. My husband, who was also a graduate student in English at Tulane, had won a Danforth Fellowship at the Shakespeare Institute. I spent that summer nursing a colicky baby, cooking for masses of institute fellows who

Susan O'Malley is a professor of English at Kingsborough Community College, City University of New York.

never seemed to leave our apartment, and thinking longingly about my dissertation, abandoned out of exhaustion. It was not surprising that when I took my daughter for her six-week checkup, the doctor said, "The baby is doing well, but the mother is not."

The next year was also difficult. I grew to enjoy motherhood, but the possibility of finishing my dissertation grew dimmer. I taught twelve hours of classes a week and shared an office with Aline Taylor, who had been brought over from Newcomb, the women's college, because it was believed that a woman should not share an office with a man. Professor Taylor was a formidable eighteenth-century scholar who, of course, had no children. At the end of the year I resigned. I simply could not do it all, and I realized I would never finish my dissertation at this pace. My marriage was also unraveling. To complicate matters my husband's graduate advisor and our close friend told me not to finish my dissertation because it would ruin my marriage. Shortly afterward, he made a pass at me that I graciously evaded.

Because we never had enough money, I agreed to teach part-time the following year at Louisiana State University, now known as the University of New Orleans. If you had asked me to list my priorities during 1968–69, I probably would have said, "kids, politics, graduate work, and marriage."

Then somehow in February I got pregnant again while using birth control pills. We had wanted a second child, but not quite so soon. Not knowing I was pregnant, I had already agreed to teach full-time again the following September. Because I knew that I would be fired if it were discovered that I was pregnant, I held in my stomach the rest of the term and told no one. In September with my baby due in November I couldn't hide it. The chair of the English department reacted in dismay, but I assured him that I could handle it. The baby would be born during Thanksgiving, and my husband would teach any class I might miss. And that is what happened. Brendan O'Malley was born at 6:00 P.M. on November 18, 1969. I had taught the previous evening and was preparing to go to work on the day he was born when I felt the familiar twinges. That day my class was called off, but no other classes were canceled. My husband took over my classes, and I was back teaching in two weeks because there was no maternity leave. I was exhausted, but I did not know what else to do.

When my son was a few months old, our car ceased working, which was disastrous since my breastfeeding schedule was dependent on it. Once I took my infant son with me and let him breastfeed under my shawl while I was going over a paper with one of my students. I pretended that there was no baby, but unfortunately Brendan smacked his lips while he sucked. My young male student looked quite alarmed, but I refused to acknowledge the presence of my baby. Too often the experience of mothering in academia for me was pretending my children did not exist.

I continued to teach, the women's movement with its liberating energy erupted in New Orleans, we bought a house and lived in a commune that started a free school, our marriage continued to unravel, and I simply couldn't finish my dissertation. It seemed to me that to be happy I needed children, a career, and an intimate relationship, but I knew no woman who had managed this.

Finally in May 1971 I decided that if we were not doing better, I would leave my marriage on September 23, the date of my first fall adjunct paycheck. Of course, agonizing chaos erupted as soon as I left with the children. I thought my life was over (there was no divorce in my family; in fact, my mother told me succinctly, "marriage is to endure"). But somehow my leaving gave me permission to finish my dissertation. I knew I would have to support my children financially, and I would need a full-time university position to do it. We were poor: my adjunct salary was only four thousand dollars a year, occasionally supplemented by my husband's one hundred dollar a month contribution.

Nine years after I had begun my degree, I finally received my Ph.D., amid cheers of "Yea Mummy!" by my children and their friends seated in the audience. As soon as I knew my Ph.D. was imminent, I made a half-hearted attempt to secure a tenure-track job. I accepted a position at Kingsborough Community College, much to the disgust of the Tulane English department. R. P. Adams sneered at me: "At least if you are getting raped, you're doing it for a good salary." I held my tongue, realizing how little older tenured faculty knew of the job situation. In fact, my initial salary was pathetic: I made $13,970 for the first four years because of the financial problems of New York City and because I didn't have enough sense to bargain. The following year I received a call from the Tulane English department urging me to apply for the Renaissance position at Millsaps College in Jackson, Mississippi, but by that time I was too enamored of New York to consider leaving.

I was adamant that I wanted a "mother's" schedule: no teaching before 9:00 A.M. or after 3:00 P.M. Teaching at a community college was probably more compatible with raising children than teaching at a four-year college. My children did not need to be as invisible as they had been, for I was definitely not on the fast track. But I insisted that they get sick only on Thursday, my day off. If the doctor demanded that they stay home, I would carry their sleeping bags into my office, where they would spend the day. With fifteen hours of teaching many composition and few literature courses, I worked until 2:00 A.M. four nights a week to prepare for classes and mark papers.

I had arrived when New York City threatened to go bankrupt. For the following five years my reappointment was always uncertain. There were forty tenured professors in the English department, and no one was hired after me for six years. I lived in a state of perpetual uncertainty. My chairman, worried about my leftist, feminist politics, said that I had to write a book on the Renaissance for tenure and that articles on pedagogy or women studies wouldn't count. I had become editor of the socialist/feminist journal *Radical Teacher*, which was criticized as poorly written and a waste of time. I heeded the warnings: My dissertation was published as a book, I received university research grants and an NEH summer seminar grant, and I never mentioned *Radical Teacher*. I chaired every committee I could and achieved superlative ratings. Then in October 1979 I was denied tenure, much to the shock of my colleagues, who had supported me unanimously.

In the spring I managed to get a substitute line for the following academic year in the American studies department at SUNY–Old Westbury. This took some of the pressure off. In July the employee's union, which had previously been optimistic about getting my job at Kingsborough back, said the situation was hopeless and that I should try whatever contacts I had. First, I wrote to Carol Bellamy, who was chair of the city council. Next, the union arranged a meeting for me with the president. I was finally granted tenure on the condition that I leave Kingsborough for four years to teach at LaGuardia Community College, a campus with fewer tenured faculty and much more radical politics.

Now thirteen years later a full professor tenured at Kingsborough, I have developed a varied academic life of teaching composition and Shakespeare at Kingsborough, women's studies at City College's Center for Worker Education and occasionally at the Graduate Center, editing a newsletter for the CUNY Faculty Senate, chairing the local union chapter, and becoming more involved in Renaissance women's studies. My children are doing well. Ragan, the mother of two daughters, is in a doctoral program in comparative literature. Having graduated from college, Brendan teaches in Mississippi.

Should I discourage my daughter from an academic career? When she wanted to state on her graduate application that she had a baby, I cautioned her not to. Although there are maternity and paternity leaves, having children is still not looked upon positively. Somehow we need to revive a sense that children are the responsibility of the community and not an impediment to a woman's life. Above all we need to develop the awareness that raising children is an important part of many academic women's lives and that children should not be rendered invisible.

Initially, I didn't want to write this account of parenting and the academy. I felt I didn't have much to say; besides it all happened so long ago. But I think the real reason I didn't want to write my story is that it was too painful. While I was writing this, I would cry quietly, and I don't cry easily. Why was it all so painful when raising my children and my teaching are the two things I'm most proud of in my life?

Today I Couldn't Get Here from There: A Latina Mother's Journey

Mercedes Lynn de Uriarte

I was a teenage mother, statistically among the most unlikely to become the highest ranking Latina in mainstream print newspapers or a tenured professor at one of the nation's respected universities. But in another time and political mindset, enough components of assistance allowed not just me, but also my two children, to become college graduates with advanced degrees. Now I watch the deconstruction of all the programs that meant self-sufficiency and accomplishment for me and for my family. Today I couldn't get here from there, where I began. Nor, I doubt, could my children and I have become significant contributors to society and to our professional fields.

About thirty years ago, I entered a local community college in Orange County, California. It was the early years of the women's movement, which later endorsed such ventures by nontraditional students. But then I was an anomaly. Born in the United States and raised in Mexico where my father's family had been since 1838, I felt most comfortable surrounded by Mexican customs. Almost a decade before, I'd graduated from high school in Mexico and in the interim had two children and a troubled marriage. I was then in transition to single head-of-household status and, although I did not know it then, would soon become sole support as well. Along with a stack of new books and a craving to absorb them all, which surprised me with its intensity, I carried a great many insecurities. As I tried to cope with conflicting

Mercedes Lynn de Uriarte is an associate professor at the University of Texas at Austin.

demands and desires, I discovered a growing outrage at the gap between cultural mythologies and social realities.

Enrolled at the time were three other women older than the recent high school graduates who filled the typical classroom. All of us were oddities in a system with little give for the unusual. Financial aid was restricted to those who would graduate before the age of twenty-seven. Scholarship applications provided space for recent high school triumphs. Some majors required courses not offered before 3:00 P.M., when those of us with children had to be home. Most faculty were male and many had little or no tolerance for deadlines missed because of family responsibilities. When illness forced my aging grandparents to live with me—an eventuality long before agreed upon—a number of people offered unsolicited arguments on the practicality of convalescent hospitals. Fortunately, the older doctor that I turned to for health care posed a simple question: "Which is better: that your grandparents live a little shorter time among loving family members or have a few more months in institutional surroundings?" So I remained true to Latino family values in making my decisions. I often did assigned reading with my grandmother dozing in a nearby chair.

But acquiring an education repeatedly became a matter of juggling cultural imperatives that warred across a gap widened by Latino, white, female, parental, aspirational, and survival components. At the core was a struggle to keep from being overwhelmed by cultural values hostile to family responsibilities as much as a struggle to internalize necessary subject matter. Try explaining to a Spanish-language professor whose test you missed that your son's favorite snake had impaled itself on a jagged wire in its cage and had to be freed before it thrashed itself to death. Social assumptions, like media images, made difference odd. Women with families stayed home and contemplated the wax shine on their floors. They didn't spend hours in research libraries or march in protest against the Vietnam war, Watergate, voter limitations, proposed citizen identification cards—or debate the merits of Chicano studies. On the other hand, stay-at-home wives didn't have a chance to cross the chasm between 1960s students and the older generation whose values they scorned. It was a time of applied theory—textbook democracy, social studies exercises kneaded daily. Altruism was not uncommon. Not since has course content seemed so relevant. Although many attribute my success to personal ambition, the truth is that my aspirations were mostly generated by a desire to provide my children a life of wider choices and a determination to spend as much time as possible parenting. Absent role models, my children became my incentive, they and an idealistic faith in what this nation could become. It was a time to practice courage.

Close in age to both Cristina and John, I loved doing things with them and planning things for them to share with friends. Divorce moved us a step away from welfare. Two years later, when my former husband moved leaving no forwarding address, court-ordered support, or health insurance coverage, the fragility of single-parenting security was a nightly worry after Cristina and John went to bed. The possibility of financial disaster was terrifying. In that pre-homelessness epidemic era, I conjured visions of having to wander in search of shelter. Even today, I cannot pay bills, balance budgets, or discuss expenditures in the evenings.

One recurring question then was whether I had the right to go to school instead of taking a menial or dead-end office job to assure a constant, albeit inadequate, paycheck. In the end, one of the determining factors was the ability to structure an academic schedule that allowed more parenting time, to be at home when they returned from school, for instance. When I began attending community college classes, I did course assignments between 3:00 A.M. and 7:00 A.M. every day. Five years later, the week I graduated with one B.A. degree in comparative literature and one in American studies, my daughter received her high school diploma and my son finished middle school. My father flew up from Mexico for the occasion and helped us begin packing for Yale, where I had been granted admission.

Two months later, our U-Haul truck pulled onto a national highway bound for New Haven. On the sides, Cristina and John had painted slogans: "Yale or Bust!" "Eastward, ho!" All those I held most dear and all we owned were aboard. Towed behind was a Volkswagen bug, with a cat, a dog, and two snakes riding east. We were an unlikely sight for those awaiting gothic college structures—but we were on our way. Silently I tried coping with simultaneous feelings of exhilaration and irresponsibility. Before us, I was convinced, lay endless possibilities, no guarantees, and perhaps pitfalls. We were headed out with no more than the barest of resources and the boldest of assurances.

A Ford Foundation Fellowship for minority graduate students made advanced education possible. For those who survived a national competition, Ford paid tuition and provided a $300 book allowance and a stipend of $350 a month, plus $50 additional for each child. Within my group of Ford Fellows were the sons and daughters of farm workers, janitors, small businessmen in minority communities. We were all the first generation in our families to attend college. Most of us would not have been there without the progressive and liberal activists of the past. Personally, I have never understood how educational issues could be perceived as radical politics. Empowering individuals to work for a living seems like conservative common sense. Still, a lot of Americans define education as a privilege and try to keep it to themselves.

From that era of financial aid came the Latino educational, business, and political leaders of today—former California legislator Gloria Molina, former New Mexico governor Tony Anaya, former cabinet member Henry Cisneros, Department of Education attorney Norma Cantú, historian Rodolfo Acuña, CBS correspondent Juan Vasquez, editor and writer Elizabeth Martinez, playwright and movie producer Luís Valdez, and many more.

For almost all minority students, financial aid was necessary to bring income up to subsistence level. We used the Pell grants now under threat of being eradicated. For us they bought groceries, shoes, and winter coats. But they also provided an ironic slice of humor—although they were created to open access across class lines for the nontraditional student, their originators had a rigid view of the nontraditional. Within three years, all three of us were in college and each academic term, when I filled in the Pell form box that asked the size of the family and how many were in higher education, I carefully answered: 3. With an asterisk I footnoted the entry and added an explanation. Regardless, each year the applications were returned for correction since the programmed computer check did not accept that all members of a family could be in school at the same time. Money was always delayed.

But computer forms were the least of direct and symbolic resistance to a changing world where expanded opportunities changed the demographics of the campus. At Yale, during the early seventies, alumni objecting to the admission of women and minorities withheld their donations, plunging the institution into financial crisis and forcing a redesign of student-loan packages. In 1972, when I arrived with almost 5,000 other students, fewer than a quarter of the undergraduates were women and fewer than 200 were minorities. I was 1 of 11 Latino graduate students; 10 were male. Then, nationwide, only a tiny percentage of all graduate students were Latinos or African American. In fact, when a census count was begun by the American Council on Education in 1981, of the 31,357 Ph.D.'s granted that year, 1,013 were awarded to African Americans and 464 to Latinos. Ten years later, of the 37,451 doctorates awarded, 993 were to African Americans and 708 to Latinos—ample testimony to the slow, lumbering effect of affirmative action.

Sometimes minority graduate students, surrounded by a wealth with which we had no previous experience, would wonder if all this was a good idea. Was this education provided by a foundation and a university hoping to empower its marginalized groups? Or was it embracing its best students knowing that the experience would assimilate and co-opt potential future minority leadership? All those hallowed halls, where would they lead us in the end?

Resistance to diversity didn't always come from anticipated quarters. In a preview interview at Yale, a female dean of students had suggested that I reconsider graduate school there. "You people do better in the Southwest," she said. And the idea that I was bringing children with me met with her strong disapproval. I was a rare sole-support, single-parent, female graduate student in Yale's history, although females had been attending Yale officially since 1892. Signals that I was unwelcome often came from expected directions. Within the first few months, white women in my department sent me a multipage letter on yellow, legal notepaper advising me that I was not Ivy League material. Perhaps the foreshadowing of our estrangement began in roundtable discussions of feminism where they typically focused on equal pay for equal work issues and I focused on equal rights to housing, decent schools, credit access, and the opportunity for minority women to be more than someone's domestic help while others did "real" work. Their greatest complaint, besides my alleged cultural incompatibility, was that I put my family first. To prove my worthiness of Yale, they suggested that I limit interactions with my son and daughter to certain periods of the day, to be determined by a sign-up sheet on my bedroom door.

As isolating as these experiences were, they provide insight into the current academic scene, where the situations of minority women have remained virtually unchanged. The proportion of white female faculty women jumped from 24 percent to 28 percent between 1981 and 1991, while the proportion of nonwhite women rose from 3 percent to only 4 percent. Moreover, the future promises a similar pattern: Of all doctorates earned by women in 1981, white women earned 86 percent and African-American women earned 6 percent. In 1992, they earned 88 percent and 5 percent, respectively. Latinas earned 189 Ph.D.'s in 1981 and 353 in 1992, even fewer than those earned by African-American women ("A Troubling Picture"). As Nancie Caraway notes in *Segregated Sisterhood,* there is a need to "'subvert the culture of whiteness' which feeds on a supremacist ideology" (22). In the workplace, some management consultants say that tensions between minority women and white women are a serious issue. This is particularly troubling as the nation's demographics change, heading toward a population that will soon be 50 percent minority.

My decision to go to college kept us in a financially fragile state, constantly suspended somewhere between pending possibilities of disaster and the next financial aid award. Although getting an advanced degree in the interest of a better future sounded reasonable in a society greatly controlled by culturally fostered ideas of deferred gratification, it made a lot less sense in the daily world of parental responsibilities to children dependent on adults for security. And even less in a homogeneous youthful, affluent, campus society.

Mostly it was lonely—both intellectually and socially. Aside from a brief romance with an administrator, my company was mostly family. Like many of my counterparts, one of our largest expenses was the phone bill for calls back home. The joint Latin American studies/American studies program I devised was as much a search for reaffirmation of self as it was an academic experience. On the pages of Mexican novels I found echoes of my family, its historical context, and the nation's assertive women. In American sociology I found labels for the alienation I felt even as I looked for access to a gratifying professional role. My personal and intellectual life was full of contradictions. Yale provides its students a richness of special programs in the arts, research opportunities, political forums, and assorted role models enviable anywhere. My children were surrounded by assets none of us had imagined. Nevertheless, the role of parent became entwined with feelings of guilt. Parents on limited income become the naysayers to even the smallest pleasures that other children enjoyed—no vacations, limited Christmases, few new dresses for a pretty teenager going on dates, no driver's licenses that would bring higher insurance rates, and no margin for emergencies.

My Ford stipend didn't stretch across all my expenses. Yale discourages graduate students from working except in assistantships, so I had loans. Despite the best planning, emergencies happen. On the second day of my second semester at Yale, my car was hit head-on by a drunk driver who crossed into my lane. Both my son and I went partly through the Volkswagen windshield, newly purchased groceries flying from the back seat to pummel us. We were both injured. The loss of the car made life significantly more difficult. We had to give up our cheaper-rent house to move closer to campus. But that was nothing compared to the disruption of family the accident caused. There was no institutional support system. No one inquired after us. No one offered to help or pointed out services or benefits of which we might take advantage. We truly lived on the fringes of Yale, an institution that had no need to provide safety nets for its elite clientele.

Yale had no medical-leave policy. But even if it had, there was no way that I could stop attending classes and forgo my stipend. I navigated through that semester on pain pills and spent the summer in traction therapy in Mexico. And then, with an agony I can still feel as I write, I left my thirteen-year-old son with my parents so I could continue to bring in an income but otherwise restrict my activities while I healed. The loss of that year with John was the greatest price I ever paid for an education. Psychologically, I still seek ways to recover that lost time.

That fall, however, brought another satisfaction. My daughter began her studies as an undergraduate at Yale in the second of freshman classes to admit women. Today she not only holds a cum laude degree in intense sociology from Yale but also a Harvard Ph.D. She is now an associate chair at California State University in Los Angeles. In 1978, she and I were the first mother-daughter team to ever share Yale graduation ceremonies, mine a master's and hers a B.A. By then my son was in one of the first Vassar classes to accept men. Now he is working on a Ph.D. in visual anthropology.

Although I eventually completed my doctorate, I left Yale in 1977, when job offers were scarce and when I could no longer justify the financial stress created by my continued study, especially since both the academy and financial aid policies worked against the impoverished. So I accepted a job offer from the *Los Angeles Times* before finishing my dissertation. Like most minorities who did not complete Ph.D. programs, economics made the difference. Had it not been for Ford, for Pell grants, and for National Defense Student Loans, none of us would have ever gone to college.

I leave behind a trial of firsts that testify as much to absence as to accomplishment. While at the *Los Angeles Times,* I was the highest ranking Latina in mainstream journalism, the first to receive an Alicia Patterson Fellowship (one of the most prestigious awards available to journalists), the first Latina journalist to receive a Fulbright or a Kellogg Fellowship. I was the only minority in the College of Communication when the University of Texas hired me away from the press corps. Because I hold an elected office in the Association for Education and Mass Communication, I have been the highest profile Hispanic in journalism education—a field where, according to academic surveys, fewer than two dozen Hispanics teach nationwide. I am now the senior woman in the journalism department, the senior minority in the college, and one of five tenured Latinas on a faculty of more than 2,300.

This statistical profile of silence and absence, shared by many underrepresented professors, has as its subtext the isolation of being different in a largely conformist society. Missing is the discourse that acknowledges the translation of risk-taking into the loneliness of sole responsibility and the worry that your ambition could cost your children's security and initiative. At what point does one generation's liberation come at the cost of the independence and originality of the next? Can children put at an early age into child care, for instance, resist conformity? If not, from where will society's rebels come?

As a nation, we are still far from comfortable with diversity, far from accepting difference. What we have seen most often in the past twenty years is only a limited inclusion on the easiest terms: genetic distinctions with intellectual conformity and conservatism, people who look different, but think the same. The rise of Justice Clarence Thomas and Texas attorney general Dan Morales are among the best known examples of this phenomenon.

Inequity breaks severely across class lines, with American minorities disproportionately represented among the poor. Since the United States has become the most stratified of industrial nations, I am struck again by how narrow the passage to opportunity and how short-lived it was for those of us marginalized by race, ethnicity, and economic limitations.

WORKS CITED

American Council of Education. *Minorities in Higher Education.* Washington, D.C.: American Council of Education, 1982.
———. *Minorities in Higher Education.* Washington, D.C.: American Council of Education, 1992.
Bernstein, Alison, and Jacklyn Cock. "A Troubling Picture of Gender Equity in Academe." *Chronicle of Higher Education* June 15, 1994: B1.
Caraway, Nancie. *Segregated Sisterhood: Racism and the Politics of American Feminism.* Knoxville: University of Tennessee Press, 1991.

Motherhood Is Not an Entry-Level Job

Karen Brodkin

At college in 1959, I was very much a child of the suburban fifties. I married at nineteen, young even for those days. Marriage was really less a decision for me than an expectation, a necessary part of the way one became an adult and a woman. But my mother worked at something she loved and I saw marriage as giving me the space to have a career I enjoyed without being pitied as unattractive or excluded as uncoupled. Graduation marked my entry to adulthood and its responsibilities. My parents, my mother-in-law, and my husband all let me know they wanted me to have a baby. I felt selfish, immature, and not a proper woman because I was not ready for motherhood.

I was determined to be a good mother but was scared and not at all prepared for it, having little sense of myself as an adult outside the world of school and political activism. My life changed radically with motherhood. Guilt at not having a child was replaced by a guilt (still with me) at being a bad mother and a selfish person for pursuing—really for *enjoying*—my work.

I was determined to prove myself as a mother. I wanted to do it right, starting with natural childbirth and nursing. My husband and I took a Lamaze course and were well prepared. The University of Michigan hospital, however, was hostile to my agenda. Partners, even if they were of the opposite sex and certified by the state, were not allowed in the delivery room, and I was wheeled off, hands strapped down, feet up in the stirrups, glasses removed, to "deliver" my baby.

Karen Brodkin teaches anthropology and women's studies at UCLA.

Benjamin was stunning and I was quite entranced with him, but I was also scared because he was so little and seemed so fragile. When Benjamin was ten days old we discovered that he had a birth defect for which he had to be hospitalized twice.

Even the early women's liberation movement, though not exactly anti-motherhood, in practice treated mothering as if it were a woman's private issue. A feminist machisma underlay our attitudes. Machismo was a disease of the student Left, but women shared in the general romanticization of toughness—one had to be willing to sacrifice, to glory in it. Even as feminists criticized these aspects of male progressive politics, we also bought into them. I was certainly at war with myself. I could not let go of either motherhood or my academic and political identity. I needed to be a mother to be a woman and a mature grown-up, and I needed an academic and political identity to save me from being boxed into the truncated life that I saw as the fate of a proper mature woman.

I was recruited for my first tenure-track job at Oakland University before I'd begun to write my dissertation. I took it because it had excellent medical benefits, which were important because I was pregnant with Daniel, my second child, and because it was a leftist, activist-oriented department. The senior sociologist in the department was anything but progressive. He told me shortly after I was hired, "I always like to hire lefties and women; you can get 'em cheap and they work hard." He was right on both counts. My salary of $9,500 was $500 less than that of a male colleague with the same qualifications, hired at the same time.

One late August afternoon I returned from a new faculty orientation to find that Benjamin, who was then almost two years old, had been hit by a car. He was in the hospital, and Bill, my husband, was with him. I was in shock at first, but somewhat reassured that Benjamin was conscious and that nothing was broken. But he wasn't getting better and he wasn't looking or acting normal.

In desperation I called Benjamin's most regular pediatrician at Wayne County Hospital, the nearest clinic my student insurance paid for. When the receptionist told me the doctor wasn't available and wouldn't give me his home number, I got hysterical. The next thing I knew, Benjamin's doctor was on the line. Benjamin went by ambulance directly to surgery.

Benjamin remembers some of his hospital stay; so do I. After he got out of intensive care, he was in a crib in the nursery, a big, open room with many cribs and many very sick and dying infants. Bill and

I were at the nursery from the time Benjamin woke up until he went to sleep for the night. During the day we took turns leaving to teach our respective classes at our respective universities. In those years hospitals did not have facilities for parents to stay with their children. Then and now, I feel as if I abandoned Benjamin by sleeping at home. I also feel guilty that I continued to teach. I asked for a leave, but my chair said I would have to take the whole semester without pay or meet my classes from the beginning of the semester.

My waking life consisted of the nursery and my classes. I was always on the edge of fear when I went home at night and anxious to get to the hospital in the morning. Months later, I had a conversation with the wife of a radical faculty member. She said she was pleasantly surprised that I was such a nice person. She had surmised that I must be a monster to go calmly about teaching while my child was at death's door. I don't remember what I said, but I felt like I'd been stabbed.

Daniel was born two months after Benjamin came home from the hospital and just after I'd graded about one hundred essay exams. My request for maternity leave was shrugged off as unreasonable by my chair. However, my colleague Peter Bertocci offered to teach my classes for as long as I needed to rest. It was a lifesaver. I took two weeks. I remember Daniel's birth as unalienated labor and quite intimate despite the hospital setting. The real center of my life in Daniel's early months was trying to mesh his nursing schedule with my teaching schedule. I can't remember what I taught or whether I did a decent job. Fortunately, Daniel was a very happy, easy baby.

The next year, when three students in my introductory anthropology class, all returning women, proposed to persuade the university to set up a child-care center on campus as their class project, I was delighted on personal as well as political grounds. Their project soon became a major campus issue involving faculty and cleaning staff. My job was to solicit the support of the campus maids, most of whom were in their forties and fifties; half were African-American and half were white. Child care was not an issue for these women, although they supported the idea. They really wanted student and faculty support for equal pay with male janitors, who did basically the same work. Child-care activists expanded their demands to include equal pay for maids and janitors.

The campaign heated up when the administration refused to expand the center despite a petition with several thousand signatures. Instead they called an all-campus meeting to present their position.

Those of us who worked on the campaign planned to seize the microphones to explain our position.

I asked the campus maids to participate. Some said they would if they could; others said they would like to but the meeting was on their lunch break, and they did their errands during that time. Some said nothing. I knew from the discussion that no one was going to show up. Finally, one woman said, "Look girls, you know either we're all going to go or none of us will; so which is it?" One woman said, "We only have a half-hour lunch, so we'll have to miss eating." Another asked me if the students could bring them sandwiches. When I said yes, the de facto leader said, "Okay, so we'll all be there and you'll have lunch for us." When they walked into the gym in a body, they seated themselves right in front of the microphones the students had just seized from the president.

This meeting expanded our support greatly. Students then created a one-day child-care center in the president's office to show the need for all-day care. I remember it well and with pleasure; so does Benjamin. Years later he told me that it was the child care he liked best.

This campaign was my first lesson in women's grass-roots decision-making. The maids decided to participate as a group. They had their own informal leader who spoke for them but only when she perceived a consensus. Also, by joining with others for a child-care center, I began to believe that I really was entitled to social support and that it wasn't whining or political to demand it.

The rise of pro-choice politics, of single motherhood among heterosexual women, and of lesbian motherhood among singles and couples indicate that the institution of motherhood is being reconfigured more as a choice than as a defining duty. That is good. But these changes also imply that motherhood is still an entitlement for middle-class women. Talk about women's biological clocks reinforces old notions of birthing and motherhood as defining a woman's life once again. Sometimes it is hard to distinguish women's struggles to reshape motherhood from anti-feminist sanctifications of motherhood.

NOTE

I thank Emily Abel, Sondra Hale, Katherine King, and Nancy Strout for all manner of nurturance and supportive critiques, especially our talks about mothering.

Paul Lauter Interview

Constance Coiner and
Diana Hume George

Paul Lauter: I started graduate school literally the day after I got married. [My wife] finished her dissertation two weeks before our first kid was born. Though we were both in graduate school and we were both on the same career track, we never really thought about the possibility of her getting a job and my following her around.

Constance Coiner: Did you talk about this gendered pattern?

PL: Well, we talked about it a little but not in a systematic fashion. [. . .] As far as taking care of Danny, our younger son, was concerned, it was pretty much my job, especially at night, when he got up a lot. Tris was home with the kids all day. [. . .] I got home a little crazy from school and she was a little crazy from these two babies. I did most of the cooking. At that time neither of us had anything to do with nor any knowledge of feminist politics.

Diana Hume George: At work did you have a sense of what it was like to be a dad? Could you talk about it with your friends who were fathers?

PL: I never felt any awkwardness about that; it's just something you never talked about. It wasn't an entirely male department; there was at least one woman. Feminist ideas weren't even on the screen. Nowhere in sight, certainly as far as we were concerned in the late fifties and even into the sixties. [. . .]

Paul Lauter is Allan K. and Gwendolyn Miles Smith Professor of Literature at Trinity College. This interview took place at the American Studies Association Conference, Pittsburgh, October 1995.

DHG: [. . .] You and Tris broke up in what year?

PL: Summer of 1963. The kids were four and five.

DHG: From then on you were a weekend dad?

PL: They were with me on all school holidays, including summer.

DHG: And neither of you thought in terms of Tris having a Ph.D. from Yale or your following her to a job.

PL: Well, *I* didn't think differently, and if she did, she didn't say anything.

DHG: I know it's hard to explain to someone else, or even to oneself, how you didn't think of these things. You have called that a function of historical amnesia.

PL: If you don't have ideas, an alternative to what exists, then you're stuck in what exists. If you don't have those alternative ideas available, then you must be really a remarkable person to be able to think through alternatives for yourself.

CC: And of course those alternatives had been systematically erased from education.

PL: Yes, in particular, for an example of that, when I was working as the director of this community school project in Washington in 1967, one of our problems was, as far as the parents were concerned, that they knew what school was: the students sat in their places with their hands folded, kept their mouths shut, answered if they could when they were called upon; otherwise, they sat and were good little boys and girls, and that was the beginning and the end of it. We wanted to introduce a much more open classroom, much more interactive, get the kids involved. It was very hard to get the parents even to consider those ideas, because those were not ideas they were familiar with in any way. [. . .]

On the other side, for me, in part because my mother was such a strong figure, the notion of doing such things as cooking was no problem. I had to do it for myself during the summers, during high school when I was alone. [. . .]

CC: Talk about your mother. What kind of effect did she have on your life?

PL: She's a very strong lady, a strong person who when I was young worked outside the home and then went back to work before my father died, which was in 1959. She worked as a librarian for many years. Even within the household it was likely to be my mother who took the tool box and fixed things. So it wasn't that I had a model of my father doing things like cooking, quite the contrary. I have the model of my mother playing a more traditionally male role.

DHG: Sort of cross-gendered mothering.

PL: Yes. It seems to me that I didn't have very strongly fixed notions of gender.

DHG: So it was possible, when these ideas finally got out there, for you to be among the first generation of men to not experience much resistance.

PL: That sounds reasonable. There's another element to this thing which has to do with the intensely repressive character exemplified by the use of the word *queer*. There once was a time when such things really limited what you did. [. . .]

DHG: So you would do your job wherever you were and you would come home and participate in daddying when you were in your marriage and differently when your marriage ended—but you never thought you had to choose between being a father and having a career.

PL: I did, too, in a sense. The kids were with Tris during the school times, so the everyday life and problems of child rearing were hers. [. . .] We made the divorce agreement that I would be sending them $200 a month. I then left to go to Chicago in 1965; they started coming and staying, and I had to have an apartment big enough for them to stay. It was a process of working it out. It didn't just happen. It seemed natural to me that they would be with me during the school holiday, and they would retain my name even after she got remarried. What I'm saying is that they were with me during those times that it was easiest for me to deal with them.

CC: Did they stay with you during the whole summer?

PL: They would generally be with me during the whole summer. [. . .] It was a situation in fact when they were mine on demand. It was not a situation in which Tris could say, "Here, take them for such and such time." In that sense it was fairly one-sided.

CC: So did you continue to have a good relationship with both of your sons?

PL: We have a relationship. I don't think it's terribly good—it's pretty good in a pretty distant way. We go literally sometimes a couple of months without talking to one another. We don't write very often. I correspond with David now on e-mail. The way things emerged, the way they developed as they grew up, we did not talk regularly during the time that they were with Tris because, you see, for me to talk regularly with them would have meant calling her, and I found that hard. So there would be substantial periods of time in which we just didn't talk, so I was really not a participant in their daily life at all. We were very distant from that.

CC: Do you feel that had you had daily contact, you would have an intimate relationship with them?

PL: I'm not saying that, I'm just saying that it didn't work out that way. It may well be that they didn't want that kind of intimacy, and I didn't either. On the one hand, you are saved the agonies of dealing with adolescence. The downside was that I really wasn't involved in their lives.

DHG: Your not having been involved deeply in their growing up— well, you do seem to feel as though this is still costing you in your relationship with them?

PL: I think it does.

DHG: The either/or dilemma that women encounter—the rap is that men don't have to choose, they get to have it all. Your case supports that generalization. But you didn't get intimacy.

PL: Yes. They got used to my not being there and not being involved with them. And it's carried over into today.

DHG: So you, Paul Lauter, American academe's premier male feminist good-guy, have that paternal intimacy problem with your sons.

PL: I probably have a problem with intimacy in general. You know I have a lot of friends, but they're spread across the globe. There are very few that I am close to physically.

DHG: Talk about the line between homosexual and intimate male relationships.

PL: Well, it's related to the question of gender behaviors that are and aren't possible. What I said about cooking, it's okay for a guy to cook because that was like a possible vocation for a man. But if I had brought up the question of a job for my wife in the 1950s, I'm sure the answer would have been that we discourage couples, or nepotism, and even asking for it would probably have been a no-no. The notion of my following a job that she got would have been equivalent to outwardly homosexual behavior. It would have marked a crossing of the line. Now you have notions of bisexuality being, if not accepted, then somewhat tolerated. Until recently it was rather black and white. You either were or you weren't. There were lines that we would cross and we couldn't come back, whereas now you can cross all sorts of lines and come back tomorrow. The tendency in the fifties was to classify "queer" as homosexual. Back then the definitions of what was homosexual were very clear cut.

DHG: And the category of the aberrant would have been sexually defined and would have that in common with sexual orientation. So the lowering of homophobia has led to a greater freedom for what a man can do.

PL: Yes, there's been a relaxation of gender definitions.

DHG: Let's get concrete about effects on policy. Maternal leave is now parental leave. Men and women both can take it. But men statistically *don't*. Is it going to become acceptable for men to take these leaves as well as women?

PL: It depends on what you mean by acceptable. Are you saying that there will not be costs in terms of career possibilities and advancement and that sort of thing? No. In the same way that women are not able to do it without cost. If a man takes parental leave for six months or a year or something, it would not be coded as aberrant or queer, but the result would not be positive for career development.

DHG: He would be perceived as not being all that serious about his career, the same as women are?

PL: Not necessarily a question of being perceived unless he's very good. It's taking time away from work when you're young and aspiring and you have to get out the article and do the reading, go to the conferences—if you're lucky and you get a child that sleeps a lot and with your computer set up at home, the costs might be lower. If you had a kid like mine, if I was staying home to take care of him, at that point it would have meant taking the time out of my career development.

CC: Did you take care of the kids on the weekends along with Tris? So you didn't have time for scholarship, teaching during the day, and taking care of kids at night?

PL: Yes, but once they went to sleep, I would stay up and read and during the day at the office I would go at it.

DHG: Increasingly any serious career track and parent track are becoming incompatible. The institution demands all your time. Realistically speaking, as a former union leader, Paul, during these tight budgetary times, what do you think we can ask?

PL: Like any other policy the question of possibility and affordability is really a question of where you put available resources. There aren't resources to do every- and anything in the world, but there are always resources to do some things, like the federal budget always involves a transfer of funds from any tax policy. So the issue is whether or not the institution chooses it—to do x, how much do you have to take from a and b? Are you willing to do that? What goes along with that in a situation involving a tight economy, but a superfluity of available personal resources is this: So who the fuck cares if so and so wants to be a mommy or a daddy? The difficulty is that if you want to develop a humane policy, then you have to be willing to figure out places in which you are going to withdraw funds in one way or another. [. . .] I think you have to always recast the question—it's not a question of economics, but one of politics. The enormous expansion of colleges and universities during the sixties was for me personally profitable in a direct and indirect way. It meant that I could get a job even if I got active in the antiwar movement. With my Yale Ph.D. and the job market the way it was, I could get a job, but the consequence was that there were too many Ph.D.'s produced for what was to be the future market and now we've got a lot of people.

CC: In this cluttered market, is there any way to put pressure on universities?

PL: I really think it's very hard. I think it puts the burden back on people who are tenured. The problem is that it is a very debilitating process. When Annette Kolodny became dean in Arizona, she cracked a lot of eggs and a lot of people disliked her. [. . .] I think there is a shift in the ideological superstructure that keeps things fixed in the way they are. When I was younger, the ideology had much more to do with gender roles, and that really inhibited change. Now it's got much more to do with the bottom line, notions of economic competition, the global market. Nobody asks why don't companies and nations get together and stop the competitive cycles and try a different path.

DHG: How appropriate is it to ask the university to change their policies, given that parenting is partly a narcissistic decision? People's motivations for having children don't seem to me to be necessarily large-minded. Should we ask colleges to support people's decisions to replicate themselves?

PL: We have to historicize it. For instance, for a female full professor coming out of a Jewish working-class family the idea of becoming a mother was big, you could not be a real woman without being a mother. It's the other side of the gender divide that I was describing before. Tris was absolutely devastated when she had a miscarriage. The very first thing when we moved to Dartmouth was she wanted to have a child. She absolutely had to get pregnant, and she had to have a child. Part of [my next partner's] rage at me was that we didn't have children. Having a child is still considered a necessary part of perpetuating the race and the nation. Then the question is, whose responsibility is it? The choices are very limited. It's either private, workplace, community, or national. There are good things to be said about all of them and bad things.

CC: So you think there's an equally good/bad case to be made for its remaining a private matter?

PL: No, I think that as long as this is seen as a national service, that to privatize the costs of birthing children is to dodge the issue for the state it serves.

CC: It is easier to have children if you have money than if you don't have money.

DHG: I don't know whether it is the academy's responsibility to support it or not, but I do think it must be equal for men and women.

PL: Hmm . . . I don't think about it as the academy, but as the workplace.

CC: Do you think things have not changed in the quality of higher education in the past few years?

PL: It's not that things have not changed in terms of quality. What it means is that the quality of life in American higher education is still a hell of a lot better than whatever else is out there.

CC: But you wouldn't argue that this term *crisis* is a smoke screen.

PL: No, I was talking to Jane Marcus last night. Jane says, for example, nothing works where she teaches in CUNY, bathrooms, escalators, etc. Meanwhile Hunter is spic and span and there's a lot of money going into that. They're draining money off from City College because only blacks go there and putting it elsewhere.

CC: So there is a crisis?

PL: Most definitely, but that isn't to say that American higher education is not better than what else is out there. It is only to say that it is not as good as it was in many places. The line between bottom and top is getting much sharper.

PART TWO

Analysis and Theory

Carolyn Forché Interview

Constance Coiner and
Diana Hume George

Carolyn Forché: Most discussions addressing how women childbearers function, in the workplace and domestically, ignore the larger socioeconomic and political issues and individuate the women and transfer the onus of responsibility for achievement in these areas of life to the individual. That transferal is a species of blaming individuals for predicaments that are socially constructed. Erosion of the sustaining of contemplation and critical thought necessary to academic work is something that serves certain economic forces.

Constance Coiner: Could you identify those forces?

CF: The French poet and intellectual Paul Valery began to identify them when he discussed the evolution of industrial production and analyzed its effects on societies and on human communities and proposed that there would be less and less play in the machine and less and less room for eccentric expression and individual choice. As the twentieth century's agenda has been the will to power, as best thought by Nietzsche, the twenty-first century's agenda will be social control, in the interest of maximizing production, maximizing profits, minimizing loss, and speeding up the machine. To ignore the effects of macroeconomic forces on communities and individuals is madness. I am not interested in advising women about how to adjust to a situation that is fundamentally unjust and inequitable. One of the things that angers me is that there are no solutions acceptable to hegemonic power. [. . .] We're constricted in our thinking when we begin with

Carolyn Forché teaches at George Washington University. This interview took place at Pennsylvania State University at Erie, the Behrend College, October 1995.

the supposition that the task is adaptation rather than resistance and refutation. I don't think I will outlive the period of denunciation, the period of bringing the sin to the eye. I can't begin by advising women that there are artful ways of "having it all," or artful ways of adapting to a situation that is fundamentally unhealthy.

If we talk about women in the academy in the United States, we're talking about an institution that is at once the site of replication of societal structures and a potential site of resistance and disclosure. We're discussing a group of relatively privileged women. One of the things that's so infuriating about the message of the mass media toward women and toward their roles and capacities in the society is the absence of consciousness of the social construction of these conditions. It's as if the past did not create the present and decisions were not made that have had certain effects and results.

Diana Hume George: The academy is taking on corporate values more nakedly. Anyone who doesn't see this is not looking.

CF: There is a national movement to challenge the traditional structures of higher education. That movement would like to corporatize and privatize the structures of the academy, to dismantle structures within the academy which promote and sustain faculty self-governance. They would like to duplicate corporate structures in higher education. They would like to divide higher education between management and labor. They would like to develop a system whereby the professoriat are reduced to contract employees, each negotiating individually their terms with the administration, what would then correspond to corporate management. And they will achieve this on a number of different fronts. Tenure could be abrogated legislatively and that's already been proposed. Everything that I'm saying is based on something that has already happened somewhere. I would suggest that one examine the Pima community college system in Arizona. I would suggest that the professoriat that doubts this take a look at the Arizona system of higher education in general and what has been proposed in California and elsewhere. And one might look at Connecticut and New York as well, in terms of what's been proposed in the legislature. But we're talking about abrogation of tenure, we're talking about the redefinition of the terms of employment for the professoriat, the professoriat not being in control of curricular matters, the erosion of faculty self-governance, and curricular decisions being made much more in accordance with projections concerning the vocational utility of degrees. And those projections are a matter of social engineering as well. What we're going to "need" in the future is an identified need based on corporate projections. We're living in a period defined by corporate culture, which has its own nature, and that's not widely enough examined, in terms of its secrecy, in terms of its hierarchical structures, in terms of its imitation of and usurpation of progressive rhetorics to mask what it is doing.

DHG: Female professors and some of our male colleagues are so exhausted from the demand that speed-up makes in the corporate academy, that they're left too tired to organize effectively. How intentional is this machine?

CF: We all know about the manipulation of statistical data, and one of the interesting aspects of this, for me, is the sheer growth of the ratio of administration to professoriat within the universities. So, we have a growth in administration, and increasing administrative drain on resources available to higher education. And one of the ways in which the professoriat has been fixed for dissection or pinned down has been to reduce the definition of academic labor to FTE [full-time equivalent] equations, which have to do *only* with FTEs and the course-hour student-contact credit ratio. So that the professoriat, no matter what course load and no matter what FTEs emerge in or are part of that equation, everything else that the professoriat is expected to do is submerged and rendered invisible. All the advising, all the thesis supervision, all the dissertation supervision, all the committee work—and there has been a tremendous growth, while we've had a growth in administration, there's been also a tremendous transference of administrative labor to the professoriat, but in an unpaid way. The professoriat is involved with and responsible for many extracurricular activities, most of the symposia, conferences, speakers, and so on that really enrich and nurture academic life on campus. And none of this is counted when academic labor is weighed, when salaries are determined, and when the public is given to examine the life of the professoriat. This gets exponentially worse as you move down the ladder of rank, so that by the time you get to so-called restricted positions or adjunct positions, the vast majority of them women, they work without benefits, without job security, for very low per course payments. And often they are disenfranchised within their own departments and are not given even a modicum of university support. Some of them don't have their own offices. If someone were to study how much of the secret, hidden administrative labor is assumed by women, I wonder if we would find a predominance.

DHG: "Women's work" yet again—charity work—nurturing students, curricula, colleagues, programs.

CF: There are exceptions to this. But I've also noticed the way in which certain faculty begin to understand this system and this structure and the direction that it's moving in and the way that those faculty endeavor to enter the ranks of administration. Once they move to the administrative side of the equation, rather than considering themselves representative of the faculty, and representatives in terms of faculty self-governance, they tend to begin arguing in ways very similar to management in a corporate structure. So I think that the analysis that needs to be done is a euphemology of those structures and a concomitant analysis of the movement to restructure education.

DHG: You came to the academy about five years ago. The assumption would be that Carolyn Forché would do very little drudge work in the academy. You'd be a queen who is highly paid for little in return, so that you *can* sustain the life of meditation that permits your writing.

CF: I'm not denying that that is available to women academics and writers, as well as male academics and writers that have achieved a certain public notoriety. The problem is that, for me, it's not possible. Because I won't give up a modicum of political, social, spiritual, and personal integration in my life. When I was working in El Salvador, it occurred to me for the first time in my life that there were no emotionally unsustainable contradictions in what I was doing in my daily work and what I believed in and how I was living. There were contradictions, of course, but not emotionally unsustainable ones. So that if one activates one's conscience—in the Latin American sense of *conscien-cia,* which is to make conscious and responsible for at the same time, the fusion of consciousness and conscience—then the range of what is supportable emotionally narrows quite a bit. So when I went back into the academy, the last thing I wanted to do was to find myself in an unsupportable state of contradiction. [. . .] And I looked around, and I stayed awake, and I saw what was happening to the academy and in the academy, and what I wanted to do was study it and immerse myself in it, and I certainly did not want not to shoulder the burden with everyone else. The way to experience the academy is actually to do the work. And so I had many students, and what happened to me was that I began to administer and to perform a service both professionally and within my own institution that was similar to what my colleagues, especially women colleagues, were performing. [. . .] Because of my circumstances and my responsibilities to my family—economic and otherwise—I can't say no to a decent salary, but in every other respect, I work as an equal with my colleagues. The other thing is, though, that the responsibility extends to the responsibility of voice. When celebrity allows you to be one of those whose voice is heard, you are deeply responsible for what you say. And you have to say the things that are difficult for others to say because of *their* circumstances.

DHG: What about being a mother in all of this?

CF: Well, Sean changed my life, as children will change lives. For one thing, you are no longer a child. I notice that when I'm working with student poets, their orientation in the world is as children of their parents. Once one becomes a parent—and one doesn't have to actually be a biological parent to achieve this, of course—one changes one's orientation and becomes one of the parents rather than one of the children. The other thing is that to love a child and parent a child is to commend to an uncertain future a being you love more than yourself, and the psychological difficulty of that is enormous and informs everything else that I do. And that is why I have to take action now, because the present is the architect and planner of the future and will deliver to my child and to your child the circumstances in which they will find themselves. And these are not accidental, either. They are intentional, and they have intentional origins. The conscious decisions that are most powerful and those that are most efficacious, in our period, serve the interests of a very selfish economic structure.

DHG: I want to call you on something. You began this by saying that you cannot exhort women to a model of adjustment or adaptation, in an attempt to "have it all"—to have the relationship with the mate, the child, the work—and yet it seems to me that that's exactly what you are saying you have to do.

CF: But I wouldn't admonish others to do it. I would say that one does the best one can. And one tries always to be vigilant over oneself, in terms of that emotional comfort that I mentioned earlier and also one's responsibility, hubris, pride, intellectual arrogance. One always has to be open to the possibility that one is wrong or one is not seeing the picture clearly.

CC: How do women resist this, rather than adapt? Or how do *parents,* assuming we have male allies?

CF: That's why I said that I didn't believe I would outlive the period of denunciation. More people have to openly admit and discuss this and see it as their personal responsibility and concern. I see *fear.* I think that many of my colleagues simply have retreated and would like to protect themselves, and they posit a moment in the future when they will feel secure enough to take action. The problem is that that moment will not come, and that security will not be achieved in any measure that will ever allow them to take action. And that very security will elude their grasp because they fail to take action now, because they feel they have to protect themselves in the academy because they're untenured or whatever, and they're afraid to speak out and confront these issues, both in public and within their own institutions. They may have nothing to confront. In other words, they may lose their opportunity. There is no time *when*. [. . .] There is nothing other than now. And now is the architect of the future. [. . .]

DHG: What would your mate say, hearing you say this right now?

CF: Harry would say, "You must rest" and "You are pushing yourself too hard" and "You're under too much stress" and "You're Sean's mother" and so on. It's fine that he says that, because that's the corrective to what I'm saying. Then I have someone in my life who can remind me of mortality and fatigue and other responsibilities—and that's a balance. But what I see around me is a significant retreat. People are fearful. It is very difficult on my own campus to get any sort of dialogue going regarding these matters.

DHG: So they vote against unionization.

CC: Twelve to 13 percent of labor is unionized in this country.

CF: When shops, plants, or factories had such a struggle to unionize, it was because people were afraid that if they were identified with the union, they would lose their jobs.

DHG: And the professoriat's doing that all over again.

CF: Well, because they also have this peculiar notion of exemption from labor. They don't see themselves as labor, and they *are* labor. And the reason they don't see themselves as labor is because they have bought into Class X conceptualizations. [. . .] Just because they're professionals and because they work with their minds does not mean that they own the means of production and does not mean that they are any more than wage slaves or that they are any more than a paycheck away from the street. And the fact of the matter is that their fears are genuine, and they are the fears of labor.

Out of the Mouths of Babes; or, A Sophist's Choice

Suzanne Diamond

If we are to trust the contemporary social commentary, people are angry, disgruntled as an era of belt-tightening closes down the hopes encouraged by a previous era of possibility. We are informed that we should be concerned about the "angry white men" out there, and perhaps we should. But what about the women? Specifically, what about that supposedly hypothetical woman beating a daily circuit from day-care center to supermarket to the two or three institutions of higher education at which she teaches several sections of an introductory course or two? Where in the pages of our newspapers might we find *her* anger? More pointedly, what has feminism or the academy—two institutions we have come to assume are synonymous with progressive social consciousness—done to speak to this marginal woman's plight?

In this belt-tightening—and crowded—world the idea that one is *entitled* to reproduce is justifiably under scrutiny, though institutions are slow to own their participation in the discouragement of parenting. Would-be professionals who dare to complain about constrictions on either their career or their parental ambitions are vulnerable to the charge that they are just spoiled baby boomers gracelessly confronting the subsequent bust. But neither economic constrictions on parenting, in general, nor professional reactions to such constrictions, in specific, is exactly my topic. What I mean to focus on are the roles that feminism and the academy are playing in this historic shift. I am trou-

Suzanne Diamond is an assistant director of the writing program at Rutgers University and director of its Livingston College Writing Center.

bled by the idea of a contemporary academy that could be accused of knowingly participating in—much less profiting by—students' historically delusionary hopes to one day combine parenthood with academic careers in any traditional definition of the latter category. Ultimately, it would seem, parenthood is institutionally ghettoized, despite rhetoric to the contrary. Being a successful academic, now as ever, usually entails displacing the social labor of reproduction onto a structurally excluded service class. What is most troubling is that the deluded young college population—the economic lifeblood of financially flagging academic institutions—is strikingly, in fact disproportionately, female. This state of affairs proposes not just a feminist dilemma but an ethical one as well. Is it consciouable for academic institutions to accept young women's tuition dollars without being absolutely frank regarding the systematic relegation of mothers to adjunct teaching status? To those who might reply that female would-be academics might "choose" not to parent, I would reply in this way: We cannot turn our backs on the systematic exclusion of mothers from the academy by convincing ourselves that the parenthood that makes them marginal could be the result of anything like free choice. In the first place, women who opt not to parent can hardly be said to have exercised anything as benign as "free choice." In the second place, higher education is dependent upon the reproduced population to which this pertinent sector of its adjunct class contributes. In short, the building numbers of women joining the academy and its ostensible promise of cultural enfranchisement are making the academy's conflict of interest regarding biological reproduction more apparent than it has ever been.

In exploring the dilemma faced by would-be parents in graduate school, I am reminded of a discussion of schizophrenia and depression that occurs, ironically enough, in Ernest Becker's *The Denial of Death*. Schizophrenia, Becker suggests, is a condition characterized by excessive notions of possibility. Depression, on the other hand, is a state of mind induced by an excessive sense of necessity. I suggest that the hidden and diabolical curriculum for an academic would-be parent begins with schizophrenic delusion and progresses to depressive actuality, as Becker characterizes the two.

The delusion persists late into college. In a study of Berkeley students Arlie Hochschild discovered that although most senior men did not intend to share child care and housework equally or to relocate to accommodate a partner's job, 80 percent of senior women anticipated having careers as well as partners and children. According to Hochschild these men do not recognize that most of them will have a partner who works and these women have not seen their future as superwomen (see Smart and Smart 37). Mollie S. Smart and Russell C. Smart contend that "students can be taught about these realities, not only through courses, but also by the example of their professors" (37). To begin with, even casual research indicates that women are in college now in globally unprecedented numbers. As of the late 1980s the Organization for Economic Cooperation and Development has reported that women make up at least half of all students in higher education in Canada, Finland, France, and the United States and at least 40 percent of the enrollment in most other Western industrialized nations (Scully). This report, headlined in the *Chronicle of Higher Education,* goes on to warn in finer print that "there is little reason for complacency over the status of women in education" (Scully 1). Ultimately it suggests that relatively few women attain what it deems the highest educational levels—top scholarships, for instance—even though, according to Liz McMillen, women reportedly now earn more than 50 percent of the doctoral degrees in education, health sciences, psychology, and language and literature (25).

Perhaps this caution against complacency is an attempt to speak to the bleak prospects inevitably faced by women in higher education. This report does not attend, for instance, to a later phase of the educational elimination process: How many of this minority who attain, in the report's terminology, the highest levels of education actually move on from that point to the next logical step: meaningful, full-time, academic employment?

According to Mary W. Gray, professor of mathematics, statistics, and computer sciences at American University and president of the Women's Equity Action League, not many do. In a 1986 interview, she indicates that the picture gets even worse when one looks toward meaningful postgraduate employment. "I strongly suspect," Gray comments, "that there won't be any great influx of women [into academic jobs] in the 1990's." She points out that "the last time there was a big surge of hiring in the 60's and 70's, women were not hired in numbers equal to their proportion" (qtd. in McMillen A1).

When they manage to get hired, moreover, women continue to encounter an academic version of the "glass-ceiling"; "today, women tend to be concentrated in the academic 'proletariat,'" Liz McMillen observes, "in part-time, temporary and non-tenure-track appointments. Nationally, they make up 27.5 percent of the full-time faculty and only 11.4 percent of the full-professors, according to the U.S. Department of Education's Center for Statistics" (25). One need not resemble the proverbial rocket scientist to perceive that something is wrong with the figures. If women are in college in unprecedented numbers, as studies indicate, and if they are achieving some 50 percent of the graduate degrees conferred, what is happening to them between degree and career? Though far more statistical evidence is necessary, the converging anecdotal evidence suggests that they are becoming mothers who wish to combine parenting with professional careers but are thwarted by a culture whose habit is to frame career or motherhood as a mutually exclusive choice.

One striking factor in the analysis of parenthood is the degree to which the job becomes, even in presumably "liberated" circles, a woman's job; Although men are increasingly involved with their children and housework, some commentators argue that they manage far less of the family work than women. According to Arlie Hochschild men in dual-career couples do only about 25 percent of the housework and manage only 20 percent of the domestic affairs. Fathers contribute the same amount of time as mothers toward socializing and educating their children but they spend less time than mothers physically caring for them. For the three types of family work—housework, parenting, and managing domestic life—only 18 percent of the fifty husbands surveyed completed 45 to 55 percent of it (see Smart and Smart 34).[1]

But this was the situation that—at least according to our undergraduate students—feminism has supposedly cured, was it not? That this situation no longer prevails is one of the reasons for all these young women in higher education, right? In fact, feminists within the academy seem at odds about how to classify and understand the phenomenon of pregnancy, often sharing in the cultural assumption of maleness-as-health to cast pregnancy in the light of illness. One sees various forms of cultural male identification, for instance, even in the shifting pronouns of the AAUP's Lesley L. Francis, who resists tenure-clock delays for candidates who have recently given birth to or adopted a child. "If the woman continues to draw a full-time salary and continues to teach, *we* think the clock should continue to run," she claims, endorsing this logic with the good old "give 'em an inch" adage: "Once *you* let *them* take some time out, *they* may ask for all kinds of extensions. Maybe *they* just didn't publish enough" (Mangan A17; emphasis mine). And sometimes the insult of such inhumanity is sanctioned by the misdirected hostility of non-tenure-track members of the academic underclass. Katherine S. Mangan solicits the opinion of Eula Booker, a specialist in programs for women and minorities and non-tenure-track teacher at Michigan State's School of Labor and Industrial relations, and reveals to us this form of hostility. Booker was back in her job three weeks after her child was born. Perhaps understandably, therefore, she is short on sympathy for tenure-track women who seek extra consideration after giving birth. "I don't think the clock should stop," she proclaims, calling on the inept metaphor of pregnancy-as-sickness; "why should a woman who has a baby be any more severely affected than a man who had appendicitis or another major operation? Pregnancy is like any other *illness*" (Mangan A17; emphasis mine).

Shifting to part-time teaching might seem like a sensible option for academic mothers, but part-time work usually does not count toward tenure and may hurt a career in the long run as well. The Smarts observe that

> many of the wives of the older dual-career couples we spoke with who now work full-time worked part-time during the early years of child-rearing. They reasoned that mothers and children should be together for several hours a day, that the arrangement would result in less stress for all, and that it would pose little or no financial disadvantage given child care costs and other expenses. Today, however, young women are wary of working part-time because they can see the effects this choice has had on the careers of others, particularly in academia. (35)

This is the sad lesson—the diabolical double bind—that younger women students who are considering motherhood might learn from their older counterparts. Why is the academy—so often lauded as a vanguard social institution—not crystal clear about its complicity in this state of affairs? Along these lines, the Smarts cite the example of "Henry and Barbara." Both finished Ph.D.'s and then married; Barbara took time off to give birth and then returned to teaching extension courses. "Twenty five years after their marriage," the Smarts observe, "Henry is a full-professor with a substantial bibliography and ongoing research projects. Barbara is a full-time temporary lecturer who, for the past fifteen years, has taught all four sections of freshman biology. Henry told us proudly what a wonderful teacher Barbara is, as did some other members of the department. Yet her days, packed with students, lectures, and labs, leave no time for research and writing" (35).[2]

I contend that academic feminists ultimately cannot afford to participate in the business-as-usual casting of pregnancy as individual illness, particularly in the face of two present social realities. The first is the already mentioned unprecedented numbers of women in undergraduate and graduate education. The second factor, however, brings wider social pressure to bear on this matter: the public perception of an academy that is out of touch with "family values." This angry age is ever fond of polemics and ever drawn to the sound bite for its sense of important issues, and these sometimes troubling trends have swept up the academy as well. A front-page headline in the *Chronicle of Higher Education* proclaims that "Philosophy Professor Portrays Her Feminist Colleagues as out of Touch and 'Relentlessly Hostile to the Family'" (Jaschik). The story prefaces its coverage of this charge, launched by Christina Hoff Sommers of Clark University in Massachusetts, with the idea that Sommers is skillful in divisive politics, but this assault—perhaps misdirected— is one that the university system, if not feminists, might have seen coming. Sommers terms herself a "Liberal Feminist" in the tradition of Mary Wollstonecraft and John Stuart Mill, and she assumes the self-consciously essentialist stance of advocating for equal access to jobs for women and against crimes such as rape and domestic violence. Collectively caricaturing feminists who have thought their way past "equality" issues as "gender feminists," Sommers assails them for disrupting "the traditional family." Her complaint is essentially that "gender feminists" systematically exclude more "dissident feminists" such as herself—a crafty adjectival co-optation—because they support "the traditional family" (an aspect of Sommers's work left conspicuously untouched by the article). Perhaps not surprisingly, Sommers is lauded in her efforts by Camille Paglia, who deems her "deft, incisive and learned" and applauds the presumable dethroning of "all of the wildly overinflated feminist reputations sitting there like big fat ducks in academe" (A18).

The sensationalism of such charges is damaging both to the academy and to feminism. It should come as no surprise that mothers, trained by feminism to anticipate broader social possibilities, call feminism to account when those possibilities are shut down. When non-tenure-track mothers feel motivated by their own pressures to argue against more humane policies toward their tenure-track colleagues, when family-oriented feminists come to frame themselves as "dissidents," and when academic policymakers freely refer to a gender majority as "they," it would seem that women in the academy are in an abject state indeed. The sophisticated state of feminist thought by this historical moment tells us nothing if it does not say that to frame parenthood and career activity as a "natural" opposition is, in effect, to make of parenting a sophist's choice.

NOTES

1. I do not mean to overlook the way culture defines the roles of fathers. It is probably more accurate to say that these domestic gender inequities are culturally *enforced* rather than to assert that they are universally *embraced* by individuals of either sex.

2. I do not mean to underrate the importance of teaching as an integral part of an academic's work. But when inordinate portions of a department's introductory coursework are shouldered by part-time faculty with large course loads, a class structure and a potential for abuse begin to be apparent. Ominously, moreover, the Smarts observe that "having children *before* earning a Ph.D. leads with even more certainty to temporary status" (36).

WORKS CONSULTED

Becker, Ernest. *The Denial of Death.* New York: Free Press, 1973.

Bloom, Lynn Z. "Teaching College English as a Woman." *College English* 54.7 (1992): 818–21.

Chodorow, Nancy. *The Reproduction of Mothering: Psychoanalysis and the Sociology of Gender.* Berkeley: University of California Press, 1978.

Jaschik, Scott. "Philosophy Professor Portrays Her Feminist Colleagues as out of Touch and 'Relentlessly Hostile to the Family.'" *Chronicle of Higher Education* Jan. 15, 1992: A1, A16, A18.

Mangan, Katherine S. "Women Seek Time Off to Bear Children without Jeopardizing Academic Careers." *Chronicle of Higher Education* Feb. 3, 1988: A1, A16–A17.

McGivney, Veronica, and Beryl Bateson. "Childcare: The Continuing Debate." *Adults Learning* 2.7 (1991): 203–4.

McMillen, Liz. "Women Flock to Graduate School in Record Numbers." *Chronicle of Higher Education* Mar. 12, 1986: 1, 25.

Rich, Adrienne. "The Domestication of Motherhood." *Of Woman Born: Motherhood as Experience and Institution.* New York: Norton. 110–27.

Scully, Malcolm G. "Women Account for Half of College Enrollment in U.S., Three Other Nations." *Chronicle of Higher Education* Sept. 17, 1986: 1, 42.

Smart, Mollie S., and Russell C. Smart. "Paired Prospects: Dual-Career Couples on Campus." *Academe* (Jan.–Feb. 1990): 33–37.

Not the Feminism I Want My Daughter to Know

Valerie Begley

In our not-so-distant past, female faculty were often warned that children were a barrier to tenure. Such warnings were intended to convey the all-consuming nature of the profession and the hence "necessary" personal sacrifices women needed to make to advance. This specific warning has not entirely disappeared; prejudices against having children persist, and they do so in surprising ways. Ironically enough, professionalization is an instance in which academic feminism meets up with a right-leaning dominant culture in an endorsement of anti-family, anti-children, give-it-all-till-you-drop careerism. When I decided to raise a child while continuing in graduate school, this decision was taken as a mark against me as a feminist and as a scholar, as a betrayal of my politics and my ambitions, since the roles of feminist-scholar and parent are somehow "obviously" at odds. But it is that kind of reading that is short-sighted and fails to examine the apparent incompatibility of lifestyle and professional choices. For there are material as well as intellectual reasons that these two roles should be thought of as partially related even as they appear to be mutually incompatible.

Buttressed by an anti-family, pro-careerist dominant culture, the feminist position that emphasizes the oppressive aspects of the institution of the nuclear family gives careerist scholars an alibi for attitudes that favor lifestyle conformity to the profession. So when I complain that The Academy in general does not support graduate student parents, this is not to dismiss or overlook the support I have received from faculty and colleagues; it is instead to try to point to a problem

Valerie Begley is completing her dissertation at Carnegie Mellon University.

in the ways in which our professional practices sometimes operate in contradiction to our personal choices, our scholarship, and our politics. I am not interested, that is, in complaining about the gaps between these arenas; rather, I am interested in thinking about the ways in which it is "naive" to "complain" that my private life choices inhibit my social and professional life.

To challenge the ingrained binarisms between professional and personal obligations, we can question the notion of "difficulty" on two levels. First, at the level of practice: Why *must* it be difficult to raise children or care for elder parents while managing a career? Second, at the level of social discourse: In whose interest is it to maintain these as mutually exclusive—or at best simultaneously difficult—practices? How are "we," collectively or professionally, as feminists or not, complicit in sustaining what we like to call the "challenges" of our careers? That there are tensions between private and public dimensions of everyday life has everything to do with the organization of private life in relation to productive forces in the late twentieth century; what I question is the willingness to comply with these divisions from the very people whose livelihood depends on producing that critique. Why do (some) feminist materialists, especially those who have a critique of capital firmly in place, enact what appears to be the wholesale adoption of corporate-culture values? In what ways does it remain in our interests to sustain the borders between the personal and the professional, instead of transforming institutional practices so as to accommodate diverse subject positions within the professional ranks?

It is a historically recent and extremely classist view that childbearing should be put off until one's career is under way. In addition, it is a view that denies ethnic, religious, and racially different attitudes toward private life.[1] The assumption seems to be that we leave those cultural differences behind at the door and adopt in their place the ethos of the professional-managerial class.[2]

The fundamentally liberal impulse that remains at the bottom of contemporary transformations in scholarship seeks to convey, for example, the multiplicity of positions from which historical subjects understand and enact their lives. If cultural studies locates the sources of meaning not in individual reason or in subjectivity but in social relations and forms of cultural reason that transcend individual subjectivity, then why does the simplistic "explanation" of students who chose to parent in the academy focus on choice: "bad choice; too bad." If scholars have become sensitive to the complexity of terms such as *subjectivity* and *identity*, it is one more instance of the gap between politics and practice.

Macho Professionalism

"Motherhood" remains, rightly, threatening to many feminist positions: since the late nineteenth century it has been the social justification for the structural removal of middle-class women from the work force; and second-wave feminism fought hard for our freedom from the belief that motherhood is the source of a woman's fulfillment. So opposition to child rearing should remain an important part of the refusal to participate in compulsory gender roles. And despite all the pleasures in which I indulge as a parent, I continue to believe that resisting the cultural imperative to reproduce is, finally, the more contestatory gesture.

So I concede that there remain important reasons for not jumping onto the pro-natalist pro-family bandwagon. But for those of us on the Left who do choose to have children, we must take back the rhetoric of family values from the conservatives, who have nearly emptied it of discursive power. One way of doing that is implied in my critique of "corporate" academia: significant opposition to capitalism can come from reimagining the temporal relationship between labor and nonlabor practices as a way of defining and ordering our desires. If we continue to privilege our careers over our private lives (indeed, for some, the two are indistinguishable), then we are indeed engaged in reproduction, but of a different sort. Feminists would do well to open the debates around reproduction with an eye as to whether we wish to promote the reproduction of social relations under capitalism.

Individualism in the Middle-Class

The refusal to imagine the subject of the "middle class"[3] as potentially complex, as contradictory a subject position to occupy as any other, seems an unnecessarily defensive reaction. Indeed, Marxists have already pointed to the failure to take seriously nonresistant cultural practices.[4] In the age of "post-feminism," the embrace of counterdominant sexual practices, lifestyles, and orientations may bring with it (perhaps predictably) the policing of politically incorrect lifestyles and sexual practices. Which is another way of saying that we are not "beyond" class any more than we are beyond gender.[5]

There is a failure to understand the middle-class subject as complex. My own middle-class upbringing is but one example of the crosshatched nature of such a position: If I love to cook and garden today, it is because I learned these passions from my father, not from my mother, who resents these and all other domestic tasks, her self-image notwithstanding. The point is that the supposed "legibility" of my class upbringing as an index to my subject position mystifies, by oversimplifying, precisely what it is supposed to explain.

I spent a great deal of my twenties resisting the structures of my socialization. I lived the cliché—dressed in black, hung out in cafés. Then one day I decided that I could raise a child alone and continue in graduate school—full-time.

I spent the next few years trying to understand this seemingly insane decision and my complicated responses to it, trying to explain the appeal for that which I had been previously contemptuous. I began to track the intricacies of gender training as they intersect with class background but emerge as decisions seemingly based on a kind of individualism. Many mountains of plastic toys later, it became clear that this "explanation" is itself what needs explaining, that recourse to individualism is another of the ideological legacies of my middle-class upbringing, as well as fundamental to the humanism upon which the academy rests. The rupture in the narrative of my twenties is an example of a desire that flourishes in contradiction to intentions that needs to be addressed.

So individualism is (still) falsely imagined as the chief basis for choices. Feminists are somehow supposed to be immune to the effects of their historical subject positions. To moralize against someone who makes a choice/wanders into her life script is to make a categorical error. To dismiss politically incorrect choices as self-evidently reflective of class and gender positioning, and therefore uninteresting and unworthy of academic and political attention, is to repeat that error.

Child Rearing Qua Inquiry

Child rearing is seldom acknowledged as an intellectual endeavor. But it is and always has been, for me, a kind of philosophical inquiry, as I have indulged in the psychological dramas played out before me by my daughter and in my head/body as I interact/remember/observe/admire/shrink from these moments. The failure to imagine child rearing as intellectually productive, compelling, or worth taking seriously as an intellectual is a key source of my anger and frustration.[6]

Parenting has made me a better scholar, and not only for the reasons typically cited: yes, I am better organized (sort of), yes I appreciate what I have. But this life-shift has made me a better scholar because raising a child has made me a better materialist. It has been impossible for me to avoid confronting the material conditions of my life, the conditions of possibility—in the most literal ways—of my professional development. I have a pronounced sense of the temporal relationship of my cognitive processes and my productive output—where I fall on the learning curve in relation to my daughter's weekend play schedule. Most of all, I understand too intimately the relationship between fatigue and money. Money buys time savers; money buys health; money buys, in the form of nice clothing, the approval of those superficial others that so densely populate the academy.

So in graduate school, I've gained an unpleasant reputation for wearing my "baby politics" on my sleeve—a practice I intend to continue because I want to expose the material conditions under which we do our work: in this respect, I am suggesting that while my position is different, it is also a more elaborated version of the conditions of life and work in the humanities, for it is not just that most of us are "overworked and underpaid" but rather that we are supposed to love our intellectual life at the expense of everything else. But to be honest, the smartest thing I ever learned in grad school was to cease to locate solely in my work my sense of pleasure and self-worth.

Future Feminisms

However fragmented, or widely imagined, the social body of feminism has become, it must be safe to assume that feminist politics remains committed to addressing the exclusions and oppressions that relate to issues of gender and sexual orientation. This is, for me, the bottom line. The issues to which I am committed in my work always depend to some extent on rupturing those boundaries between my work and my private life in an effort to constantly make clear the material conditions of everyday life.

I am weary of the way that my complaining is taken as a form of victimization, rather than as a call to transform the academy. I can feel certain that my decision to raise my daughter while continuing graduate work was right for me, without liking that I seldom get enough sleep. Instead, I am expected to maintain a warriorlike (or is that a "professional"?) stance in the face of these "challenges," an attitude that smacks of arrogance and antipolitical machismo.

I don't mean to claim that what I or other students-who-parent do constitutes a radical political gesture. It is not "radical" for a white middle-class suburban-raised feminist to raise a child—and, for a time, in a heterosexual marriage no less—but I do want to claim that it is contestatory because in this particular moment it enacts the antithesis of the professional image and resists scholarly reproduction in its proscribed ways. The social body of the academy is rapidly changing, and feminists would do well to recognize this and head up the changes, rather than fall into step with the accelerated pace of a professional life that increasingly resembles corporate work life.

I suggest we aggressively undertake the transformation of our hiring practices, our publishing schedules, and our curriculum agendas to reflect a concern with what is really important, which is how can we live in a different and better way. At a time when our published scholarship is dense with calls for complexity and multiplicity, our experiences give us a rare opportunity to negotiate those values in the moments of their actuality, to theorize our experiences, and to renarrativize our desires. By suggesting our feminist work starts with ourselves, I am not suggesting that every decision made by a feminist in the name of feminism is necessarily contestatory. But I am arguing that thinking alone won't undo the decades of work the culture has done, and this is a necessary lesson in humility for every feminist who still thinks that consciousness-raising alone will make it so (as in "that'll never happen to me") and for those who have abandoned such work altogether.

What I want to convey is that "decisions" are both passive and active, structured by external forces and differently inflected by moments of agency: in my case, the desire for a child (which itself needs much explaining—I am aware that I utter that phrase without any real sense of its scope and depth) and the sense that this would be manageable for me and a good experience for her; guilt and responsibility (emotions that also need theorizing); but also watching too many soap operas, succumbing to the melodramatic tragedy of it all. This mixture, this all-of-these-things-at-once quality of anything we think we can still call a "decision" is precisely what is worth thinking about, if we have any investment in understanding what it means to be culturally engendered. But if we are not willing to take risks and enact the unthinkable,[7] then there really is no point in continuing as feminists. The feminism that such an atmosphere can produce is not a feminism I want my daughter to know, though in all intellectual honesty, she'll have to know where she's come from.

NOTES

I would like to thank Lori Shorr and John Groch for their careful readings of earlier drafts of this essay.

1. Many ethnic, religious, and racial groups favor starting large families early. The wholesale rejection of the social formation of "the family" as bourgeois

has rendered many leftists unable to adequately account for the needs and interests of groups who hold such different worldviews from their own. As Barrett and McIntosh put it, we need to understand the appeal of the family before dismissing it as simply oppressive.

2. The argument for the historical development of a "professional-managerial class" and its fundamentally contradictory mission is elaborated in Ehrenreich and Ehrenreich.

3. Following the work of Stuart Hall and others, *class* in my usage is an unstable category. Class position is not the predictable monolith typically imagined, and that ever-ready target of analysis, "the middle class," is a complex and unstable place from which to hail.

4. Angela McRobbie's work in Britain in the late seventies is but one example of work undertaken in part as a corrective to the then-current practice of theorizing resistant boys' culture to the exclusion of nonresistant girls' culture, which McRobbie pegged, rightly in my view, as partially symptomatic of the misogyny of classical Marxism.

5. For a recent critique of the notion that professional gender imbalances have been sufficiently redressed, thereby obviating the need for hard-line feminist politics, see Modleski.

6. I transmute Lisa Heldke's phrase "cooking qua inquiry." Heldke theorizes cooking as a form of antiessentialist inquiry that merges theory and practice in a self-reflective and interactive mode. She eschews the strict dichotomy between "knowledge gaining" (theory) and "getting things done" (practice), which are not, of course, the only ways to define theory and practice, but for my purposes do quite well in the translation to child rearing. Heldke rightly warns against considering cooking as simply analogous to philosophical inquiry, and I, too, offer my disclaimer against simple homologies between child rearing and theory. Like cooking, child rearing warrants its own practice-specific philosophical investigations.

7. And I mean here to play on the many-layered pun on "unthinking": the unthinking characteristic of ideological beliefs enacted as if "second nature"; the way pregnancy is "unthinkable" for professional scholars because antagonistic to ambition; and the way women are still imagined as unthinking creatures of desire. Think here also of that classic statement of mock horror, "How *could* you think such a thing."

WORKS CITED

Barrett, Michele, and Mary McIntosh. *The Anti-Social Family.* London: Verso, 1982.

Ehrenreich, Barbara, and John Ehrenreich. "The Professional-Managerial Class." *Between Labor and Capital.* Ed. Pat Walker. Boston: South End Press, 1979. 5–45.

Heldke, Lisa. "Recipes for Theory Making." *Cooking, Eating, Thinking: Transformative Philosophies of Food.* Ed. Deane W. Curtin and Lisa M. Heldke. Bloomington: Indiana University Press, 1992. 251–65.

McRobbie, Angela. *Feminism and Youth Culture: From Jackie to Just Seventeen.* Boston: Unwin Hyman, 1991.

Modleski, Tania. *Feminism without Women: Culture and Criticism in a "Postfeminist" Age.* New York: Routledge, 1991.

PART THREE

Mentoring and Metaphorical Mothering

Mentoring, Mothering, and Mayhem: Costs of the Superwoman Syndrome

Trudy Christine Palmer

The majority of the demands placed on me to "parent" students have come in my capacity as a mentor for black graduate students. During my two years at the University of Pittsburgh, I worked closely with five of the six black women graduate students in residence. I'm still mentoring some of them, although I left Pittsburgh several years ago.

I take mentoring seriously for a number of reasons. I know how much it would have meant to me to have a mentor on campus during my graduate school years, but there were no prospects. Second, I know how much it meant to me to have a long-distance mentor, one with whom I remain in close contact. And finally, I think that what will significantly effect a less racist academy is the presence of large numbers of black and other "minority" faculty and administrators. To that end, I work very hard to support students of color, in particular, through the often alienating, sometimes unfamiliar, and seemingly irrelevant hoops and hurdles of graduate school.

I advise them, unofficially, on their course selections; I listen to their concerns about the provincial parameters delimiting most of their classes and suggest ways for them both to talk with their professors and to subvert canonical syllabi; I read drafts of their papers and help them interpret professors' feedback; I counsel them about how to read and respond to the tensions caused by their presence in the classes they take and in those they teach; I assure them that they were not admissions mistakes, invited to the program simply to add a bit of

Trudy Christine Palmer is senior staff editor for the *Christian Science Sentinel*.

color; I remind them of their reasons for getting themselves into this mess to begin with and assure them that they'll get to pursue what interests them eventually; and I encourage them to dedicate themselves to the work without becoming consumed by it—to "have a life," in other words.

In addition to these more or less academic issues, I listen to their longings for a black community or a black church or even a decent black beauty shop; to their stories about being called names by strangers on the streets; to their fear of becoming utterly alienated from members of their families and communities who are vaguely proud of but ignorant about their endeavors; to the difficulties their families face, difficulties exacerbated, in some cases, by their own absence; and to their persistent feelings of loneliness and alienation. I also do my best to help them through the incidents of racial harassment that inevitably occur. Finally, and in a way most importantly, I provide a safe space where these students can share, not shed, what Du Bois termed "double consciousness." Where they can speak within the veil, not through it. Where, in short, they can express themselves without having to tailor or interpret their words for white listeners. To this end, the students I mentored at Pitt dubbed my office the "Culture Club" and literally let loose there—shrugging off the white world, speaking in nonwhite rhythms, and signifying on all that lay just outside my office door. Naturally, this kind of mentoring is extra—extracurricular, extraordinarily draining, and extraneous—as far as getting tenure is concerned. Yet it is, it seems to me, one of my most important contributions.

I want to share just one incident that demonstrates the blurry boundaries between this kind of mentoring and motherhood. One day, the student whom I had been mentoring most closely sat, despondent, in my office. I'd rehearsed every possible pep talk I could think of to no avail. Finally, after a silence, she said to me, "But does being a black woman in this profession mean you have to be single?" I must admit I was unprepared for this. I know that graduate school is a lonely proposition for almost everyone, and I know that it's even lonelier for black students in predominantly white schools. But I hadn't realized how long-term that loneliness looks to a twenty-three year old accustomed to an active social life in her predominantly black college and hometown.

"But does being a black woman in this profession mean you have to be single?" she asked. What's a mother/mentor to do? "No," I fumbled, intensely aware all of a sudden of my own single status. Was this the time to pull out my one-needn't-be-married-to-be-happy lecture?

No. I sensed that her comment wasn't so much a challenge to my happily single lifestyle as it was a hope that being single hadn't moved from the category of choice to that of necessity upon her decision to enter graduate school. Next, I mentally flipped through the faces of the black women I knew in the profession, searching for examples of happily married ones. None came to mind. What surfaced instead were all the statistics about the shortage of marriageable black male professionals. Clearly not the time to drag those facts and figures out. Finally, I thought of a black woman scholar whom we both knew who was, at the time, romantically involved, at least, if not married. Believe me, I leaped at it, though I knew nothing at all about the quality of this relationship. Quality be damned—I needed to restore hope before launching into reality.

This sounds funny in retrospect. It was even, in a perverse sort of way, funny at the time—to me at least. But I write about it here to make two serious points. First, responding empathically to a question like this is hard work emotionally. Being a mother is hard work. Sometimes being a mentor is similarly difficult. Second, this woman's concerns were real and reasonable. As this student sensed, the costs of being black in this profession are steep. One cannot, it seems to me, mentor those preparing for the profession without acknowledging these costs. Yet to do so means embarking on a relationship that is all but tidy, that is full of surprises, and that inevitably unleashes a memory or fear you'd just as soon have kept bridled. Hopefully, however, it also means embarking upon a very rewarding relationship.

The same student who popped the question about being single wrote me a lovely letter soon after learning of my decision to leave the University of Pittsburgh: "It means a great deal to me to see you hold fast to your commitment to being not just alive, but 'well' (emotionally and spiritually) and in this profession. . . . Know that you are inspiring me to continue doing what I enjoy professionally without sacrificing my spiritual well being." Most days I wonder how anyone could look at *me* as a model of "spiritual well being." She is right, however, about my unflagging commitment to being whole in this profession.

Though I try, of course, to spark my students' intellectual curiosity and to hone their critical skills, I hope most of all to pass along the goal of wholeness to a few of the next generation's black scholars. Can it come as a surprise, really, that to do so takes a bit of mothering mixed in with mentoring?

Recently, however, I've found myself doing less mentoring and more literal mothering because just as I was leaving Pittsburgh, I adopted a baby girl, Gracey. Her arrival was the realization of a long-held (seventeen years) dream. Needless to say, she has altered my life enormously—and enriched it immeasurably. I adopted as a single parent determined to spend as much time as possible with her until—at age six or so—the schools lay claim to her days. I know I swim against the current in my refusal to employ full-time day care, but I wouldn't trade my time with her for any amount of money or any number of extra articles. Her skin is too soft, her smiles too warm, her growth too swift, and her words too precious to miss. I offer below a portrait of Gracey's and my first two years together simply to present one (admittedly imperfect) alternative to the use of full-time day care for those who believe, as I do, that the flexibility of the professor's schedule can be a boon to parent-child bonding.

Through a combination of summers, a postdoc year (arranged long before I knew of Gracey's arrival), and a negotiated term off at Tufts, my then-new teaching post, I was fortunate enough to be free of teaching responsibilities during Gracey's first eighteen months. For the first twelve of those, she wasn't very mobile and napped well, so I was able to write at home and could get by with very little child care. After that first year, though, she started walking more and sleeping less, and my duties at school increased. I hired 15–20 hours of child care a week for the next six months, increasing it to 20–25 hours once I returned to full-time teaching. Of course, that didn't cover much more than class time, office hours, and a meeting or two, so I did the bulk of my work at night.

The first semester was tough. Here's how I got through it: My rule was that whenever Gracey was asleep, I was working. That meant, of course, that any socializing (including phone calls) had to be done with Gracey in tow, so I never (not an exaggeration) went out at night and chatted in only the briefest of snatches with friends on the phone (good for my phone bill, bad for staying in touch). The minute Gracey went to bed (7:30ish), I would sit down to work. Usually, I'd fall asleep in my chair around 10:00, napping there until 2:00, when I would start back to work until 5:00 or 5:30. At that point, if I was lucky, I'd slip between the sheets for a nap until Gracey awakened at 6:00 or so. That was my schedule five or six nights a week.

It's not a schedule I recommend exactly, but it has its advantages: I didn't have to wash the sheets very often since they got used so little, and I got to spend a lot of time playing with Gracey. I was tired much of our time together, it's true, but one needn't be at peak performance to enjoy building with blocks or bouncing on the bed. I was, admittedly, a little more short-tempered than I would have been with more sleep, but reminding myself that it wasn't Gracey's fault I was tired restored my flagging patience more often than not. Naturally, I hope that, with fewer new courses next year, I'll be able to sleep a normal number of hours (in bed) on a nightly basis. If not, so be it. My time with Gracey is worth more to me even than sleep.

Obviously, this wasn't a semester when I got a lot of writing done. I did, however, serve on several department and university committees as well as on the program committee for the American Studies Association, so I certainly wasn't professionally inactive. In short, I simply cut out all adults-only socializing and slept insufficiently to guarantee my time with Gracey. Petty sacrifices in the scheme of things. Gracey and I have four more years before she goes to school full days. I'm looking into morning programs as she begins to need more time playing with her peers, but until she's in first grade, I plan to spend most of her daylight hours playing, learning, and laughing with her.

In making Gracey my first priority, I have necessarily chosen to limit not only my social life and my sleep but also my professional aspirations. The temptation these days is to believe that one can have it all—a personal life, a family life, and a career all functioning at peak performance. I entertain no such illusion. Choices have to be made, priorities set. I am happy having focused my life on my child, willing to make the sacrifices that focus requires.

It's no coincidence, of course, that my time spent mentoring has decreased as my time spent mothering has increased. I am simply less available than I was before Gracey arrived. Instead of meaning that I am of less use to my students, I hope this means only that as they witness me struggling toward wholeness, they will find my example worth following.

A coda. A year or so after I first wrote this (and about three years before coming up for tenure) I reached a moment of decision: either I had to get busy revising (yet again) my dissertation into a book or I had to start looking for another profession. I chose the latter. When Gracey turned four, I ended my life in academe and began what has turned out to be the job of my dreams. My hours are not as flexible as when I taught, but I keep time in the office down to 30–32 hours a week. To do that, I still work at home well into most nights. And, as before, I rarely socialize sans child. It's not a balanced life, I suppose, but it's a happy one.

As for mentoring black students, I'm still in touch with a few. I leave it to them (and their peers) to mentor the next generation—even if that means tossing some good old-fashioned mothering into the mix.

Lavender Labors or Activist Mothering

Rebecca Mark

As an out lesbian professor on a university campus, I have had the unique and often difficult task of balancing my role as teacher, professor, "master" of the subject with my role as advisor, activist, friend, role model. I think this is a struggle many women and minority faculty face daily. I originally entitled this essay "Lavender Labors: From Midwifing My Gay Students to Mothering My Son." At the time I conceived it, I was literally going into labor with my first child. I was convinced there would be a dramatic difference between mentoring and parenting. One year later and much older if not much wiser, I am helping my son go off to day care for the first time. What the experience of literal parenting has taught me about the surrogate parenting that I have done for so many years is not the dramatic differences between the two, but the need to recognize the profound contribution that "activist mothering" is making to the university. I now believe more than ever that we can transform the academy by recognizing mothering as a pedagogical alternative to the patriarchal fathering that has ruled the classroom and the campus. Because our society has such a stereotyped and belittled notion of mothering, embracing this term means negotiating a difficult theoretical terrain.

There may in fact be more stigma associated with being a mother in the academy these days than with being gay. Professors who are themselves mothers have consistently faced the impossible task of separating themselves from their mother role when they enter the academy, hiding their pregnancies throughout tenure decisions, giving up the possibility of being a mother so that they may appear to be

Rebecca Mark is an associate professor of English literature at Tulane University.

serious scholars, or giving up the possibility of being serious scholars in order to mother. Professors who have chosen to mother their students face ridicule, the assumption that they have fewer brain cells than their far more intelligent and detached colleagues, and little or no recognition of the work they do. Because those of us who are members of minorities spend long periods of time talking to students who seek us out to explore the difficult issues of classism, racism, sexism, and homophobia, we must address what it means to be a mentor to these students. But this is not an issue that only minority faculty should be discussing. The problem of a disenfranchised, deeply troubled, often addicted youth should be everybody's concern.

Over the past nine years I have listened to at least fifty students come out and helped many more find ways to articulate their difficult passage into adult definitions of sexuality against a backdrop of extreme homophobia. Going directly against what I was told to do—stay out of the way, don't get too involved—I did what I knew had to be done: I sent students to therapy for issues and problems that a therapist needs to address; I sent them to drug and alcohol programs for addiction; I sent them to support groups for coming out. What I did myself can go by no other name than mothering, but it is a different type of mothering than what I do for my own son. It is "activist mothering," the mothering many of us bring to our roles as teachers, lawyers, and doctors but that has been banned from ever being discussed. It is the kind of personal involvement that anyone who understands the now clichéd phrase "It takes a village . . ." will necessarily embrace. The university as a village is in crisis. Patriarchal fathering—a combination of academic crime and punishment, hands off approaches, and male bonding over beer, football, and sex—has obviously been an overwhelming failure. We need another model.

In many cases when I have chosen to parent, I have saved lives that desperately needed to be saved. Mothering students is not the touchy-feely-cookies-'n'-tea pampering that so many of my colleagues conjure up. It is not being a best friend and it is by all means not to be confused with being a lover. It is instead strong guidance, respect, willingness to listen to and support a student through a period of often devastating identity crisis, loss of a parent or grandparent, discovery of addiction, remembrance of child abuse, rape, abortion, or any number of difficult life passages. It is political action in its most important manifestation. When I parent a young person, I am teaching them to parent themselves. I am reminding them of values and ways of acting that will benefit the whole community.

Friends cannot risk what a professional mother must risk—that the student will actively rebel against you, even at moments hate you. This rebellion is part of the learning and developing. It is a political, intellectual, and emotional process. The terms of the agreement are mutual respect. When these terms are firmly in place miraculous changes can occur. Activist mothering means giving an enormous amount of encouragement for what has been accomplished and expecting more when one goal has been reached. As any great mother knows, mothering does not mean helping to excess, pampering, smothering, or any of the other demeaning terms that have been used to describe this profound acceptance of responsibility. It means mirroring health in your life, revealing ways of solving problems that do not create crisis, being willing to feel the pain of the most difficult moments without turning to drink, drugs, excessive exercise, shopping, work, or any other addiction. It means listening when you are called upon to listen. It is difficult, it is time consuming, and in the academy it is not rewarded; in fact, it is actively discouraged. It is time that we encouraged and respected activist mothering as a valid pedagogical technique as we have for so long respected the more patriarchal method of control.

What has struck me most this week is that going off to day care is not unlike going off to college. When students go to day care and to college for the first time they are faced with enormous demands, including meeting a new peer group, getting used to a new environment and a new set of expectations, and living away from parents for the first time. What makes college a lot more difficult than day care is that students must set their own rules. Some of the decisions they will make will effect them the rest of their lives. It is so easy to fall into drug addiction, alcohol abuse, accidental pregnancy, addiction to computer games, and a thousand other landmines of modern youth culture. It is not so easy to get out. The four years of college, in a culture that has done away with rites of passage, becomes one of the most difficult and profound rites of passage many people encounter. As the guardians at the gate, as the only adults in the predominantly youth defined culture of the university campus, professors are put in a unique position, a position we rarely talk about, rarely even acknowledge.

Bob Dylan taught my generation to be suspicious of their elders. His words "Get out of the way if you can't lend a hand, your home rule is rapidly aging," still ring in my ears. My generation is so worried about being cool and accepted we forget that human compassion might not follow a particular set of rules. Sometimes being decidedly uncool is a much more radical political position. Dylan's words make many people fear the tyranny of age, butting in where we are not wanted or needed, but the phrase "*if* you can't lend a hand" is the key. We can lend a hand and it is a hand that is needed in this demoralized and dazed society more than ever. Both gay adults and adults who were raised in the sixties spent so many years rebelling against the status quo, we have spent little time learning how to be the older generation, how to set the standards and teach the lessons. Get out of the way if you can't lend a hand, but if you can then, as my one year old would say, "Do it."

Even as I write I can hear a chorus of colleagues saying, "I don't even have time to get my syllabus done and you want me to parent? Leave the parenting to the parents." Professors who spend a large number of hours advising are sensitive to the fact that their intellectual skills have been downplayed while they get taunted by their colleagues with such terms as "mother figure," "father figure," "friend," "too close," "lack of boundaries," and "tries to be a counselor." While I am acutely aware of and in fact quite conservative about the issue of boundaries, I think we should distinguish between true professional parenting and inappropriate ego investment. I am totally against teachers who try to play best friend to their students or teachers who get their own emotional and social needs met in the classroom or teachers who share too much of their personal life issues with their students or teachers who cross sexual boundaries and harass their students. If we substitute "parent" for "teacher" in this list you can see that it would be equally wrong for a parent to engage in any of these activities. Responsible parenting actually moves toward disengagement and independence.

The professor who has served in the role of advisor knows the difference between herself and her student, the difference between herself and the biological parent, the difference between herself and a trained counselor, the difference between herself and a best friend. The professional parent serves a much needed and little spoken of role. We are the front line, sometimes the only adult a student will see all day except the staff, serving people, janitors, and security guards, many of whom have also stepped in as front-line parents. When the extreme pressure of the college years hits crisis proportions, those in the front lines need to have their ears and eyes open for the student falling sleep in class, the student who can't get work done, the student who appears at your office door day after day and needs to tell you something. Only those who are aware of the boundaries I have just mentioned can be secure enough to provide the modeling and mirroring that needs to take place.

This dance is complex in all circumstances with all students but with gay students it is even more crucial and more difficult because they have different circumstances and issues. For one the student is coming into his or her own in a turbulent political/cultural climate in which he or she faces extreme pressure from the outside to please the world by deciding to be heterosexual. Those students who choose or who recognize in themselves their gay identity must rebel against the authority of family, state, church, community, and forge a new community. Often they must go against their parents in a way they never have before. As a gay professor you are part of this new community, the accepting gay "parent" and simultaneously part of the establishment they are negotiating. What I have found is that like a parent you become the sounding board for independence. I am like you but not like you. This is one reason why each generation of lesbians, gay men, and bisexuals do things differently, rejecting wisdom and experience along with fashion and style often with great personal loss.

But the rebellion is part of the parenting and any investment in helping the transition into the new gay community should not get in the way of fulfilling our role as a wiser and safer adult. Another problem with the issue of identification is that when that identification changes, a student will still need you to be a scholar, a mentor, and an academic advisor. Therefore you cannot be invested in their sexual identification anymore than as a parent you can become invested in your child's becoming a doctor or lawyer.

It is time that we came out of the closet about mentoring issues and began to find a terminology with which we can feel comfortable. It is no secret that young adults in our culture are not in good shape. Recent reports have shown the highest incidences of alcoholism ever on college campuses; almost 50 percent of the students are binge drinking. In the gay and heterosexual population AIDS cases are on the rise and the general sense that there is nothing to live for is demonstrated by high suicide rates. Date rape has reached epidemic proportions and we have stood by and watched without making this a number one priority. Hate is epidemic. Homophobia is epidemic. Racism is epidemic. Under these conditions no one can learn and there cannot be anything that even approximates equal educational opportunity for gays, women, and people of color.

What is most appalling is that it is often the radicals, leftists, feminists, and activists who have kept aloof in their ivory towers avoiding and often sneering at activist mothering. What I ask these friends is this: If our students, our children are not the cause worth fighting for, the obvious site of our struggle, then what is? How can we discuss cultural studies and queer studies and feminist studies and performance studies without looking at the representation of despair that has become our college classroom? We can say it is not our responsibility. We are hired to teach. But then I would ask you, how can a student who has just been raped or is remembering childhood parental abuse or who is drunk learn? Yes our first priority is imparting and disseminating knowledge and the skills to learn but we can engage in this task in a way that will help heal the wounded children we face every day. We have a serious task on our hands and if I get accused of having fewer brain cells than my colleague down the hall because I feel comfortable mothering my students than I can live with that. I can live with that because I have a strong sense of my own adulthood and I want to see my gay, straight, male, female, black, white, Asian students leave my classroom with the ability to think and reason and love their way out of this mess. My experience as a gay parent in all its manifestations has taught me a lesson about my responsibility to the next generation that I think should extend to all professors and all parents.

When *Mother* Is a Four-Letter Word

Claudia Limbert

I have four children. All are now ed-
ucated, grown-up, and working full-time away from home. So it's not
as if I were teaching my classes while rocking a cradle with one foot.
Looking at me, you wouldn't necessarily connect me with active motherhood. I do everything possible to keep the focus on my academic
life. I publish widely. I serve as the chairperson or director for campus
committees and groups. I even try to dress in what I perceive as a non-
motherly way. My friends are right. Being perceived as a mother is
negative for an academic career. It means that your accomplishments
probably will not be taken seriously.

Many of my women friends in academic careers tell me that their
success was dependent on their hard decision not to have children
and, in some cases, not even to marry. Because mothers still bear the
primary weight of child raising and housekeeping, not only are female
academics often exhausted, but also they are unable to take part in
campus life in the way that most of their married male colleagues can.
Such a woman cannot be a member of an important committee that
meets late in the afternoon nor can she have a casual, after-hours
drink with the others in her department. She may also be denied tenure on the grounds that she was "not collegial enough."

An unexamined issue that keeps many women from achieving
honors and senior rank is their activity in what could be called campus quality-of-life programs. Who are the people running the film se-

Claudia Limbert is the chief academic officer at Pennsylvania State University at
DuBois.

ries, serving as editors for student publications, acting as advisors for student groups, chairing charity programs? Who most often have students sitting with them long after office hours, seeking help with a paper (sometimes for a male professor's class) or asking for advice about a problem—a woman with a bruised face who wants to talk about her battering husband or a young man whose father wants him to become a state patrolman when he wants to be a poet or a woman who suspects that her child may be using drugs? Our female colleagues most often deal with these matters, possibly because female academics are often seen as surrogate mothers by their students and possibly because they are seen as less threatening than male professors. All these activities take huge amounts of time and inner personal resources and provide little or no career payback. Such activities take time away from publication and conference presentations, where emphasis is placed for tenure and promotion.

What if we decided to treat the term *mother* as positive, refusing to see it as a four-letter word and refusing to accept second-class citizenship in both literal and symbolic respects? On the professional level, there are many things that we can do to make the academic community more hospitable to mothers as well as to women and men who value qualities often perceived as maternal. Here are ten suggestions:

1. We must make sure that interviewing committees understand and honor the intent as well as the letter of the law regarding the rights of potential employees who are female and, if possible, we should sit on such committees and insist that they include females. There must be no indirect loaded questions, no elimination of female candidates because of their reproductive possibilities, and no preconceived notions of what women are "really" looking for in a position.

2. We must find a way to deemphasize traditional academic male-style work patterns as the norm and realize that there are many ways for men and women to succeed. We must insist that the work day be adjusted to fit the needs of faculty mothers. Course schedules aren't cast in stone and can be readjusted to allow a female academic with heavy family responsibilities to teach at times that will mesh with her home situation.

3. Team teaching should become more common. The advantage to academic mothers would be that one team member could assume additional course responsibilities when the other team member needs time because of pregnancy complications, childbirth, or children's illnesses.

4. We should press for an official maternity leave policy for female

academics instead of leaving it to be decided on a case-by-case basis. Stopping the tenure clock for childbirth should be standard in maternity leave policy, but that's only the beginning.

5. Parental leave, as opposed to maternity leave, should be an option not only for adopting mothers but also for male faculty members who wish to take a more active role in the early days of their children's lives without being subjected to job discrimination.

6. We should individually and as a group make our feelings known about the need for on-campus, affordable, decent day care that is not only open to faculty but also to students and staff with children.

7. Quality-of-life programming on campus should form a measurable portion of tenure and promotion review. Not only will the women who typically take on these responsibilities be rewarded, but their male colleagues, seeing benefits for themselves, will become more willing to share some of these responsibilities.

8. We must improve the work climate not just for female academics but for females in every career by educating males about the dreary circumstances of most women's lives. This is best done by requiring all students to take women's studies courses. Male students' brief encounter with issues concerning 51 percent of our population is just as important as requiring computer literacy.

9. We need to find more ways to fund scholars both in undergraduate and graduate school. We need to make the academic community more hospitable to our nontraditional women students—most of whom are mothers working at least part-time outside the home and who are often trying to survive as scholars under almost impossible conditions.

10. We should lobby within our professional groups for women's caucuses and meetings devoted to the topic of motherhood in academia as well as to feminist criticism on motherhood—literature sections that focus on mothers in literature, how motherhood affects the work of women writers, and women and motherhood in history.

PART FOUR

Apprenticeship Issues

The Discursive Production of Student-Parents: Theory, Class, and Coalition Politics

Lori Shorr

> As the arena for negotiating values,
> meanings, and identities, representation
> authorizes ethics and social practices; it
> stages the workings through of the dom-
> inant ideology.
> —Mary Poovey,
> "Scenes of an Indelicate Character"

With my youngest child now in kin-
dergarten, I have had the time to become both emotionally and intellectually intrigued by the decision I made several years ago to become
a graduate student and a parent simultaneously. What hails someone
to such a decision and what are the implications to the academy in
having that someone around? I want to look at how I came to recognize myself as a working-class student-parent and how "being" those
things affects the type of scholarship and theoretical investigations I
chose and now understand as important political work.

On July 4, 1991, the *Pittsburgh Post-Gazette* printed a picture of me
and my two children. The picture shows me literally trying to juggle
my three year old, Eliot, and my one year old, Sadie, on my lap. Trying
to keep them still for the picture before I had to rush out the door to
teach. My eyes half-closed, my head titled back slightly, my mouth
opened in nervous laughter. This was, iconographically, the picture of
the "woman doing it all." This happy and shining picture, as well as the
accompanying article, constructed me as a victimized yet brave fighter
for the rights of student-parents. In the Coalition for Childcare at Pitt,
the organization I founded in 1991 to get the child-care needs of student-parents and low-income employees recognized, this publicity

---

Lori Shorr teaches film at Villanova University.

meant everything. From it we received monetary donations from faculty members and a steady stream of support that did not end until 1993, when the university agreed to open a new center, hired a new director committed to the needs of student-parents, and implemented a sliding scale fee and flextime care.

Part of my identity as student-parent was constructed for me by newspaper journalism. In the article the student-parent was constructed through the discourses of crisis ("the child-care crisis"), underdog heroism (with its attendant commitments to individualism), and female victimization. I became the "poster child" (infantalized in my maternity) and instantly interpretable to many. It is only by participating in these discourses that this newspaper article was politically efficacious. And, indeed, I sometimes voluntarily took on the position of victimized underdog for just this reason. The makeup of the Coalition for Childcare at Pitt is an example of temporary identities between constituencies, as it did not reinforce what one might expect, an exercise in identity politics—hassled graduate moms united. Instead, our membership was highly diverse in gender, sexuality, nationality, and reproductive choice.

A large part of the success of the coalition was based on the conscious manipulation of images. The photo on the front page of the *Pitt News* in September 1991 pictures me as "radical" graduate student running a meeting, complete with bleached hair/dark roots, frozen in midsentence, and aggressively gesturing with my hand. Here I had become configured as the isolated leader of the "CCCP" (the abbreviation used in the article) exposing the economic injustice of the current child-care system. This is a recognizable image to the university community: irate graduate student agitating for change. The radical disjunction between these two discursive treatments of my identity, one in the *Pittsburgh Post-Gazette* and one in the *Pitt News*, exemplifies the parallel disjunction inherent in many student-parents lived experience.

Hearing over twenty administrators of a large research university talk about student-parents invited me to think of the way class is implicated in the construction of this identity. I cannot remember the words "working class" ever being mentioned in those meetings. Differences in class values and lifestyles were never considered as even a descriptive, let alone an explanatory, category when discussing family formation. Instead, students who had chosen to have children and be in school were not different from other students due to class-inflected choices but clearly marked as academically and even morally questionable. They were obviously less committed to their school work and therefore less valuable to the university. In listening to discussions of whether the implementation of a sliding-scale fee might not encourage students to have more children, it was clear that like the mythical "welfare mother" the student-parent was scheming and anxious to cheat the system. In discussions on the uses and abuses of drop-off care, evening care, weekend care, the student-parent was imagined clearly as a bad parent, one who if given the opportunity would leave the child in the center indefinitely. And why not? The only way most of the administrators could understand "this situation" was as an unfortunate mistake.

On more than a few occasions several female administrators proudly announced: "Of course, I waited to have my children until I had my career established." In the men's cases, it was mostly irrelevant. This clearly middle-class understanding of family was unanimously marked as the "right" choice. In fact that choice—waiting until one is married and thirty-five to have one or two children—describes a very small but powerful group of people. That *when* one might choose to have children is based not just on class but also on ethnicity, religion, race, and nation never entered the conversation. But we were all good liberal humanists and as such we were there to try to help those who had made "bad" choices. It was an unquestioned assumption that "we" did not condone those choices. And clearly if these students had made this bad choice, they would make others. Systems were put in place to safeguard the university from this element. The only other student around that table made an important observation. The possibility never existed in any discussion that student-parents might be an asset to the university community, that the university might actually *want* to recruit and retain them.

In these discussions there was also no space to say that my picture of a parent is different from theirs. Everyone in my family has children in their early twenties. That is how I learned to understand parenthood, to build a family if I chose. My mother had her first child at nineteen, my sister at twenty-four, my brother at twenty, my cousin at twenty-four. Women in my family always worked and raised families, so I did not imagine these choices to be mutually exclusive. Being from the first generation of our family to be college educated, I did not understand that the job I chose was substantially different from those of my mother, grandmother, and aunts. I was uninformed and did not realize that the university was not set up to make me, a young woman with children, as comfortable as it made the nineteen-year-old men I teach.

It is only in retrospect that I can understand the position I had been assigned and accepted in these discussions. The frequent verbal and nonverbal reiterations that I was unlike the portrait they were painting of the "typical" student-parent did not at that time always ring false to me. It is appealing to think of oneself as "exceptional." Yet these reiterations did not operate to separate me from this sometimes negative portrait/identity. Instead, they highlighted the ways in which I did not read this picture/portrait in the same way they did. This disjunction led me to further identify myself as one of "them," those "student-parents." So it was in these discussions where I first heard, recognized, and identified a part of my identity, working-class.

Despite the monumental changes that resulted from these meetings—which made it possible to finish my degree—despite the support, and despite some administrators' efforts to champion our causes, good intentions are beside the point. My critique is of a pervasive discursive formation in which everyone, myself included, participated. My bitter tone emanates from how insidious these classist attitudes are, even among the most well-meaning. My tone comes from the realization of how mentally disabling these attitudes were to me and are to many others.

The Theory and Practice of Working-Class Scholarship

*In general, however, I don't believe that
anyone undertakes any kind of cultural
study—chooses an object of study—that
one is not personally invested in. All
such research is deeply autobiographi-
cal—how can it not be?*
　　—Andrew Ross,
　　　"New Age Technoculture"

How does one bind together with coherency and clarity lived experience and academic theory? Our discipline mandates clear separation between intellectual work and personal life, clear boundaries between the pure space of theory and the messy hybridity of lived experience. Although this separation myth is being questioned more and more often, frequently it is still a foundational principal in the daily workings of graduate school. It is a split one must respect to be respected. But as many other marginalized groups have outlined, not all lived experience has been seen as valueless to theory. The experience of the straight white Western man of property is instrumental in the shape contemporary theory has taken. The very definitions, the boundaries, of theory change when *any* person's lived experience can be valued. Indeed, if one were to value a lived experience such as mine, these foundational dichotomies would be impossible to maintain. Even to write this essay I find myself negotiating scholarly dichotomies such as social constructionism versus essentialism.

As I trace the relationships between my experience outside the walls of the Cathedral of Learning—the literal name of Pitt's main academic landmark—and the theoretical positions I have taken, it is clear to me that they are interconnected. The "bad" choices I had made, having two children while in graduate school, were indeed an important part of my graduate education. The rubbing together of these two usually separated worlds moved me to be theoretically curious and intellectually committed. Major shifts occurred to my critical position as my life became more and more demanding.

My first clear theoretical stance in graduate school was as a pregnant lover of the French feminists who embraced via their brand of psychoanalysis the maternal as subversive and outside patriarchal constraints. This essentialism was comforting and enabling, opening up possibilities for an "outside" from which I could be certain of the evils of patriarchy. In these theories I found the makings of a corporeal subjectivity, an identity based on the immutability of the body. I trace my political commitment to feminism from that point, for the advantage of this theory is its innate ability to build collectively, as differences are wiped out in privileging an idea of the body as immutable and universal.

The beauty of *l'écriture féminine* faded fairly quickly as I became the harried mother of a toddler living on a teaching fellow's salary. I came to experience the material conditions of my life as the structuring force that mediated how I interacted in the world. I was told around this time that Julia Kristeva employed a full-time nanny to care for her child in an adjoining, but separate, apartment. This universal nature of how women actually experienced "the maternal" became suspect to me in my one bedroom apartment—desk, crib, and bed within five feet of each other. I decided then that the material conditions of life had to be accounted for in any theory for it to be valuable. Such an understanding allowed me to see the larger structures that were, in many ways, defining my life. My perspective shifted from the intrapersonal (i.e., the "body") to the global (i.e., the circulation of capital). The work of British feminists became important to how I understood the world to work.

Two years later, though, with a new baby and a toddler but no child care, I needed a theory that allowed for some sense of agency and could account for how change might occur. I no longer needed to understand myself as merely the product of some larger uncontrollable structures of capital circulation, although this had served me well. The work of such post-structuralist theorists as Gayatri Spivak, Judith Butler, and Donna Haraway offered me the idea of "partial and fractured identities." This was a way of discrediting monolithic ideas of "mother" and "student." These ideas resonated with the dissident moments in my life—when I tried to talk with a professor while keeping one eye on my kids by the ditto machine or presented a paper on the construction of the female body in instructional childbirth videos. By leaving behind the straitjacket of categorical purity, the idea of "strategic essentialism," the collectivity of the coalition was possible; and learning to "*negotiate* the structures of violence" that we find ourselves inhabiting was invaluable in the political strategies the coalition used.

I've just laid out a narrative about the construction of a scholar and the renegotiations of authority involved in growing as an intellectual. The place of theory itself shifts in my narrative from a "stance" I took as a French feminist to a map I used for a political end. The class-inflected choices I made to have children while in graduate school led me to not only constantly realign the theory I read and wrote with my rapidly changing life but also shift my relationship to theory itself.

While I strenuously echo sentiments concerning the difficulties of being both a graduate student and a mother in the current university setting, my focus has been turned recently (as my kids have gotten older and I have completed my degree) to the complex and beneficial dialectic for me in this coupling. As for the benefits to the academy, it seems clear. If our lived experience of the material world always informs and structures the scholarship we choose to participate in, then the inclusion of people who negotiate various material realities can only strengthen the academy and the scholarship it produces.

NOTE

I thank Christine Ross not only for the insightful readings she performed on drafts of this essay but also for the countless hours of work she performed in helping to secure child care for students at Pitt. I thank Valerie Begley, Carolyn Ball, and Stephen Parks for their insights into being a parent and a scholar. Constance Coiner's encouragement and validation will never be forgotten. I also want to acknowledge the support of Chancellor J. Dennis O'Conner, Anne

Levinson, and Professors Carol Kay and Jonathon Arac for the Coalition for Childcare at Pitt as well as the hard work of literally hundreds from different segments of the campus.

WORKS CONSULTED

Butler, Judith. *Gender Trouble: Feminism and the Subversion of Identity.* New York: Routledge, 1989.

Haraway, Donna. *Simians, Cyborgs, and Women: The Reinvention of Nature.* New York: Routledge, 1991.

Kristeva, Julia. *Powers of Horror: An Essay of Abjection.* New York: Columbia University Press, 1982.

Kuhn, Annette, and AnnMarie Wolpe. *Feminism and Materialism: Women and Modes of Production.* Boston: Routledge and Kegan Paul, 1978.

Ross, Andrew. "New Age Technoculture." *Cultural Studies.* Ed. Lawrence Grossberg, Cary Nelson, and Paula A. Treichler. New York: Routledge, 1992. 531–55.

Scott, Joan. "The Evidence of Experience." *Critical Inquiry* 17 (Summer 1991): 773–97.

Shorr, Lori. "Performing Birth: The Construction of Female Bodies in Instructional Childbirth Videos." *Velvet Light Trap* 29 (Spring 1992): 3–14.

Spivak, Gayatri Chakravorty. *In Other Worlds: Essays in Cultural Politics.* New York: Routledge Press, 1989.

———. *The Post-Colonial Critic: Interviews, Strategies, Dialogues.* New York: Routledge, 1990.

Beware the Silence: The Risks of a Commuter Marriage

Maura Doherty

I take the risk of telling my story—unsure of its impact on my career or my personal relationships—because I believe that silence prevents the empowerment of women and stalls the revolution. Despite our privileged status as graduate students and later as professors, women who enter academia need not let their pioneering status "silence" them or their experience.

While I have always challenged traditional gender roles, until now I have benefited from a generation of feminists before me who have taken on the patriarchal establishment, making my own journey easier than theirs. These women have been admirable pioneers to whom I am gratefully indebted. However, their monumental task of gaining entree into higher education has silenced many of them into accepting the institution as it was created by elitist men. They are on the defensive seeking tenure and the legitimacy of their academic voice; they do not, perhaps cannot, seek a radical restructuring of the institutional processes along their way. My generation is heir to the task.

Because I was in a women's history graduate program, most of the professors and students I came in contact with my first year were women. I initially thought this was a sign of the "feminization" of higher education. I imagined it was all part of an institutional plot to pay professors significantly less than they had been paid in the past. I soon learned I was quite far from the truth (although possibly not about the attempts to lower professors' salaries). In actuality, I attended an ex-

Maura Doherty is an assistant professor of history at Illinois State University.

traordinary liberal/leftist department filled with talented women who had managed to break into the field.

In my classes we spent week after week critiquing patriarchy and deconstructing women's experiences. Our discussions emphasized the need for historians to listen to women's voices in assessing their status and experience. We gave women agency, we emphasized collectivity, we even dared to criticize the early women's rights activists for not being radical enough. Yet there was no dialogue on the difficulties we as women would encounter pursuing Ph.D.'s; there was no discussion of the political nature of our personal lives. Old-fashioned mentoring did not exist. Perhaps our female professors were overly burdened with a disproportionate share of departmental and familial responsibilities. How ironic, though, that we were silent about these issues and completely on our own or even in competition with each other in trying to work our way through the academic maze and the outside world.

During my second year, as Rich and I were planning our wedding, I found myself desperately in search of female role models whose personal lives combined career and family in a way I could emulate. Because women were more abundant in my department than at most schools, I had many examples to choose from. However, I felt quite alone as I discovered most of their circumstances had little bearing on my situation. Most came from extremely privileged economic backgrounds that undoubtedly cushioned their experiences. Two had pursued graduate studies later in life after their children had matured. Two were near forty and had chosen never to have children. One started her family in her forties. Three routinely commuted 250 miles from their "home," where their husbands' jobs were. I have only respect for each woman's decision, but I was left trying to combine marriage, a family, and the pursuit of my degree and career without the comfort of an example showing that it was possible.

The following year, I attended a symposium at which women described the obstacles they faced as women and mothers on the tenure track. It was disillusioning to discover that corporate America has made more concessions to women regarding childbearing and rearing than have most academic institutions. Later, when I asked a question about pregnancy leave at a history roundtable on women's careers, I was surprised and dismayed by the responses. One woman discounted my desire to have children in my early thirties because *she* had *her* first child *after* she got tenure at forty. She could not understand that I was not obsessed with my biological clock, that I was ready and eager to start my family *soon*. Another tenured faculty woman asked if my husband had a job and then told me to stay home, take care of my children, and not worry about my career yet. She added, "Honey, you just want to have your cake and eat it too." My question was about *childbearing*, not child rearing. A matriarch in the profession even scolded the entire audience, saying that women had the *right* to have children, as several recent lawsuits had demonstrated. That lawsuits were still necessary was not comforting to the younger, childless women in the room. I was uncomfortable with the lack of empathy and the authoritarian silencing of my generation by these women who had finally "made it." Nobody answered my question; yet everybody felt the need to scold me and tell me what to do. At least the silence was broken and an intergenerational dialogue had begun.

After delaying for more than a year, Rich and I realized that I needed to begin the dissertation process. It is not completely clear to us now why we chose a commuter marriage as our solution to the dilemma that my research required me to be 250 miles from my husband's place of employment. We talked ourselves into commuting between two separate residences; after all, most of my married female role models *appeared* to commute successfully. This influenced what we thought was possible. Rich worried about the loss of income and the impact on his career if he moved. I was afraid to ask him to leave his job. Knowing that in the future he would have to follow me in my search for tenure, I did not want to push my luck. We never dreamed how difficult and destructive this choice would be.

The tension was thick as my in-laws disapproved of me "leaving" their son to take care of himself. Friends, family, and near strangers subtly and overtly expressed disapproval. Oftentimes people marveled that my husband was "allowing" me to do this research. He was labeled "modern" and "supportive"; I was "lucky" and "ambitious." I grew to resent the innuendo that Rich was a hero and I was the castrating wife. Our grandparents harbored the notion that we were truly separated. Others who were more sympathetic toward our situation offered their condolences for our "difficulties" despite our attempts to assure them that we were "happy" and comfortable with our choice to commute. We became defensive about our arrangement and overly sensitive to any hints of criticism. We also grew less "happy."

Out of a sense of guilt that I was not fulfilling my "wifely duties" I spent close to ten days each month with Rich and twenty at my research site during the first nine months. Much of my time was spent driving back and forth, packing and unpacking, managing our households, and cleaning two apartments. After several months, the commute began to take its toll and my low level of productivity became evident. Despite my meager progress, I put my dissertation on hold once again so that we could spend the summer together. As I looked to the upcoming year of commuting, I grew depressed. I pleaded with Rich to look for a job near my research. After much soul-searching he agreed to start a job search and to be there by January. Until then, we agreed, it was Rich's turn to do most of the commuting. We saw each other less this time because he found it too difficult to commute and hold a full-time job.

During this time I was more productive but grew increasingly apprehensive and defensive. Rich continued to worry about the impact leaving his lucrative job would have on his career. He also worried about the loss of income we might face when he relocated. He found that his job and his income were part of how he defined himself as a man and a husband. Because moving would challenge who he was, he did not look for a new job as promised. He soon grew depressed in his solitude. In my loneliness, I became active in my community and in several creative projects. I made a life separate from my husband and began to grow and change without him. He admired what I was doing but felt left out. Increasingly, I felt betrayed and rejected by his unwillingness to truly support me by living with me. My self-esteem plummeted and my anger soared.

The commuter marriage, which is becoming increasingly more common in academia, is a modern solution for the dilemma facing the dual-career couple. Until recently, state laws *mandated* that women reside in their husband's domicile. Cultural prescription considered it part of their wifely duty. The extent to which commuting is a successful partnership or a mere compromise determines the amount of strain inflicted on the marriage. Most commuters I have met consider the husband's place of income as their home base. The wives do the majority of the travel and have the task of managing (and cleaning?) both households. The amount of financial comfort also determines the stress level for the couple. Most of the women I know in commuter marriages can well afford it. Perhaps it was more stressful for us that my "absence" was not for a well-paying job but for unpaid, costly dissertation research.

For now, I remain unconvinced that *most* commuter marriages are more than a poor compromise to allow a woman a career without challenging the male gender role. Most are *not* a new form of feminist partnership. Why do so many women commute long distances to have a career? Are our men unwilling to follow us? Are we unwilling to ask? Can a new couple start a family in such circumstances or is it only viable for the childless or older couple? My commuter marriage was clearly the result of my husband's refusal to reverse traditional gender roles and my inability to challenge this. It was only when our marriage was severely threatened that Rich left his job to come live with me. By then, we were married nearly six years and had commuted on and off for three. As I write, many issues remain unresolved and our future together is uncertain.

My hope in telling my story is that academic women will no longer be silent about their personal lives, including their pain; that couples in commuter marriages will be honest about the difficulties; and that the female vanguard of academia will not silence my generation as we raise legitimate concerns about the personal impact of the politics of academia. Together, the two generations can create a more humane academic institution.

Maneuvering through the Cultural Borders of Parenting: Egypt and the United States

Pauline Kaldas

It was August 14, one day past the due date, with no sign that the baby would emerge anytime soon. I had followed my doctor's instructions. "Walk," she said. So we walked from our apartment in Garden City to the doctor's clinic in Mohandessein, a distance of about five miles through Cairo's broken sidewalks, heavy August heat, and a chaos of traffic. Our return tickets for the United States were set for August 25 and school started August 30. We had tried to communicate this vital information to our child, but she seemed oblivious to our sense of urgency. She was born on August 17, the same day as her grandfather. Apparently, she had a plan.

My plan took shape from the lives of the women in my Egyptian family and the suggestions of my American friends, as well as my fears regarding my new roles. My family had this advice to offer:

"You're too small; eat more."

"Don't let your feet swell like your cousin's."

"You can't go back so soon after the birth. Let your husband return. You stay with us for a while."

"You can't go to school. Who will take care of your child?"

After my mother became pregnant, she withdrew from college. After my cousin gave birth, she quit her job. Most Egyptian women leave

Pauline Kaldas is working on her dissertation at Binghamton University.

their jobs or education once they become mothers and remain at home for several years, at least until their children are of school age. In Egypt, it is possible for women to resume their careers after a long absence, something that is very difficult in the United States. Some women elect to work in government jobs because, in addition to a three-month paid leave of absence after delivery, they are allowed two years of unpaid leave per child for a maximum of three children, a total of up to six years. This is referred to as a child-care vacation. During this unpaid leave, the company continues to pay social security for the employee so that her pension will not be affected. Maternity leave policies in private industry vary and are usually not so generous.

In the United States, it is rare to receive more than six weeks of maternity leave. To continue child care, our technology offers us the breast pump. Our position as an advanced country valuing freedom and equality seems precarious if we are unable to provide parents with sufficient time to care for their children. For me, freedom includes the right to nurture my children before placing them in the care of others. Perhaps the problem of child care can't be solved through technology but requires a change of policy, comparable to that in Egypt.

I don't mean to imply that combining a career with motherhood is always easy in Egypt. There are many factors that affect the options available to women and the choices they can make. What is assumed to be temporary sometimes becomes permanent.

My cousin sits next to me, her shoulder leaning awkwardly against the back of the sofa. Her two young daughters, one five and the other almost three, are lying down on the rug in the other room. A few streaks of the hot afternoon sun sneak through the closed shutters as the girls create a melody on the red toy pianos. My two-year-old daughter watches them intently, occasionally extending her hand to offer a different note. My cousin begins to tell me how she wants to find a job but wonders how she can enter the work force with her outdated knowledge of computers, her lack of job experience, and her husband's reluctance to have the youngest girl attend nursery school. She wishes that thirteen years ago she had had the courage to finish her M.A. in computer science, but her family had strongly advised her to quit the program and join her husband, who was working abroad. They assured her that soon there would be children to occupy her, no one guessing that the children would not arrive for many years. Her voice moves away from tiredness, becoming more solid, and I hear her love for her children along with a frustration for the lack of intellectual and creative work in her life.

In my sixth month, waiting to hear from graduate schools, I was determined that nothing would deter me from starting the Ph.D. program. I saw no reason why having a child should change my career plans. I turned to my American friends for support, but their advice was not what I expected:

> "Graduate school is too hard. You can't take care of the baby and do well in school."

> "You can't start school just one week after having a baby!"

No one, American or Egyptian, suggested that my husband should stay at home or defer his graduate studies. Everyone cautioned me about trying to do both at the same time, one side claiming that motherhood was all encompassing and the other that graduate school was all encompassing.

By the time we were finalizing our plans, the commotion of voices in my head, along with my husband's—"I'll support you whatever you decide to do"—made me feel only doubt. One friend suggested that the graduate school might be upset when I arrived with a baby and perhaps could not work up to their expectations. I began to wonder if I should tell before accepting an offer, taking a chance it might be withdrawn, or show up and hide the baby? During the last phone call with Binghamton University, feeling my palms sweating on the phone and my heartbeat rising, I decided to explain my pregnancy. The graduate chair, without hesitation or surprise, offered me a semester's deferment with my teaching assistantship guaranteed. (If it had been another school, a man, or a woman who was not a parent, would I have been given the same choice?) Her offer gave me permission to again believe that I could be both a good mother and a good student. Our decision to attend Binghamton was based on that offer, which I hoped was indicative of a welcoming and understanding university environment. In recruiting graduate students and faculty, universities might benefit from understanding that, due to cultural beliefs, some people might be unwilling to place their children in day care. Offering a flexible schedule or a deferment can be a strong recruiting device.

My secret plan of taking one course the first semester quickly dissolved once the baby was born. Spending those months nursing her on demand (which sometimes meant all day), hearing her first cackling laugh, and watching her crawl upside down on her head and feet—that was a luxury that I now realize is rare for women in this country. Not only did that time enable me to enjoy my daughter but it also made me feel less guilty and apprehensive once I started school.

In graduate school, I am tormented with trying to get all the work done. Often, I feel disconnected from other students, most of whom are single without children and whose priorities and lifestyles are very different from mine. I work around my daughter's schedule, never sure when I will have time. That first semester, I was hounded by my insecurity about returning to school after six and a half years, as well as everyone's warning about the impossibility of accomplishing all this. Once she would fall asleep, I would pound the computer keys at manic speed. I am amazed that I handed in everything on time, that I was always prepared. Time was more precious and I couldn't take the chance of waiting until the last minute because my daughter might be sick or irritable or just need more attention.

My husband is also a graduate student, and our work with school, house, and baby is equal. Often we manage with little babysitting and do the "baby swap." But time becomes the source of tension.

"Well it's not two yet so it's still my time."

"But yesterday you took some of my time."

We are left with little time for each other or to spend together as a family. There is also the added pressure of trying to survive on our meager student stipends. I never knew a two year old could eat so much peanut butter or that starting preschool (another major subtraction from our income) would require so many additions to her wardrobe. As I watch her latest stomp foot, swing hip dance, I wonder whether we will finish graduate school in time to encourage these precious talents.

At Binghamton University, I have met several professors, men and women, who have broken the silence of parenting in the academy. One professor told me that my husband and I reminded him of the way he and his wife were caring for their first child while they were both in school. In another course, the professor required us to read an article about parenting in the academy, an assignment that enabled me to see my situation in a wider context. More recently, a professor was explaining that her early critical work and that of many other African-American women was in the form of articles, whereas African-American men were producing books. In class, she discussed the difficulty of combining parenting with the demands of an academic career and told us how she was able to write a book only when her children were older. Besides articulating my fears regarding my future, her insights made me review the way gender roles affect academic production.

My husband and I struggle to establish new parameters for living our lives in academia on an equal basis. Yet, on particularly busy days, I feel guilty as I think of my female relatives who dedicate themselves to the care of their children and consider how far I am from my own cultural legacy of parenthood. I am constantly juggling caring for my child, reading for my exams, and teaching my students, often spending less time than I would like with my daughter. However, when I speak to my family members, who tend to ask me only about my parenting, I feel a desperate determination to finish my education before those opportunities bypass me.

I have watched friends go through comprehensive exams and writing dissertations with possessed looks on their faces. For me, the desire for academic success is constantly placed in perspective by my daughter, whose insistent demands that I read *Horton Hears a Who* remind me that there are other important matters in the world. As I try to teach her Arabic and English, I live between cultures, between languages, and also between childhood and adulthood, a place that allows for continuous enlightenment and appreciation of how we live our textured and varied lives. At the age of two, she has just discovered the pronoun "I" and the possessive "mine." Teaching her my two languages pushes me to an awareness of my cultural legacy and my cultural present as I muddle through parenthood.

I have met with what I believe to be unusual support and understanding at Binghamton University. At times, the experience of parenting has been articulated in more subtle ways than what I've said here, such as seeing my graduate chair walking with his daughter on campus or watching my professor coach her daughter's baseball team in the park. I have tried to follow these models in my classroom, whether by mentioning my daughter, bringing her to class, or being sensitive to the needs of my undergraduate students who are parents, often single parents whose financial and emotional responsibilities exceed mine. To have professors articulate their experiences as parents and teachers/researchers is valuable for all students, not only those who are themselves parents.

I believe flexible deadlines for exams and other requirements is essential for those whose primary responsibilities go beyond their schoolwork. Also, discussions about beginning a family and a career at the same time are needed since so many graduate students are in that position. Some put off having children indefinitely out of fear that they will lose their careers. As one fellow graduate student hesitantly asked: "If you're pregnant, does that hurt your chances of getting a job?"

As I walk on campus, I am struck by the limited segment of the population I see. I wish there was a children's play area on college campuses, a place where parents can sit with their children. Such an area would serve as a physical and visual reminder that children are part of our world; it could also inspire discussions about being a parent in the academy today.

NOTE

Special thanks to Constance Coiner, who encouraged me to write this essay.

Reading around the Kids

Michael Rectenwald

The books are everywhere, stacked like barricades between me and my family, on coffee tables, end tables, the kitchen table, dining room table, chairs, desks, dressertops: *Social Semiotics* by Robert Hodge and Gunther Kress; *The Predicament of Culture* by James Clifford; *The PostModern Condition,* Jean-François Lyotard; *Madness and Civilization,* Michel Foucault; *The Field of Cultural Production,* Pierre Bourdieu, to name just a few. All of them interlibrary-loaned—I couldn't afford to buy them, I have three kids to support. Gretchen waits tables evenings. When I come home, I pass the car keys; she tells me what to cook and goes. I have tomes to read, so I slap something easy on the stove, like macaroni and cheese, feed them, and then descend to the basement.

The kids watch Nickelodeon game shows while I read Adorno's "The Culture Industry: The Enlightenment as Mass Deception." After a few hours, I come back up for air, find kids slouched all over, lighting too dim, two-and-a-half year old's diaper loaded; toys, plates, sundry items scattered all around the floor. Flip on lights, straighten up, change the baby, milk and cookies on the house. I give them the old tirade about TV, but the truth is, it's me that puts them in front of it—the damn thing's the best baby-sitter on earth. It grips them. How else could I get a Ph.D. in English than by exposing them to such hypnosis? For every book I read some 12 hours of combined television programming are viewed by my kids, as if one activity necessitated the

---

Michael Rectenwald is a graduate teaching fellow in literary and cultural theory at Carnegie Mellon University.

other. As Adorno noted, without the formatting of leisure, total systemization fails.

But what leisure? Gretchen works all day at home, then at night waiting tables. I accepted a job running the sales department of a university radio station. This job brought us to a small town unlike any of the metropolises we'd been living in. For me a big part of the compensation for losing the allure of San Francisco, Washington, D.C., or even Pittsburgh was the chance to study for a Ph.D. in English with partial tuition reimbursement and partial sanction from my employers. Employer support for such studies is no small thing when one's work background is advertising sales. I've worked for many broadcasters for whom even a modest interest in intellectual matters makes one suspect. Sales people are supposed to hustle, not contemplate things.

The university where I take classes happens to be almost one hundred miles from the one where I work. I started out taking one class a semester and then was offered a teaching fellowship the following year. So now I teach a class and take two others at one university while working full-time at another almost three hours away.

I spend some time with the kids, then put them to bed. Their mother comes home. We talk a while, questioning everything, including whether all this is pulling us apart. There is financial stress, time pressure, and, perhaps most important, the contradiction between theory and praxis. After all, *I* am the one studying feminism (amongst other things), while Gretchen labors taking care of children, straightening the business of the household, and waiting tables. As Marx wrote in *The German Ideology,* the "division of labor"—and its attendant inequities and alienation—"only becomes truly such from the moment when a division of material and mental labour appears. . . . This can only occur because existing social relations have come into contradiction with existing forces of production" (159). In terms of our dilemma, my consciousness (reified as reading) has come into conflict with my existing social relations (family), but only because I have come into conflict with my position within the realm of production. I am resisting the division of labor that I "chose" earlier in life, that of an advertising salesman. Meanwhile, Gretchen is now finding herself, naturally, in conflict with the current set-up of productive and nonproductive forces.

This theory, which is really only a reflection of praxis in the world, has come to take on the appearance of reality. It almost represents an adequate description of our life. That it actually reflects circumstances that I am helping to perpetrate even while studying it seems to me inevitable given my own contradictions: "For as soon as the distribution of labour comes into being, each man has a particular, exclusive sphere of activity, which is forced upon him and from which he cannot escape" (160). I try nonetheless; stay up reading till about 3:00 A.M., write for another two, slip into bed beside Gretchen, trying not to wake her, and get up for work by 8:00.

It confounds sense, trying to teach and sell advertising, manage eight interns for the station, read six hours a day, and do my own writing, as well as that for class and business. It all has to do with wanting out of my "original" career. It seems like it's either this or always doing "meaningless work." Francis Thompson's first lines from "The Hound of Heaven" aptly describe my flight from the Ad Man: "I fled him, down the nights and down the days. / I fled him, down the labyrinthine ways / Of my own mind" (89). Of course, Francis Thompson was referring to a zealously panoptic God and his own therefore futile attempts to escape such a God. As, perhaps, am I.

I'm in my office trying to read Friedrich Schleiermacher's hermeneutics, when in pops my boss, a punctilious administrator, asking whether I've raised any new money for the radio station. The last time he came by was about an hour ago. I was reading then too. Again, I slip the book under the desk quickly. My haste confirms any suspicion he might have had. I wish I had the hermeneutic key to unlock the meaning of this: I am compelled to work very hard at that which doesn't support me (and my family), avoiding that which does, to the point of very real danger.

Twice a week, I drive a hundred miles to teach and take classes. I hope for something exceptional to happen. Recently something did. The cultural criticism professor was talking about some students in his other class who "aren't real students . . . I mean," he said, "they have jobs." He was quick to add, not quite apologetically, "like you guys." We were, the two of us working stiffs, stupefied. "Work degrades," he was saying, just like the elitist modernists he's always ripped on. This is apparently my problem: I actually believe this. That this kind of slander still has not been adequately addressed—that the ideal of the graduate student still has ivy clinging to it—is not as fundamental as is the denial that intellectual activity itself is supported by other life-sustaining labor, whether one's own or someone else's. Likewise, a working-class background or the need to be employed are not only practical liabilities in academia; they present image problems as well. One solution to this is a kind of romanticism where one works a "lowly" job to support a "lofty" ideal. But such romanticism may not be available to those that either have no access to the "lofty" or else cannot afford to work a "lowly" job.

These images, as social constructs, aren't therefore "all in one's head." But they are there too, nonetheless. I have to keep slashing at them. But it behooves me politically not to mention that I am a husband and father, who likewise must work to help support life. These appurtenances just don't jibe with the "pure theory" of the academic, which, regardless of what is studied, always depends on labor to support it, maternal labor being the first form thereof. Like typical German ideologists, we academics like to imagine that we have no material (or maternal) history, but rather were just plopped down in the universities as full-grown students, lecturers, and intellectuals.

This kind of denial of personal history (and labor) extends itself to the children we engender. Children are the graduate student's leprosy in polite company. For instance, when recently a young Iraqi student who is also a mother met her husband and four children in the hall during a class break, the professor rolled her eyes and cleared her throat repeatedly at the slightest noises the children made. "When the voices of children are heard" in the hall, the result is not the breast-stilling awe that occurred to William Blake, but rather is—too often—ignominy. Children embarrass us because they point ever too cleverly and clearly to our denial of personal, material, and maternal history. This accounts, in part, for academia's pedophobia and the hush-hush we maintain about parenting.

I am implicated in this contradiction between pedophobia and some of the more progressive positions that I hold. This is due largely to the nature of intellectual life as a kind of self-flattering divorce from labor, in both senses of the word. While pregnancy embodies literally and inadvertently many Western ideological contradictions—the subsequent labor of which (giving birth and taking care of children) has never counted in the calculations of economists (excepting those of recent feminist economists and perhaps Marx)—such contradictions are perhaps even more prominent in academia. The sheer physicality of the event embarrasses, and the reality of human reproduction doesn't fit into rationalistic-bureaucratic schema. Leave policies are decided by bureaucrats who only yield to the fact, but never really own up to it. As an ontological event, it defies logic.

I am loathe to speak for the hypothesized Others, women, as to how this is experienced—as external pressure or internalized opprobrium or both. As for myself, I admittedly internalize what I feel is an implicit pedophobia and disavowal of parenting, denying by omission my status as a father on many occasions. My standing as an intellectual, I somehow feel, would be affected by regular referral to my children. This is, of course, a ridiculous notion. But it is no less powerful for that, until it has been exorcised. If we brought children more often into our halls, as a kind of talisman to drive away our pedophobic ideologies, we might help to make the university resemble more closely the kind of community that we expect others to become, one that accepts diversity in its many forms. And hopefully by airing our varying concerns about the suppression of parenting in the academy, we may come to acknowledge and reclaim it for ourselves and for others.

HOME

Child:

You live in my room daddy,
it's big enough for us,
I can sleep on the floor,
you sleep in my bed,
I won't talk at all, and
I won't bother your thinking
and you don't have to be
sorry for anything . . .

Chorus:

Between the children there's a father,
an absence they play with,
like an imaginary friend,
everything between the covers,
as if he were about to read them
a book not even he can construe—
there are no constants here,
they will forget even the myth.

WORKS CITED

Thompson, Francis. "The Hound of Heaven." *The Poems of Francis Thompson.* London: Oxford University Press, 1937.

Tucker, Robert C., ed. *The Marx-Engels Reader.* 2d ed. New York: W. W. Norton, 1978.

Vampires in the Classroom

April Salzano and
Thom Dworsky

April Salzano:

She has chosen to be a person. That was one of my first thoughts about Sondra Ellsworth when she walked into our first class together four years ago. Dressed in a flowing skirt and turquoise jewelry, a mane of graying hair touching her waist, she was beautiful. An odd silence filled the room, a sort of collective respect for the established literary critic, poet, and professor I later learned is an enigma. Several students greeted her by her first name, a boundary I consciously chose never to cross.

Throughout my undergraduate career I worked closely with Dr. Ellsworth as professor, thesis advisor, and mentor, but I never took the liberty of allowing myself to feel that I knew her or of taking my personal problems to her office as so many other students did. The message that she sends to her students is continuously misread. By hiding her eyes behind tinted lenses, Dr. Ellsworth attempts to create a barrier between herself and those whom she instructs. Inevitably, it is more fulfilling for each student to both acknowledge and cross that barrier than it is to recognize himself or herself as one of many—all individualizing themselves—forcing the professor into the uncomfortable role of mother/confidant. Students seem to take liberties with certain female professors that they would never take with their male counterparts. I cannot think of one male professor at my university

---

April Salzano has an M.A. from Queen Mary and Westfield College, the University of London, and is now teaching English at Westminster College in Pennsylvania. Thom Dworsky plans to enroll in a master of fine arts program.

who is called by his first name, nor have I ever seen a student cry in a male professor's office. As I begin my graduate studies in literature and move toward a career as a female professor, these are the issues I face. How much can a teacher allow a student to disclose without being interpreted as a surrogate mother by students and colleagues?

The discussion of poetry incessantly turns inward, leaving students with the peculiar burden of comprehension. In an effort to understand a poem's central metaphors or to ascertain meaning, as we are taught early to do, students often divert the discussion to their personal lives, drawing constant comparisons between their experiences and those of the poetic speaker, their perception of the dramatic situation, thereby justifying personal discourse. Inevitably, the literature and writing professor learns a great deal about students as human beings. She witnesses the manifestations of personal pain on a daily basis and is unable to reciprocate. Each fragment of her personal life that she divulges strengthens a student-perceived umbilical cord. Even though Dr. Ellsworth may have made a conscious decision not to disclose the personal elements of her past or present circumstances, anything she might say is expanded in the mind of the listener.

A brief but strangling tension filled the room when Dr. Ellsworth told the story of her recent experience watching the slow death of a butterfly. She was referring to mutability, a theme in a Blake poem we had been discussing. As she revealed the two-day incident, she referred several times to her "hiking partner," not disclosing name, gender, or relationship. The effort was conscious and, to me, obvious. For the students, the hiking partner became the focus of the story. We stopped caring about the suffering butterfly and wondered who this person was, what they were doing alone in the woods together for a weekend, where they were staying, and why. She owed us that much. We want to feel that we know her, even if only because she knows us. As human beings, we have been conditioned for reciprocal conversations. We do not wish to reveal ourselves and get nothing in return, lest we should somehow be made vulnerable by our own disclosures. Somehow, this simultaneous expected/perceived reciprocation allows students to apprehend the female professor as a mother figure. Students want to continue discussions later, for any number of reasons. And if the professor listens too intently, she begins a cycle of academic parenting.

The first years of college are a time of self-discovery. Students are learning about themselves and testing their independence. Frequently, they detach from their parents and seek new bonds. Yet immediately we are called upon to present some distinguishing characteristic that will separate us from the nameless sea of faces in our classrooms. Those who can't prove themselves academically expose their pain to anyone who will listen—anyone including a professor. Such listeners are more often female. Male professors do not need to establish the barrier between themselves and their students. For whatever reason, physical or otherwise, it is already in place culturally. Fathers are praised for being detached, somewhat cold—mothers are not only condemned for that same behavior but also valued for its antithesis. Women professors must continually reestablish barriers to discourage students from adopting the wrong role as victimized children in need of parenting.

Students project their sense of loneliness and of being overwhelmed onto the professor in the same way that they project their limited understanding of pain onto poetic speakers. They want to help. They want to be able to help. Another professor I studied creative writing with revealed her childhood poverty to her classroom. My circumstances mirrored hers and in the margin of my essay, she thanked me for writing my story. I understood the comment to be reflective of her appreciation of my emerging skill at memoir writing. I could not help but wonder if this very human act of hers, bestowed on another student, might have made the student feel thanked for somehow helping the professor comprehend her own pain. Since my piece was being considered for publication, people would "need," as we say, to read it. I did not take the liberty of assuming that my professor was one of them. What could have been seen as a (dangerous) signal of invitation, in this case, was not. I severed the perceptual umbilical cord. I have observed many others utilizing such instances as opportunities to tighten it.

As I consider teaching at the college level, I want to be able to share with my students anything that will help them understand a particular poem or enable them to write. At the same time, I am painfully aware of the implications of personal discourse and of the vampiric nature of some of the student populations, who seem to mentally consume any other among them. When we realize that a teacher is consciously holding back, even the smallest revelation comes as some sort of invitation—or as a cry for help. When Dr. Ellsworth told my modern poetry class that her closest friend had died hours before our class, I could not help but wish she had not. Of course, she only wanted us to understand that she would not be as accessible within the next few days—office hours would be cut short, classes might be canceled. But I knew that my classmates were going to knock on her office door to see if there was anything they could "do" for her. In the interim, they were going to tell her stories of their own loss. They might even cry in her office. And for a strangely predatory reason, would hope that she would cry, too. Later during my scheduled thesis meeting that day, I resisted all forms of what I knew to be etiquette and did not even ask Dr. Ellsworth how she was doing. What was obvious to me—if she needed comfort from me, she would ask—was probably not obvious to my fellow students. The sad fact is, what a male professor can say to a room full of students, a female professor cannot. And though that may very well be the reality I will have to deal with in the future, part of me has already decided that it is simply unfair. I do not want the burden of constant word manipulation to prevent anyone from feeling like my son or daughter or be forced to be cold and unapproachable simply because the alternative is worse. I was wrong in thinking that Dr. Ellsworth has chosen to be a person. In the academic environment she is as far from herself as possible, not because she wants to be, but because she has to.

Thom Dworsky:
The system of beliefs through which the college student understands education at the university level changes the teaching process and denies the female professor the freedom to express herself as both a professional and a human being. The female professor must be careful not to be viewed as an individual or she may lose the identity of a professional, at the same time forfeiting the prospect of a positive impact on her students. The myth that a youth enters college to learn new and interesting and hidden aspects of his personality while at the same time being prepared for a life in the higher levels of society is widespread and dangerous to the effectiveness of higher education. Each student has the ability to disempower college as it relates to him, creating a new college of the self, where real learning of classroom material is done passively, and in some cases not at all.

Whether or not the student knows anything of a female professor's private life, she often believes she does and will continue to seek out more personal "facts" to enhance her own self-awareness and identity. The professor's role is not to encourage a backtracking individualism in the student but a forward-stepping extension of the student's self into an area of intellectualism from which the most good can be done for society and the student. It is the parent's role to promote self-discovery, not the educator's.

The male professor does not simply have the option but the right to keep a class or office or recreational discussion focused on goals. Given the standing perception of Professional Man, a male professor can refer to a personal story without sacrificing the substance of what needs to be taught or learned. Within the schema of the myth, the student will consider the personal disclosure as it relates to his own life while the professor continues educating.

For the female professor, a solution is not as easily found. She is the strong but compassionate mother figure who is able to manage at the same time as care. There is not only a respect for her as a professional but also a vision of her as a mother who comforts. A personal story, even disclosed as an image for class material, can be an invitation for the student confounded by the myth to explore the person of the teacher more deeply. The student, once exposed to the idea of a private life connected to the female professor, is able to infringe upon the whole of that other life in such a way as cannot be done to a male professor. After the precedent is set, that the professor will respond to philosophical self-discovery topics, the student quickly widens the range of the relationship. The female professor is labeled in the mind of the student as accessible for conversations entertaining personal thoughts.

It is neither uncommon nor wrong for a professor to advise a student, but advice from a female professor is mothering in the mind of that student. The student begins to need more support until the quality of her work, which has already been that of a passive learner, begins to show a child's pout and asks forgiveness and partiality. The female professor loses the student once she is able to be delayed and interrupted and treated as Personal rather than Professional.

That the cultural construction of the mother figure suggests protection and encouragement and unconditional love mandates for the professor that she cannot, in any way, serve as one for the student. Service as mentor is the functional extent of the professor's relationship with the student. Though the student desires (even needs) knowledge of the professor on a private level, it is only on the basis of the myth. The deconstruction and replacement of the self should not be the aim of one's college experience. Friendships develop and personalities expand in college; this process should have little to do with the presence of the professor. The material taught must be the means to all college ends, and the professor should be only the intriguing medium.

PART FIVE

When the Biological and Tenure Clocks Tick in Unison

Invisible Babies

Charlotte Holmes

My son was conceived in the first months of my postgraduate fellowship in fiction writing at Stanford. I was twenty-six, had published three short stories and a handful of poems, and felt the boundless, unstoppable enthusiasm of a woman in love who can, she thinks, do anything, stare down any obstacle. I knew that having this child would complete the small, rich circle of life I'd woven with his father over four years. I knew that, somehow, having this child would change my life.

By the time Will was a year old, my fellowship had ended and my husband and I had decided that we wanted to move back East, that at least one of us needed a full-time job. We applied for teaching jobs all over the country and ended up with two eleventh-hour positions at a small liberal arts college in North Carolina. The salary was terrible, but the mountains looked serene after the Silicon Valley.

In North Carolina we rented a two-bedroom apartment from the university. When we opened the drapes in the morning, the administration building stared back at us from across the highway. We set about arranging our classes so that one of us was always home with our baby son, because on our salaries, there was no question of being able to afford the $250 a month for day care.

We'd gone to a graduate school where the money came in the form of fellowships, not assistantships—a detail that had once seemed a blessing and now felt like a curse. I had four classes to teach that first

Charlotte Holmes is an associate professor of English at Pennsylvania State University.

semester, three different course preparations, and no idea what I was doing. But the students were warm-hearted, and I stayed up until 2:00 A.M. preparing for class, then rose at 6:00 to get ready to begin teaching at 8:00. When my classes and office hours were over at noon, I raced home, where I said hello to Jim as he dashed out the door, on his way to begin his afternoon of teaching.

Will and I had the afternoon to ourselves. After lunch, I buckled him into his car seat and set off in our twelve-year-old Volkswagen down the backroads of the Blue Ridge. At the edge of the blacktop grew wild orange lilies and goldenrod, and the scent of balsam coursed through the open window, but I kept one eye on the rearview mirror and my wavering voice pitched to every sleepytime song I knew: I got a nap out of this drive almost every afternoon. Will would nod off after fifteen or twenty minutes, and I'd ease the Volkswagen home. If I was careful lifting him out of the car seat and into the apartment, he'd sleep for another ninety minutes or so, and I'd grade papers like mad or read the next day's assignment. When Will woke, there were snacks to prepare, blocks to stack, Little Golden books to read, diapers to change, laundry. Then there was supper to cook, Papa's arrival, maybe a walk in the evening after the dishes were done. Will was usually asleep by nine, and then I could begin working on my classes in earnest. I taught five days a week, so there was always a new lesson to prepare. In that time I saw my son grow from a baby to a little boy— the most critical years, psychologists tell us, of a child's life.

Shortly after my teaching career began, I realized that this schedule allowed no time for my own writing. Most of my colleagues in the department had long ago given up their scholarly ambitions, though a few struggled valiantly to produce conference papers and fewer still wrote articles and edited textbooks. Jim and I decided that the only way we could save ourselves from drowning under the wave of coursework and housework was to divide the weekend. He worked in our office at school all day on Saturday, I worked there all day on Sunday, and in that way, I published two more stories during the three years. On Saturdays while Jim worked at school, Will and I drove to the nearest town, which had a library, a park, and a McDonald's. Even as a toddler, Will loved to read, so we spent a long time picking out great armloads of books, and afterwards, if the weather was good, I'd buy lunch at McDonald's and we'd head for the park.

The spring I turned thirty-one, a few months before Will's fourth birthday, I was hired for a tenure-track assistant professorship at Penn State. Jim was offered a lectureship. The jobs were a terrific break for us. From our present circumstances, my teaching load was cut in half, and Jim's reduced to three courses a semester.

A few months after we moved to State College, I was talking with a male colleague at a department party—inconsequential talk about classes, the football team, the local schools. Suddenly he asked if I planned to have more children. I remember staring at him open-mouthed, like a parody of myself being shocked. My first reaction was not anger at being asked such a personal question by someone I barely knew, nor was it embarrassment that the personnel committee might have an interest in my reproductive habits. My first reaction was an honest, gut-wrenching sense of amazement that anyone would think I had the *time* to have another child.

Though Will attended the university's day-care center full-time, Jim and I were busier than ever. For the first time I experienced the particular pressure of writing toward tenure. I felt as if I were trying to create art with a gun held to my head, and even in the grocery store I seemed to run into colleagues who inquired how my work was going.

After a year or so, I started to enjoy the time for my own work that came with a reduced teaching load and the expectation that I'd finish a book before tenure. But Jim, caught on the lectureship track, still taught six courses a year and had "additional duties" to make up for the required seventh course. Though his poems continued to appear in reputable journals, he was informed rather emphatically that *his* publications counted toward nothing: he was not to think that publications might pave his way to a lighter teaching load or an assistant professorship. He was a faculty spouse, but the only one in our department who was both male and a lecturer—a position that left him without colleagues.

How was our son growing up? Lonely, I think, and baffled much of the time by our anxieties. Our jobs followed us home. Over dinner we talked about our classes, our students, committee decisions, which colleague had snubbed us in the hall and which had been inexplicably friendly . . . it's no wonder to me now that Will blew bubbles in his milk, played with his food, tried to keep us from talking. I'm sure he felt invisible under the torrent of apprehension.

Writing took the place of free time, so Will was once again paired with one or the other of us, rarely both together. We had no time for a social life, so we didn't develop crucial friendships with couples who had children. Will had few friends of his own. On the rare occasions when we did things as a family, he was competitive and difficult, angry when we spoke to each other instead of to him.

The long, quiet periods of introspection we both knew were necessary for our creative work did not materialize. Jim was still swamped with class preparations and teaching. Though I was now home two days a week, the pressure to *write* was overwhelming. Time spent reading, or just daydreaming, seemed suddenly "unproductive."

Now that my son is nearly a teenager, I rise early, walk the dogs, make a cup of tea, and sit at my desk to enjoy nearly two hours of uninterrupted solitude before it's time to wake Will for school. But as an infant, this child had powerful radar. If I woke at 5:30, he woke at 6:00 with a dazzling smile, ready to be fed and played with. On those mornings as I stirred his oatmeal, snapped Legos together, ran through yet another chorus of "It's a Beautiful Day in the Neighborhood," what I often felt was akin to rage, a panicky, suffocating awareness of all the time that was slipping away. And no matter how loudly I sang, I still heard voices whispering that a real writer wouldn't let this kid get in the way. But only in the last few years has Will developed the trick of sleeping through soft footsteps outside his door, the tick of my fingers on the keyboard.

Should we, like doctors, train ourselves to operate on no sleep? During the semester Jim regularly sleeps between four and five hours a night. If the early morning is my quiet time, then the small hours are his. At the end of the fifteen weeks he collapses and only gradually comes back to himself, as if returning from a long journey. I tried this, too, for a few years in North Carolina, until I learned that sleep is the glue that holds me together.

My colleague who asked years ago if I planned to have more children has two children of his own and a wife who stays home with them. He's a good man, well-intentioned, and I doubt now that he asked his question to pin me down, though I felt then that only one correct answer existed and I didn't know it. It seems fine for men to beget children on the tenure track. Don't fathers seem more stable, more likely to work hard, to produce, to stick around? A male colleague whose child was born shortly after he was hired enjoyed sympathy in the department mailroom one morning as he regaled listeners with tales of his newborn's sleepless nights and colicky evenings. Though I laughed, I couldn't stop wondering if a woman would have dared to tell the same story. What if her colleagues went back to their offices believing that she was neglecting her research?

A few years ago when an untenured assistant professor in our department became pregnant with her second child, a male senior professor told her that she could resign herself to writing one less book.

Given this response, it's no wonder that some women decide to defer childbearing until *after* the tenure decision, when many of them are already in their late thirties.

The year before I came up for tenure, I found myself unexpectedly pregnant. Will, at eight, was finally settling down, accepting his lot as the child of parents who were perpetually busy and distracted. And there was the tenure decision on the horizon. Would the personnel committee find me overconfident in having a baby mere weeks before my tenure file went before the department? And what would happen if I were turned back? I'd have not one but two children to support. While caring for a newborn, I'd be on a job market that was far rockier than it had been six years earlier. Would I ever finish my novel?

Still bombarding myself with questions, I boarded a plane to Dallas on Halloween afternoon, headed to a conference where I was to give a paper on Nadine Gordimer. Gordimer, the mother of five children, had won the Nobel Prize in Literature just two weeks earlier. When thunderstorms grounded us in Memphis for an hour, I stood up to leave the plane and realized that I was probably having a miscarriage. Since I was in no pain, I gave my paper as scheduled and spent the rest of the conference resting. When I returned home, I saw my doctor. The ultrasound showed that the baby was still alive. She ordered me to bed. "This one's a fighter," she told me.

I canceled my classes for a week. Since both were fiction writing workshops, it seemed impossible to arrange for someone else to read and critique the six student stories (over a hundred pages of manuscript) on such short notice. Jim handed back my critiqued copies to the students who'd written the stories and dismissed the classes. I stayed in bed. By the end of the week I felt wonderful. The rest had helped me come to terms with this pregnancy. I was thirty-five years old, and it was time we had another child—in my doctor's office I'd seen those frightening charts that showed diminishing chances for delivering a healthy baby for each year after this one. Though the doctor remained cautious, I felt sure this pregnancy would last. Who cared what my colleagues thought? As my mother always promised, things would work out for the best.

When I returned to the doctor on Thursday, she did another ultrasound and discovered that the baby had disappeared. No pain. No cramping. No nothing. "This happens sometimes," she said. "It's just been reabsorbed, like a bruise."

I went home and stared at the ultrasound photographs I'd been given earlier, the ones that showed the baby like a tiny question mark with a pumping heart. How could she—I thought of the baby as she—simply disappear? She was there, real: I'd seen her on the screen. According to my doctor I'd taken her back into my bloodstream, recycled her cells, as if she'd never existed. But in my mind she was there still—invisible, liquid, still part of me.

At school the next morning, a colleague congratulated me on my pregnancy. I heard my voice sounding cool, matter-of-fact, as I explained about the miscarriage, as if this were any other piece of information he might find helpful. He gave me a quizzical look and said, "Well, you certainly seem to be taking it well," then went on to tell of his wife's miscarriage years earlier. "I don't think she ever really got over it," he said. Dry-eyed, I listened, nodding when appropriate. When he finished I may have even smiled and wished him a nice day. But afterward I went back to my office and cried, and when a friend called later that day to offer consolation, I couldn't even speak to her.

The next week, a student whose story had been scheduled for discussion during the week I missed class came to my office. We'd been talking for a few minutes before I realized that, though he seemed polite and controlled, he was actually furious with me. I'd canceled class the day his story was up for discussion. He'd worked hard on the story, and I'd taken away his only chance to share it with his classmates. I understood his disappointment, but his anger seemed out of proportion, suggesting more at stake than a simple missed class, as if I'd let him down morally, fallen from some pinnacle. When, near the end of the term, he turned in a portfolio of writing exercises that featured my miscarriage in several assignments—exercises replete with graphic descriptions of dead babies and the deficient women who deserved to lose them—I began to worry, though I tried to grade the portfolio dispassionately, commenting on style rather than substance. At the end of the term when he sent a threatening letter, I notified the campus police.

I still don't know why this student reacted so personally to my miscarriage, but I resented having to share it with him, resented the way he'd appropriated it to express his anger. And I felt guilty, because he was right—I *had* missed class. Did this mean I was a bad teacher? Hadn't I let my personal life—worse yet, my family life—interfere with my professional responsibility toward him?

I became convinced that I'd lost the baby because I'd worried so much about the wisdom of having it. Maybe the miscarriage wouldn't have happened if I hadn't gone to that conference, if I wasn't always thinking about tenure. On the other hand, maybe my book of stories wouldn't be having such a tough time finding a publisher if I'd devoted more of myself to my writing and less to my family. In short order, I knew I couldn't do anything right.

When the department head asked in all kindness if I needed a semester off to recover, I panicked. If I took the time off, would they think I was weak? If I didn't take it, would they think I was heartless? I opted for heartlessness and trudged into the spring term wary and depressed.

Though I'd been working hard on my novel before the miscarriage, I discovered in the months following that I couldn't concentrate on much of anything. I didn't notice at first that my son was reacting, too. While I had turned inward, Will was acting out—he was disruptive at school, angry at home. He'd been so obviously delighted by the news of my pregnancy that Jim and I looked at each other in surprise. Will confessed that he'd always wanted a sibling and went on to spill out eight years of grievances against being an only child. When we lost the baby, all his dissatisfaction came roaring back.

In blessed hindsight, I see those bleak months as a culmination of all the years that came before—the crazy schedules, the intense anxieties, the clumsy juggling of parental and academic and professional responsibilities, the rampant uncertainty of our lives. When we started out together, we were in our twenties, fresh from the Ivy League, full of promise, with excellent letters of reference, sure that literary fame waited just around the next corner. A dozen years later we were exhausted, disillusioned, our family life in chaos, our books unpublished, our future at the state university up for grabs. Where, we wondered, had everything gone wrong?

In my journal from 1979, I'd copied out this quotation from Katherine Anne Porter: "I'm all for marriage and children and that sort of thing, but quite often you can't have that and do what you were supposed to do, too. Art is a vocation, as much as anything in this world. . . . [Artists] really do lead almost a monastic life, you know; to follow it you very often have to give up something."

I thumbed through the journal feeling more discouraged by the minute. What had I been trying to tell myself? Why had I thought I could do it, when Katherine Anne couldn't, when Virginia couldn't, when Eudora and Willa and Flannery couldn't, when Jean Stafford and Edith Wharton and Ann Beattie and Katharine Mansfield couldn't? But I soon began to compile another list, of women writers with children, and not just the suicides like Plath and Sexton, but women who'd come through: Nadine Gordimer, Grace Paley, Louise Glück, Linda Pastan, Tillie Olson,

Mary Gordon, Francine Prose, Colette, Edna O'Brien, Caroline Gordon. I came upon a scrap of an interview with David Ignatow, in which he said, "The most important thing is peace of mind . . . growing out of an assurance about one's relationships with others. . . . If it's a secure and loving relationship . . . then you can turn around and put your energy into a lot of different things because you can take this other thing for granted."

And I realized, finally, that I had this love, and that it was more important to me than the accolades that might be thrown my way by the personnel committee. If I didn't get tenure, if my book went un-published, neither Jim nor Will would abandon me. These were the relationships I could count on, and I needed to build from there. I might have a chance at tenure at another school, or even a chance at another career, but Will's childhood is a one-shot deal.

So, the book was published, and I did get tenure. Jim won a Ful-bright to Ukraine, where he spent a year teaching one course a semes-ter, writing poems, and working on translations—a happy time for him, and I know that sometimes he would like to go back. Here, little has changed for him: still seven courses a year "or the equivalent," no job security, low pay. His poems continue to appear in good places. I'm working on the novel again. And after four years I've more or less accepted that a second child is unlikely. I think of something else Katherine Anne said: "Everything that happens, happens for a reason."

Achieving a balance is never easy, no matter the profession. It seems a diminished life that encourages us to see our children as im-pediments to success, distractions to be dealt with or "managed," lit-tle beings sacrificed upon the altar of our productivity. In my eleven years of university teaching, I've noticed a gradual change in attitude. Some of our full professors now are women with children, and their presence has been a positive reinforcement for the rest of us.

I'm finishing this essay in my study at home, at a little past six in the morning, while my son sleeps in the next room. Will, at twelve, likes Jimi Hendrix and Indiana Jones. He loves to read and draw, spends too much time playing Nintendo, and writes stories—imagina-tive ones, with deft, witty characterizations and surprising diction. He tells me that he can't decide what he wants to be when he grows up— a police officer, a spy, or a writer. I tell him, "Be a writer, because then you can also investigate. Being a writer is like being a spy."

If he becomes a writer, I imagine that someday he will write a story about growing up on the tenure track. I wonder if he'll sympathize with his harried parents or if he'll see us in the cold, ironic light of our ambitions and small accomplishments. Perhaps, in different stories, he'll do both, the way he now alternates between liking our life and thinking it's a pain in the neck.

When he complains, I remind him that at least our schedules allow either his dad or me to be home with him after school—that if we had "regular" jobs, he'd be in after-school care until 5:30 or with a baby-sitter or he'd be a latchkey kid. And though he concedes that maybe the job has some advantages, "college professor" still hasn't appeared on the list of occupations he's willing to consider for his own.

WORK CITED

Ignatow, David. Interview. *Paris Review* 21.76 (1979).
Porter, Katherine Anne. Interview. *Writers at Work: The Paris Review Interviews.* 2d ser. Ed. George Plimpton. New York: Penguin Books, 1963.

How I Got Married, Had a Kid, Got Tenure, and Lived to Tell

Sharon Dale

Why are women in academe so tired? Our knee-jerk answer is that we are trying to balance two full-time jobs, but aren't all working women attempting this sort of thing? No, I think there is a hidden agenda, an unspoken expectation that women will bring and apply their vaunted nurturing skills to campus—the university has replaced *in loco parentis* with *in loco matris.* We are subliminally required to feel a skewed form of maternal responsibility to the ivy walls, a fealty that translates into extraordinary demands on women's time in the form of being at every concert, lecture, student club meeting, faculty meeting, sensitivity-training session, gay/women's/minority/constitutional rights rally not by choice, but by obligation. So that a male faculty member, a fine teacher and scholar who serves on a few committees but does not participate in any extracurricular events, is greeted with sympathy when he grouses that the committee work is cutting into his hunting time. Imagine a female professor suggesting that nurturing student groups was cutting into her gardening and you get a sense of yet another double standard in women's lives. It is this expectation of institutional nurturing that is so insidious, for by gender alone we are the externally and self-appointed guardians of "quality of life" on campus. We don't want to "hurt students' feelings" by not being there for them. And heaven forbid, we don't want to make our colleagues, bosses, secretaries, students, maintenance staff—anyone—angry at us.

Sharon Dale is an associate professor of art history at Pennsylvania State University at Erie, the Behrend College.

I am one tough cookie. Ask my male colleagues. Ask, in particular, the resident geniuses, those male academics whose every whim and need is catered to by a long-suffering spouse, who may have a career of her own, often as an underpaid academic stringer at the same school. My favorite resident geniuses have wives doing their typing, laundry, bathrooms, bill paying, child rearing, and any other mundane business that might interfere with the higher calling of genius. The same guys who justifiably complain about my ability to say no to extraordinary demands on my time are those men whose wives are providing the female model of self-sacrificial nurturing that I so daringly flout. Indeed, I have even been told by one of these guys that he couldn't picture me a mother. He's right, I'm not his mother. What I mean is, I won't serve as BMOC (Big Mom on Campus) by attending every lecture and concert, serving on countless committees, advising campus groups et al. and ad nauseam because I have drawn my line in the sand. I teach six courses a year and advise students while I am expected to do research, present, and then publish scholarly papers and books and write (successful) grant proposals. Kick in several must-do committee assignments a year (never fewer than three or four), and you have more than a full plate. So no, I don't participate much in the active extracurricular life on the campus. I do my job well and I leave it at that. I have to attend my kid's concerts, school open houses, and Cub Scout picnics—it goes with the parenting territory—but whenever I am faced with yet another demand on my time from my school, I do a little gender test: I find out if the resident geniuses have been hit with the same request. Rarely do the guys get tapped for the small change items or criticized for not participating; their time is too valuable. They do serve on the big-time, important committees. You know the ones—tenure, promotion, the committees on which there is never more than one woman. Get the picture? So I say yes to serious committee assignments and no to nurturing the campus community—because, in my experience, this is the stuff that really eats up women's time in academe. Has this decision hurt me? Not in regards to tenure. My publications have been held to a higher standard of review, but I think that this is the case with most women's scholarship. Going to yet another lecture would not have changed this situation, but using up my time on nonessential meetings would not have allowed me to finish any research project. Do the "boys" think I'm a bitch? Yeah, but they haven't asked me what I think of them. I don't need the love of my colleagues, I need them off my back. This is a delicate balance, for active enmity of one's colleagues can be risky. On the other hand, door-mats are tired, frayed, and cheaply replaced.

Having successfully navigated the shoals of domestic and academic life for more than a dozen years, I am living proof that it can be done without a major shipwreck. Herewith my best advice on how to survive on both tacks.

Take the Right Job for You

I began in academe at a small liberal arts college that demanded my body six days a week. That's right, Saturday classes. Seven classes a year, five different preparations. I had yet to write my dissertation at this point and the department secretary was told by the chairman that typing my thesis was her lowest priority. So I became computer literate and eventually changed jobs. I really didn't want to be in a place that discouraged scholarship. I like the balance of my current job in which both teaching and research count. Every academic institution has a corporate culture. If yours favors teaching versus research, pay attention to that call. On the other hand, if research is expected, your lecture preparation time should be rigorously controlled—you already know one hundred times more than the students do and they don't know or care that you haven't read yet another deconstruction of the text you are trying to get them to read in the first place. No matter how thorough your lectures, you won't get tenure if you don't press the right bars for your school.

Pressing the Bars

Find out what recent tenure/promotion recipients did. Talk to those people, male and female, who are "stars" in your department or in closely related departments and get concrete information on how much and where you need to publish, which conferences are vital to attend, who and what counts on campus. Don't rely on information from fellow nontenured and equally paranoid colleagues. Instead, get good information from the same people who will be evaluating your record in six years. At my school we have well-defined tenure and promotion guidelines that I followed to the letter. The advice I received when I started in my job was to publish articles and save books for later. Already committed to writing a monograph in conjunction with a museum exhibition that I organized, I wrote it on deadline and turned my attention to generating articles that would get published in short order. I went to libraries and checked on the frequency of publication of journals and submitted articles to those that consistently met their publication dates. I made a huge error with one article, submitting first to a prestigious but slow journal that wanted extensive revisions (for a turnaround of five years) and then to a middling publication with an incompetent editor, whose funding got cut just as my article was in galleys. In some major research institutions, the quality of the journal is foremost. Where I live, we count pages. So I submitted to good, though not great, journals with exceptionally fast turn around. Now that I have tenure, I have the luxury of nursing an article through two years of rewrite and I submit to the top journals. Because now I can concentrate on professional recognition in my field. You gotta keep your eye on the right prize at the right time.

It is tough, though not impossible, for a school with well-defined tenure guidelines to turn down someone who has met all the written criteria for tenure—this is usually done on the basis of collegiality or lack of same. If your school is big on collegiality, spend some time schmoozing, boozing, and generally being simpatica, but be sure they can't get you for not being published at the end of six years—tenure rarely happens to nice women with no vita. Yes, I know that nice men with no vita get tenure all the time. They aren't writing or reading books like this one, are they? Nuf said.

And beware the word *collegiality* when uttered with sanctimonious gravity by hoary members of the old boy network—in this context it is code for "white men by whom I am not threatened and therefore with whom I will play poker on Friday night." You will never pass this test. Use your energies and time elsewhere.

Picking the Right Mate

I married someone who had been married before. I got three stepchildren and a husband who was already a grown-up. He married me when I had a full-time career and so did he. Neither one of us would consider quitting a job to take care of children. If you are involved with someone now, consider the expectations of that individual. Does either of you think a wife is married to a house? What role does your prospective mate see for himself and you in the event you decide to have children? And, my all time favorite emblem of the domestic raw deal: Who cleans the toilet? If you end up with a disproportionate share of the domestic and child-rearing tasks, you are getting the short end of the stick. Do something about it.

Being a Wife and Mother

I have a ten-year-old son who is shocked to read or hear about mothers who don't have jobs outside the home. He has two parents who share domestic pleasures and pains. We split it all down the middle. We pay a housekeeper for two afternoons a week of cleaning and child care. If any of the remaining chores falls more heavily on one spouse, we negotiate. If I can't get an even shake, I become passive. So, for example, we recently modified our laundry division of labor, but only after two months of my refusing to carry the clean clothing up out of the basement and to distribute it. Eventually everyone got tired of dressing in the basement, and my husband now does his fair share. I spend more time with our son during the week, my husband does more on weekends. I cook, he cleans up. If he doesn't, I let the dishes stack up. I don't care if every pot in the house is dirty, it's not my job, and I don't do it. When I run out of pots, I stop cooking and declare "Fend for yourself" nights until they get washed. Elaborate meals may not mean a lot in your home, they do in mine. My youngest stepson (he is twenty-five) says that he grew up around our dining room table. I want my son to have the same memories. Since both my husband and I are invested in this, we both work to make it happen.

Raising the Kid

Having acquired an instant family on my wedding day and then plunging headlong into adolescence three times in quick succession, I did not have a burning desire for a larger family. One biological child is enough for me. Four are certainly enough for my husband. When my son was young, I bit the bullet and paid for in-home child care. Yes, it was expensive. It was also worth it. In exchange for the money, I knew my child was receiving good care. When he turned three, I enrolled him in a marvelous preschool three days a week and in day care the other two. Although I was home on those two days, I needed that time to do research and write. My child did much better with nurturing and involved caretakers than he would have done with a distracted and irritable mother racing the tenure clock. The following year, together with five other sets of working parents, we arranged for the preschool to provide care to our children all day, five days a week. As my son got older and more independent, a larger day care setting worked well. Currently our part-time housekeeper ensures domestic tranquility while we are at work. On the days that I am home writing, my son comes home after school. He is now fairly independent and I don't find it difficult to work while he is home. If I had more than one young child at home, I would have continued with day care.

The key here is finding the child-care arrangement that works for you and realizing that children have different needs at different times. If I had several young children, I would have looked seriously for full-time household help. You would pay out more than you bring in? Your kids aren't small forever. You have six years to get tenure. Consider the money you are paying out to be a little like tuition—it's an investment in your future.

You have to feel comfortable with your child-care arrangement or it just won't work for either you or your child. I know that my son got great social experience in a preschool/day care combination. I don't mythologize my parenting abilities nor am I a martyr. I also know that I can't do everything myself. I can obtain good child care. Ghost art historians interested in my obscure corner of scholarship are somewhat more rare. I love my child, but it doesn't mean that someone else can't do a good job at child care with him. I also know that the financial (and other) benefits of my job pay off for him too.

Making Compromises

I am haunted by an image from years ago: An obituary for an internationally revered, never-married art historian reported that she died writing with pens in both hands. Part of me envies that commitment. My saner side knows that pens make lousy domestic partners. I have chosen a very full life and I make it work. This means that I am always making choices about how to spend my time and have adopted a kind of bipolar workaholicism—I alternate intense periods of work and play. In my case, geography is destiny. I can't be in two places at the same time—literally and figuratively. Most of my research must be conducted at major libraries in the United States and abroad. Because of work commitments, my husband can't travel as freely as I can. We have mutually agreed that we will not voluntarily be separated from our son for more than three weeks at a stretch, which affects the way that I do research. If I am working at a North American library, I will come home every few weeks. On my sabbatical I needed to be in Milan so, in the middle of my stay, my family came over for a short visit.

I don't have the luxury of extended research trips so I become a research demon for the time that I do have. I plan my library visits in advance, always being certain to have alternative possibilities. This is particularly necessary for research in Italy, where strikes can and do happen at a moment's notice. I take my laptop computer. I photocopy what is possible, microfilm the rest. I seek out libraries that have liberal photocopying or microfilming policies and then shamelessly exploit them. I try to develop good relationships with sympathetic librarians who can provide me with microfilms of manuscripts by mail. I can't do as much research abroad as I would like, but I do as much as humanly possible in short bursts of time.

On the other hand, the summer after I got tenure, I didn't even go into my study. I was burnt out. I spent the summer with my son, and we had a swell time. I couldn't do it all the time and I would not have blown off months of good research time before I had tenure, but I sure needed that break. In the fall, I dove right in again with renewed vigor and without that Damoclean sword over my head.

I will never have all the time in the world for either part of my life. But I know what's important, what's negotiable, and what is fluff. By my reckoning that means things are just about right.

Recollections of a Tenured Mom

Flora González-Mandri

For my daughter Rachel, with love.

I am at Sterling Library and it's 4:00. Should I write for fifteen more minutes and then rush over to Wall Street to catch the shuttle bus or quit? I look over what I've accomplished. Eight handwritten pages on "The Aleph" by Borges. Lots of marginal notes. When I begin tomorrow, I'll have plenty to revise. Damn, it's 4:15. I must pick up Rachel before 5:00.

Rachel and her friend Fiona, who are three and a half, play Go Fish on the floor of Rachel's room. They sit with their legs spread apart, their heads bent down toward the cards. I look at them from our bedroom as I make the king-size bed, half in a daze from too little sleep. Rachel is just like her father, intense and determined as if life were just this present moment. Yet her eyes and hair are like mine, dark and beautiful. Fiona and Rachel start fighting; neither one likes to lose. I leave them alone and they eventually make up.

Orals time. I haven't slept a wink. Four male professors will come together in a room. While I wait, I run through all my prepared answers. One arrives late, the second walks in, asks a question, then excuses himself. In the meantime, the third browses through the bookcase. The fourth reads his mail. Finally, it's time for me to shine, to show how I've read all the Boom novels. Two of them get into a fight about Severo Sarduy's *Cobra*. At the end, no one stays behind to congratulate me. After all, I've got a High Pass. What else could a mom want?

I can't believe that Rachel is already five. Chris and I have divorced and he comes back for the party. It's face painting time. Rachel is wear-

---

Flora González-Mandri is an associate professor of Caribbean and Latin American literature at Emerson College.

ing a red gingham dress and her cheeks are covered with little hearts. She remembers it as the best of her birthdays.

Graduation day is coming up. The entire family arrives. Spanish spills out of every crevice of my apartment. The day is gray, but no matter. Daniel, Pino, and Papi buy yellow raincoats and the González-Mandri caravan makes it to the Yale yard. Black umbrellas cover our caps, but the mood is jubilant. Rachel is quiet, I give her a hug: "Too much Spanish, huh?"

First, a one-year job. Rachel has known nothing but New Haven. Now, it's Hanover. Mr. Mullen, in third grade, teaches her to write. "First draft, second draft, forget the spelling, just write." Disconnected from the graduate school community, I'm overcome by silence. I alleviate my loneliness with walks in the woods. Rachel is lucky. Two young women in our building take her out square dancing, dress her up on Halloween, teach her to sing and to bake cookies. Martha and Mary, for that year, are her aunts.

From Hanover to Chicago. It's my first year and I don't stop. I teach six classes and travel to conferences. Miami takes the bus from Grand Rapids and spoils the child while I'm away. Rachel gets to know her grandmother. At the end of the probationary time, three years of hard work, my female colleagues, childless all, ask me: "Flora, why didn't you go out drinking with the guys?"

I get the picture: Chicago is the Yale of the Midwest. There's no tenure for me here. I leave before the axe falls. No matter that I've created new courses, that I'm the language coordinator, and that I'm the graduate student director—that's not enough. At the end of three years, there is no book. I chose the route of language teaching. I look to Boston. It's only an hour from Rachel's dad.

"Rachel, we're moving to Boston." She looks at me in shock and says nothing. She's had enough of academe.

Juggling on an Uneven Playing Field

Cecilia Rodríguez Milanés

I'm a young mother of a young child. She was three the spring I began this essay. I am also an academic, a junior nontenured faculty member, and actively participate in department committee work (four at last count), mentor teaching associates, advise the fledgling Latino student organization, mentor minority students and English majors, and work with about a dozen graduate students on their doctoral exams, dissertations, or independent studies. Despite all that, my child's existence dominates my own.

Why does the child demand me? Her mother? What about her father? Returning nontraditional student, faculty spouse, underemployed for more than three years now, co-caregiver for our child and Latino, too, he is in a precarious place. The complexity of his situation is ever present on our minds, yet both of our Latino families seem perplexed as to what exactly he's doing. From my side of the family: Ay, you can do anything if you put your mind to it. From his side: Do you need money, hijo?

They just don't get it. That he cares for their granddaughter/niece while I'm at the university. That I care for her when he's at the university. That we take turns. That we feel, as they reared us to feel, it's important that one of us is with her most of the time. That this cold, gray place provides little comfort when we need family to help care for her, help entertain her, help nurture her. We are responsible for her (our parents modeled this behavior), accountable for her being here (we

Cecilia Rodríguez Milanés is an assistant professor of English at Indiana University of Pennsylvania.

moved here), and though we are blessedly grateful that she now attends Montessori school, even with that relief, she is a handful, a lot of work, and demanding.

My daughter is completely bilingual now—Spanish is her mother and father tongue; she will first be literate in English, as I was. She is active, precocious, and socially extroverted. How do we two deal with all that? With a child who doesn't go to bed unless you're in it with her. Who nursed until she weaned herself, when she was good and ready, at twenty months. These days we giggle when she sees me barechested and lunges in, mouth gaping for the nipple that nourishes no longer. I pull away, in time, laughing, saying, "Ya mami no tiene leche." She laughs, "No hay leche," her little hands upraised. I hurry for a blouse because I don't want to be that exposed now, that kind of nourisher now. I am glad to have my body back, glad of not having to bare my chest.

She's been sleeping in our bed for years. Sleeping between us, sleeping in the crook of my arm, the arm that held her when she nursed, the arm that then replaced the sustenance. The arm she grabbed when she started eating table food, the one she reaches for in the middle of a meal. Mi brazo, she says, my arm. This arm can sometimes be replaced by her papi's arm, though it's not as soft or pliant. Yet even the arm is not enough for her. She reaches for me in the night. Even when I put her in her own bed, in her own room, later, she gets up, soundless, comes into our bed, without waking us. It's only later that I feel her hand feeling for my face, her warm fingertips patting my forehead or neck, finding at last, the face, then the arm she seeks, eyes closed, between sleep and wakefulness.

I come home from school and she drops everything and rushes to the door. She must touch me; I need to ask for a kiss; she just wants to touch me. Sometimes she says, cárgame (carry me). Her father laughs from the kitchen, says she was helping him prepare the meal, stirring or washing or sorting. Why does she want me so? What is it about the physical that she needs?

I think about her nursing and my caring for her almost nonstop for sixteen months, my caressing of her, touching her, playing with her. Has she separated yet? Does she differentiate yet between her *self* and my *self*? Does she still think we are attached? That I am part of her, hers?

This month I've hardly written at all but I did do five observations of colleagues or teaching associates, presented a lunchtime workshop on integrating Latinas into the curriculum, gave a keynote address at a women's studies conference, wrote a grant for travel to an international conference, revised an essay for resubmission to an academic journal, coordinated and moderated a literary reading in celebration of Hispanic Heritage Month, wrote two new syllabi for the department's revision of the B.A., and just barely kept up with my three different preparations this term, two of which are brand new. And when it couldn't possibly get any worse, when my hands are already overfull, my daughter got the chicken pox. During midterms. She couldn't sleep—do I need to add that means I couldn't sleep?

As long as men are willing to give up the nurturance and upbringing of children to women, as long as competition is the essence of our society and one-up*man*ship is the basis for evaluation in academe, as long as women continue to juggle work and family on this very uneven playing field, stories such as mine will be the norm. I never wanted to believe it; I used to think women could do anything; I believed *I* could compete with any man in academia, but this essay has forced me to admit that I can't. Not if I care about my family the way I do; not if I want to be actively involved in their lives as I want them in my life. Not if I want to kiss her good night when she closes her eyes. Not if I want to make love more than once every two or three weeks. Not if I care about keeping fit by exercising or preparing healthy meals. Not if I want to love and be loved intimately.

PART SIX

Adjunct Faculty,
Independent Scholars,
Nontraditional
Careers

Letter on Silences

T. Anne Archer

Dear Constance and Diana,

Your proposed anthology certainly comes at a critical time. Institutions are retreating into themselves; entrenched is a model of academic excellence that demands of its novitiates a nunlike commitment. The injunctions of the profession are pitted against the exigencies of parenting. In such an environment, the parent who is an academic (the "academic parent") faces extinction.

I should know: at forty, I have undergone a sea change and have left academia (read: been phased out of) to open my own flute studio. In my former life as both professor and grad student, I experienced some of the insidious ways in which the academy tries to silence the parents in its ranks. Pregnancy itself is an affront to the institution. "Great" with my first child, I felt self-conscious and out of place in my alma mater and former work place, Queen's University. Was I a threat to the status quo or an embarrassment? Such blasphemy—my pregnancy—marked the beginning of the end of my academic career.

Not only are parents, particularly women, bound by some patriarchal code of professionalism to silence—I was cautioned by an older female colleague not to mention my children in the classroom—but we also lack both an adequate language and a forum to validate our experience. We are either too exhausted, too angry, or too profoundly guilty (for failing to measure up on both fronts) to attempt to articulate what it means to live at the crossroads of home and academy.

T. Anne Archer is a poet, editor, and freelance musician residing near Kingston, Ontario.

145

Rather than whine or grumble—terms that seem to characterize our concerns—we try to adapt, to fit in. If we have time to write, we labor over articles or manuscripts. Especially for adjuncts, survival depends on denial of the problem, on collusion—on silence.

While many big-name female academics seem, by example at least, to advocate childlessness as a prerequisite for professional success, my (ex) female colleagues who want to have both career and child tend to "put off" getting pregnant until they achieve tenure or are at least tenure-track. One friend, in particular, wants to play along with the system until she can subvert it. But the odds against taking the system by storm by having a family relatively late in life strike me as slim. Accommodating yourself over a long stretch of time to a particular, narrow model of excellence exacts its toll. Years of jumping through hoops often makes you curiously protective of the system. And to protect the system means that the academy comes first and baby second, colic and crises notwithstanding. Not that baby suffers; with tenure comes a certain degree of financial stability. Some tenured professors can afford good full-time child care. Though the academic parent is often an absent parent—note how absence is a form of silence—the tenured female academic mother of one (and she usually has just one) has the ability to buy requisite care, to buy teaching and research time. As long as she assuages her guilt—(show me an absent mother who feels no guilt)—she can wear two hats with relative ease.

But the untenured academic parent, the marginalized adjunct like myself, is often embittered. Family responsibilities, coupled with a schedule that left little time for research, never mind the occasional but important coffee break with a colleague, precluded me from playing the game. Yet how valuable is the game when it encourages us to hold life and child rearing at arm's length, when it reinforces a way of coping where the norm is male and conservative? I want a model where the experience of giving birth to and then raising children can be integrated into, can inform my professional concerns. Having children turned my life upside down; I feel stretched and challenged in areas my years of scholarship just couldn't touch. I also became a better teacher. I learned how to ask questions, to listen to what my students were saying, and to draw into some kind of dynamic relation their responses and my aims for the course.

It's a crazy balancing act academic parents/parents in the academy attempt. And I blew the act. Sometimes out of despair, sometimes out of a sense of commitment, often because I just couldn't afford (emotionally and financially) an alternative, I placed my children and our urgent and baffling relationship before my career. Now I'm in pursuit of something more humane than life in the humanities.

Sincerely,

Anne Archer

P.S. The following excerpts from my poem sequence, "Another Shape," speak as well to the issue of silent parenting.

From "Another Shape"

A whole new word for us
(I check the calendar daily
my ticks—compulsive—form
like geese before the prairie snows)
I've missed three months so far
We celebrate
You pour a beer
I raise my glass of milk in your direction

My belly tense, shapes
the form of waiting

Breasts swollen, belly
distended, vagina torn pulled beyond desire.

Can I prepare for
this con
figuration/

Child, mold me to yourself,
I move to your dimensions.
When my flesh reassembles
I will be pliable,

still and for
always,another
shape.

No more talk no touch, even
if I could now
another claims me
what do I want with words
and silence, your lips
in candlelight and all those dreams
you talked me into wanting

your tongue makes strange
the baby stirs, my nipples
keen to lips still
warm with the taste of me
filaments of milk and spittle
glisten in the winterlight
joining us over again

her mouth a tiny eye
greedy and open

on delicate, puckered skin
a faint breath,

                    tug

how everything flows
toward the center, toward
those lips whose tiny suck
is an answer, a still point

a silence
in the shape of
a cresting wave

Adventures of a Single Father in Academe

Alan Gross

My career as a parent began during my last few months at Stanford graduate school with the birth of my daughter Molly in 1966, just before launching my parallel career in social psychology at UC-Irvine. My first two years as an academic parent were definitely prefeminist and therefore unremarkable to me. As was the custom at the time, my wife, Becky, took responsibility for most of the child-rearing tasks. While I worked at my university office late into the evening, Becky did most of the dropping off and picking up as well as nearly all of the diaper changing, cooking, and cleaning. Many evenings I arrived home after Molly was long asleep.

Nonetheless, with my strong encouragement Becky left home to seek work when Molly was only two months old. After a short time, Becky succeeded in finding an administrative position with university extension and Molly spent most weekdays in day care. Despite Becky's full-time employment, I remained the back-up parent with few responsibilities other than playing and taking photographs. During this period, I seldom saw beyond my academic struggles, but occasionally I sensed the unfairness of my domestic arrangement and offered token gestures: agreeing to hire a weekly cleaning woman to lighten some of the household chores, joining a baby-sitting cooperative comprised entirely of young childbearing academics.

Having used my traditional marriage to shield me from any serious responsibility for raising Molly, I could not blame my stalled academic career on excessive domestic duties. After two years at Irvine, I decid-

Alan Gross is retired from academia, happily remarried, and lives in Manhattan.

ed to accept a job at the University of Wisconsin. During the standard interview/visit at Wisconsin, the faculty probably assumed that I would be arriving with a standard intact family. But only a few weeks later Becky informed me that she had decided not to accompany me to the new job in Wisconsin. As a prototypical male accustomed to a high degree of control, I found the potential loss of MY wife and MY child devastating.

Shortly after I arrived at Northwestern for summer teaching en route to Wisconsin, Becky revealed that she was planning an extensive trip to south central Asia and that she would allow Molly to stay with me during those weeks. Although several new friends offered support and occasional baby-sitting, I had no justification for exploiting them as caregivers. For the first time I was wholly responsible for my two year old's emotional and physical well-being. As Molly and I became accustomed to each other and some of the unfamiliarity of child care became routine, I began to fear the day when Becky, now my ex-wife, would return to retrieve MY child.

For all the right reasons, especially my loving bond with Molly, and for some very wrong reasons, especially my male desire to control and retain possession of at least part of my crumbling family, I wanted to be the custodial parent. I wanted to directly participate in the daily living experiences of my child, and I wanted to nurture and watch her growth firsthand. Various rational and irrational forces coalesced to stoke my fear of losing Molly. I wrote a long, tortured letter to Becky, then in Pakistan, declaring that I would not return Molly until I was assured that I would have reasonable visitation and that she would not take Molly out of the country.

This confrontation created a painful dilemma for Becky, whose fiance had accepted a job in Africa. After months of relentless arguing, begging, and guilt-tripping from me—and against her lawyer's advice—Becky finally agreed to allow Molly to live with me. I agreed to send frequent reports on Molly's development, to pay for her visits to see her mother, and to insert a clause in the custody document specifying that Becky was a competent mother and should I die, she would obtain custody.

In Wisconsin I attempted to establish a measure of family stability. Fortunately, I was able to rent a two-bedroom house with a one-room apartment adjoining the basement. Over the next three years tenants exchanged cooking, laundry, and occasional baby-sitting for free rent. Shortly before fall classes began, I located a small in-home day care center operated by Muffy, a warm supportive woman who served as Molly's weekday caretaker. Having arranged two essentials—a home, albeit one starkly furnished with two mattresses on the floor and cardboard boxes for bureaus and tables, and day care—I began to chug uphill along the tenure track.

Because teaching, research, writing, and committee work couldn't easily be completed in a standard workday, I along with most other assistant professors usually worked late into the evening. When this work required collaboration, I was often able to use my single parent status to advantage. Would it be fair to ask me to abandon my sleeping baby to travel to a colleague's house or office?

Wisconsin's almost exclusively male psychology department included only three other single men, none a custodian of children. On the few occasions when I was invited to dinner with colleagues, one of the single men was usually invited for balance. At these parties in the late sixties, academic women still tended to cluster in the kitchen to discuss domestic matters and children. Although I sometimes wanted to participate in these conversations, I usually gravitated to the living room for scholarly exchanges with the men. Despite this social facade, it wasn't difficult for colleagues to discern that I was seriously committed to parenthood. They could easily observe Molly at the office on weekends or when she was sick and they responded with comments ranging from curious to admiring.

Since my script for our family specified a little brother for Molly, I filed applications with numerous adoption agencies. In the sixties a single man was only slightly more likely to successfully adopt a child than to get pregnant. Nonetheless, after a year and a half of grueling interviews, home visits, and a rejection by a state psychiatrist who had never met us, Matthew, already one year old, joined our family as a foster placement. Thanks to a special program for hard-to-place babies sponsored by Catholic Social Services, Matthew apparently became the first adoptee in a single male–headed home in Wisconsin history.

When Matthew joined our family my dual role became even more conspicuous. Matthew arrived with multiple medical problems requiring immediate attention; he spent his second day and night with us at Madison General Hospital in a croup tent. Although I had arranged his placement during winter break, it was necessary for me to spend many nonteaching hours working at home while he adjusted to his new life.

In early 1971 when an ad hoc tenure committee was deliberating my fate, a senior colleague who occupied the office next to mine acknowledged my parental responsibilities by contending that my decision to adopt Matthew had negatively affected my career. At the point of these tenure deliberations I had already received a major research grant, my book was in press, a few articles had been published, and my teaching ratings were uniformly high. On the other hand, I had testified against the department in a dispute with teaching assistants, was one of the few to organize against the Vietnam war, and went on strike during the Cambodian invasion. The denial of tenure cannot solely be attributed to my involvement with my children.

Fortunately, Bibb Latane, a respected social psychologist, had recently received funding for a training grant at Ohio State University that allowed his department to hire a visiting associate professor for the academic year. Ohio State's need for a visitor on short notice made a fortunate fit. My family by this time had grown to four to include Annie, an English graduate student who had completed her course work at Wisconsin and was seeking a teaching job. Until I had met Annie, I had dated only women with children of their own. Most of my "dates" involved weekend home visits, birthday parties, and trips to the zoo. My involvement with Annie, who was not only childless but believed that mothers were inherently boring, derailed my traditional family script for many years.

Annie's ambivalence about motherhood, however, did not prevent her from forming close attachments to both children. She played the role of friend or big sister except during the brief period she allowed Matthew to call her "mother." Despite pressure on Annie from me and others to share parental responsibilities, I clearly would remain the primary caretaker.

The Ohio State group provided colleagueship, research space, excellent students, and talented research assistants. When my appointment was extended, we immediately converted a basement room of our small house to provide quarters for a live-in student. With Annie teaching forty miles away and returning to Columbus only on weekends, Jean arrived and began to assume many of the domestic and parenting duties. She remained with us until both children had completed high school. Jean and I, though never romantic partners, eventually became true co-parents. To this day, Matthew calls Jean his mother and Molly considers Jean a very special friend.

I reluctantly declined a third year at Ohio State to accept an associate professorship at the University of Missouri, where Annie had been hired to teach women's studies. For the next four years I frequently researched, met with students, taught small seminars, and hosted parties for visiting speakers at home, all with the sometimes unscheduled participation of the children. While my academic life prospered, however, my relationship with Annie unraveled. At the end of the first year she returned to Ohio, and a group of men became my main source of social support.

One day at lunch, Bob, an assistant dean at the University, had proposed recruiting men for weekly "consciousness-raising" meetings. It took less than a week to assemble a support group of eight to ten, about half academics. Since I was the only single parent, I often persuaded the group to meet at our house after the kids' bedtime. The weekly meetings continued throughout my stay in Missouri. A few years later I attended the first National Conference on Men and Masculinity, which eventually grew into the National Organization for Men against Sexism. A session on single fathers I sponsored at an annual meeting attracted only ten men, about half academics and half custodial parents, but the following year the group mailing list had grown to eighteen as we exchanged wisdom about fatherhood and custody.

As a temporary appointment at the American Psychological Association neared its end a couple of years later, I accepted a position as psychology department chair at the University of Maryland. Although our new house included a basement apartment for a helper, Jean, who was employed as a full-time administrator, maintained a nearby apartment.

In the early 1980s, a routine physical exam and X-ray revealed a large lesion in Molly's lung; after surgery she was diagnosed with a serious form of Hodgkins disease. While I lived at the hospital day and night trying to comfort Molly and monitor her care through radiation and biweekly chemotherapy, Jean stayed with Matthew and brought him to the hospital for visiting hours. With the help of several understanding colleagues and especially my secretary, Frankie, I managed most departmental and academic matters from Molly's hospital room phone and from a desk at a nearby nursing station. Molly somehow managed to survive months of apprehension, painful procedures, horrible nausea, and hair loss. The good news was that a year later Molly's body was finally free of all disease. Now in her early thirties, Molly is an artist living in Germany.

As Molly was entering her senior year at the local high school, Matthew became increasingly unhappy with school and with me. Our relationship, which had been intermittently tense for years, took a turn for the worse. Although I had been looking forward to spending more one-on-one time with Matt after Molly left for college, I reluctantly decided to enroll Matt at a special boys' boarding school in Virginia, where he spent two years before returning to Maryland to complete high school. Thanks to various interventions—or perhaps normal maturation—he settled down, completed high school, and is now pursuing acting opportunities in California while retaining a day job as a puppeteer.

During my years at Maryland, the standard tension between family and academia became a triangle with my travel business as the third vertex. What started as a modest attempt to sell discount airline coupons turned into a home coupon brokerage that slowly began to eat the house. After three years of tumult and profit, we moved the entire operation to a shopping center midway between home and the university. In 1985, when the university was unwilling to continue an already extended sabbatical and I desperately needed to disentangle myself from the overwhelming commitments of the business, I voluntarily resigned and chose to begin my new single, childless, nonacademic life in New York.

Now retired from active scholarship and parenting, I have often reflected on my experiences in academia as a single father. Despite the pleasures I experienced during those eighteen years, I cannot recommend mixing full-time work with serious child rearing. In my case it may have helped that I was born male. Perhaps because single men were and still are less likely to gain custody, they elicit more curiosity, sympathy, and helpfulness. I also had the good fortune to be able to afford assistance and to surround the children with enough decent, creative associates to provide many good role models. Although this nontraditional environment created some difficulties for Molly and Matthew, it almost certainly contributed to their development as self-sufficient, creative, and reasonably happy adults. Now more than two decades later, virtually every day I still feel much of the pride, hope, disappointment, and responsibilities associated with parenting.

Sitting on the Fence: Balancing Heart and Mind

Ellen F. Higgins

"Sitting on the fence," one foot in academe and the other in the outside world for some twenty years, I have been on the margin for a long time: as a woman in a masculinist institution; as a feminist in a male-dominated field; as a heterosexual in lesbian-dominated departments; as an adjunct in a system that exploits and doesn't respect me; as a lower-class person in a status-conscious world; and as a mother in a "business-only," product-oriented culture.

In the twenty years I've been attached to academia, I have made repeated forays into the "real" world, influenced by both the working-class ethic and by the feminist ideal of effecting change. In the last half dozen years, I have defined myself as an independent scholar in English and women's studies. Though someone recently said that this meant "unemployed," to me it means the *choice* of employment.

When I started, I had no knowledge of the "business" of higher education and I had no guidance. Ironically, though I pursued education and knowledge, I did not pursue them wisely. I followed the good student model that everyone, but especially women, learn in our educational system: If you do your work well, eventually you'll get noticed. While that sometimes works in a classroom, it does not work elsewhere. By accumulating three master's degrees, I was showing what a good student I was, but not that I had the right credentials for a position in the academy or that I had the "smarts" to know what I was supposed to do. My naivete was encouraged by my acceptance of

Ellen F. Higgins is an independent scholar of English and women's studies.

the feminist rhetoric that everybody counted and that people should be valued for what they are, not what they do. If class and the lack of practical, political smarts were not enough, my decision to give priority to my mothering was fatal. When I chose motherhood, I was seen as not committed to my scholarship, which was the only important work. Moreover, as a radical feminist I had to confront society's baggage attached to mothering.

Yet, mothering and feminism need not be seen as fundamentally and uncomfortably opposed. Understanding the complex and contradictory forces that shape a woman's experience as a mother is important. And, though mothering can reinforce patriarchy, it can also be an extension of feminist activism. In contrast to the alienated labor of the public world of work, parenting can be humanizing labor. To stay home to care for and nurture one's children, to enjoy being one's boss, and to experience a measure of control over one's day would be a luxury to working-class women. Mothering, in particular nonsexist child rearing, can resist patriarchy. With a feminist program of education, mothers can experience self-liberation and can create a feminist environment for their children. Women can come to terms with their own power and achieve dignity.

My academic work slowed down while I focused on mothering, but I never gave up my goal of finishing my Ph.D. Though I am now working on my dissertation, I continue to sit on the fence. Part of me would like to have a regular teaching job at a college or university, but I'm still reluctant to commit. I see my full-time colleagues overworked and unhappy. I see them giving lip service to feminist ideals but playing the same games as the good old bad boys. I appreciate the need to understand an institutional system and the skills needed to survive in it. This is the one thing that is taught to men who have access to established hierarchies of power by virtue of their gender. Though they are the principal place where feminist scholars can realize the joys of an intellectual life, colleges and universities *are* institutions, patriarchal and bureaucratic. The academy seeks to maintain the status quo of human and institutional relationships. Though some academic women may support their peers in garnering tenure, promotions, and honors, I have seen powerful women push out other women who were not of their "party line." With their lower status staff, they often try to get the most possible work with the lowest possible remuneration, showing that they've learned the administrator's game well.

Indeed, this "lesser" treatment of female support staff occurs when they are automatically expected to perform housekeeping duties, ranging from creating a home (running a smooth office/work environment) to providing decorations (self or objects) for departments and the administration. When female, especially feminist, bosses continue to replicate this behavior, they have bought into the status, class, and sex hierarchy despite feminist theory to the contrary. Wives and mothers are also the unpaid and unacknowledged "emotional workers" of society. Socialized to be good listeners, women workers are asked to lend a sympathetic ear to their male bosses' woes or to bear the brunt of misplaced anger and frustration. In the college setting, female faculty are not exempt, since male faculty sometimes expect this listening of their female colleagues, with these services rarely reciprocated.

Though it requires a tough balancing act, I believe we can use our female and feminist skills, even masculinist ones, honorably and with our values intact. We must learn to bring our "mothering" skills to our intellectual and institutional work. I choose to call it "mothering" because I learned these skills in my mothering, because women still represent the principal caretakers of children and others, and because these qualities have been traditionally ascribed to females. But they are not innate to women and can be gained by anyone through practical experience or conscious practice. The teaching and practice of fair-fighting techniques, belief in the innate worth of every human being, respect for another's beliefs and values, and recognition that there is no single right answer or truth are the foundation of multiplicity and diversity and the true basis for multiculturalism.

Mothers who are feminist scholars, even those who are marginal in academia, need the courage to practice mothering skills with our colleagues and co-workers, and we need to insist on their use by others. We need to model them, in a sense to be "mothers" in the academy.

Some might question my "sitting on the fence" perspective as sour grapes, status envy, or criticizing what I can't get. For me the fence offers a better position, a view outside, not inside the academic institution.

PART SEVEN

Caring for Children with Disabilities

A Weaning

Lucia Cordell Getsi

The day in intensive care had been particularly nightmarish. My daughter lay stiff as a wax doll, nine tubes of various circumferences snaking into the holes punctured in her body—some to feed or medicate her with morphine, never enough, to keep her from going mad with pain like burning tuning forks vibrating in nerves that futilely, without the insulating myelin, tried to transmit messages to muscles; some to drain off air from her left lung to keep it from going down again; the biggest blue one from the respirator to get air back into the lungs. Two days before this day—after four months of total Guillain-Barré Syndrome paralysis and crisis after crisis, each moment of escaped death leading into the next moment of possible death; of keeping her alive for one more hour or day or night or week until the slow, agonizingly painful, but steady regrowth of myelin down the stripped nerves would allow enough of them to begin to mobilize the wasted, emaciated breathing muscles so that we could disconnect the respirator and she could breathe herself down the years-long road of functional recovery this particular autoimmune neuropathy promised if the patient but lived through the respiratory paralysis and concomitant arrhythmia, tachycardia, hypocardia, palpitations, fibrillations, hyperthermia, and all manner of organ dysfunction—just two days before, I would have almost let myself say (knocking on wood, crossing my fingers, heart, and brain, and

Lucia Cordell Getsi is Distinguished Professor of English and Comparative Literature and director of the master's programs in creative writing at Illinois State University.

practically hiding under the bed so that the furies, fates, and gods did not hear me) that *now* she was almost safe, that *now* at last *soon* she would be free of the ventilator and able, even, to talk to me again without the agency of my voice spelling her blinked-out alphabet code.

But that was two days ago, and this had been today, which might not ever end. Again. Yeast, that fungus we all carry usually unawares, that will break our bodies down when we die and return us to Mother Nature's dust, had decided that Manon was close enough. For months, yeast had been culturing on her tongue so that I peeled and scraped off the furry stuff each morning when I arrived in her blinking, whooshing, beeping room to kiss her teary face (the tear ducts were the only things of her that consistently worked besides her mind) and began suctioning her mouth every five minutes between passive therapy exercises on her stiffened and twisting arms and legs and the half-hour-long processes of turning her and positioning each part of each painful limb every two hours of every twenty-four. It had cultured everywhere there was a natural orifice, from the first moment, way back across the last four months of horror-love-holiness, the doctors had administered the first antibiotic to try to rid her of the infection that never would be cured. (All women know about this—most of those who still believe in the power of antibiotics reach for the antibiotic with one hand and for the Monistat with the other to treat the yeast infection that will follow the ravaging of the body's own protective flora.) It cultured around the tracheotomy, around the stomach tubes, around the catheter. Now it cultured around the Hickman arterial catheter straight into the heart, the cardiac specialist told me, *a dangerous sign.* I slept with dangerous signs. My sympathetic and fascinated students, during the Tuesdays and Thursdays into which my whole teaching schedule had been bunched so that I could be at the hour's-drive-away hospital five days and parts of six nights a week, knew that we discussed or I lectured past the dangerous signs I let overflow to them the first five minutes of each class and which had become the vehicle of my every explanatory metaphor's tenor. I ate dangerous signs, negotiated the minefields they mapped daily and nightly. This dangerous sign? *We'll see,* the doctor said. At midnight of this today, I arrived home after the 47.5 minutes' drive to my waiting husband and a phone message (*I was just there, for chrissake!*)—I was to be back at the hospital at 5:30 A.M. *Yeast probably culturing in the bone marrow, a condition Manon cannot survive without amphotericin B administered like chemo.* I knew this new powerful antifungal, knew as well as the doctor that Manon was too weak to survive its effects. *Bone mar-*

row excision at 6:30 A.M. You need to be here to sign the permission (another document that could kill or save her) *and to act as her comforter.* She had been too weak for anesthetic, even a local, for almost every one of the now uncountable surgical, diagnostic, and support procedures.

When the phone rang again at 12:30, of course I left my bed to answer it. I answered the phone in terror and hope every time it rang. It was my student D., who had decided to kill himself.

I need to explain what I said to D., perhaps to justify causing the irreparable breach in the relationship that had developed between me and suicidal students and friends stretching back some twenty years, a relationship caused in part I am sure by the suicide of my mother, whom I could not save, when I was in college, which made me the Red Cross Knight for everybody else to assuage my own Despayre hung like a noose around my neck. As a sophomore, D. had walked into my office as though treading on holy ground. I had translated Georg Trakl (who committed suicide), *his* poet, psychic guide, sacred *doppelgänger.* Not knowing a word of German (or about Xerox machines either, it appears), D. had found and typed a copy of my entire bilingual book of translations, both German and English, after he discovered the book was out of print and available only in libraries. Thus began a mentorship of the most brilliant student I have ever taught that lasted through three years and several of my courses in comparative literature, the last of which he was taking at that time, and even beyond the phone call of this particular evening though the terms of the relationship were altered forever by what I said: *D., I said something like, I cannot listen to this now, cannot have anything to do with your romanticized love of death, some sort of masturbatory necrophilia. Do you know where I have come from, where I am going again in a few hours—that my daughter would give anything for your flagrant freedom to choose, that I have spent the last four months in hell trying to drag, bargain, beg my child out of it? If you really want to kill yourself, then go ahead* (there was a loud receiver slam somewhere here), *my thoughts are willing, praying, supplicating my daughter's life, I do not dare think about death.*

I cannot describe the sense of vertiginous reeling, the whiplash of mental and emotional energies that I was experiencing at that moment, sandwiched between coming from so many exhausting and terrifying days and going to yet another in four hours that would be worse because I had allowed myself to hope that they were almost over (oh, inconceivably worse, that bone marrow excision on my skeletal, eighteen-year-old, paralyzed girl turned in silenced agony into my arms that could not protect her while the surgical screw twisted in and in and in and uncorked her unanesthetized hipbone and the bright red marrow spurted up—the imprint is branded permanently on all that I am, that she is).

People who have had enough encounters with BPDs (Borderline Personality Disordered people—D.'s diagnosis two years later) will recognize that D. was completely unable to empathize with my situation or my daughter's. She was in his way. Because I was taking care of her, I was not taking care of him. And instantly, I became ashamed and fearful that he would actually kill himself (BPDs always know, somewhere, the effect of their grandstanding) and phoned him back, only to find out from his roommate that he had slammed the phone down and run out of the apartment. I begged the roommate to run after and find him and bring him back. Then I called his psychotherapist, a woman about my age from a neighboring town whom he, I realize now, had seen to it I meet over lunch and whose name he had carved in my memory by repeating it often enough that I could dial information and easily find her number. Which I did, frantically. The calm voice that answered was what I needed, a woman in charge, *go to bed and get what little sleep you can before the morning, I'll take care of D.*

In another life, that voice had been mine.

Silver Linings: Forging a Link between Mothering a Child with Autism and Teaching/Scholarship

Celest Martin

*Dwell as near as possible to the channel
in which your life flows.*
—*Henry David Thoreau*

October 7, 1986. It is the quintessen-
tial fall day. The air is crisp, but the sun is warm enough for just a sweater.
The sky is the blue I associate with a poem I recited for my fifth grade class,
"October's Bright Blue Weather." I am driving past Sprague Park with its little rolling hills and musical brook. I want to turn the car around and go
home to my daughter and bring her here, to this color-washed park and the
baby swings that delight her so. It is her first birthday. Pregnant with my
second child, I know that it is the only birthday I will have alone with her to
celebrate the wonder she and I shared one year ago today at 2:00 P.M.

But I am an academic and I have a graduate course until 7:00 tonight.
Unlike other state employees, I cannot take a personal day and follow the
dictates of my heart. There are at least fifty-five human beings who have
paid for my presence today and who deserve my undivided attention. So I
tell my caregiver to sing "Happy Birthday" to Katie at exactly 2:00 and
content myself with that. "Besides" says red-haired, ebullient Sue when
she arrives that morning, "She doesn't know what a birthday is yet."

But I know.

March 1, 1990. "What we're seeing with Andrew . . ." The hairs on the
back of my neck prickle and I shiver in this stuffy little room. ". . . is pervasive, across-the-board delays."

Pervasive. It is an ugly word. And soon more words, words like "brain

Celest Martin teaches nonfiction workshops and literature at the University of
Rhode Island.

damage" and "appropriate placement" explode in the air and shred the ideal every parent cherishes, the ideal of an intact, undamaged child. My sunny little son, blond and blue-eyed and everybody's darling, is going to need special education. In two weeks he will be three. I have taken this academic year off, partly to deal with my newly diagnosed lupus and partly to uncover the mystery of this child's scattered development. It will be the most absorbing detective work of my life.

December 12, 1990. "What is all this stuff?" "Where are we going to put it?" I ask, dismayed by the mess in my living room two weeks before Christmas.

My husband is moving his office home. Two years ago, he had a thriving construction business with thirty-seven employees. Now, it is only him. We owned land worth $300,000 and I had been thinking about staying home to write full-time and raise my family. But all that has been lost in a bankrupt condominium project. We can barely pay the mortgage and, of course, we argue about money. I would like to be supportive of my husband on this traumatic day—to stay home, to help place his office furniture, to soften the sting to his pride.

But . . . I am an academic. We are in the middle of finals and I teach writing. I have three stacks of projects to read and comment on—the least is twenty pages; the greatest, seventy-five. And a search committee to work with trying to finalize three hires before the Modern Language Convention and before statewide budget cuts. And two little children who are shortly expecting Santa Claus. And a dirty house because we can't afford the cleaning person anymore. And now, an at-home husband with a personal crisis of his own.

What to do? I will surely come asunder if I continue to fragment myself. Learning about autism has become my second career. My husband is home more and that helps with child care, but his self-esteem is plummeting and together we research alternative career choices for him. The lupus exhausts me and I feel as though I'm holding onto the edge of a well with my teeth and fingertips. If I move a muscle, the blackness will suck me down and I will never get out again.

So I read and I think and I remember that a long time ago, I got into this whole academic business because I wanted to write. I had wanted to be a feature writer, but the only undergraduate college I could afford, Rutgers, didn't have a journalism major. Well, now what? "I'm forty," I say to myself. "It's time to find a way to write what I want to write and to teach that kind of writing."

My son has provided the subject matter for my writing. I just have to figure out a way to work it into my courses so that I can talk about what I'm writing. I look to my students' writing and I begin to see trends. In the creative writing class I see trends. I am reading "fictional" accounts of children of divorce, life with alcoholic parents, choosing between abortion and adoption, coping with mental illness, broken hearts, and shattered lives.

"There's a lot of pain out there," I said to myself, "and these kids want to write about it. Probably to read about it, too. What can I do with this?"

For years, nonfiction had been my leisure reading of choice. Pretty much ever since I had put the last period on the last sentence in my Ph.D. qualifying exams, I had bolted to the library for some books I "didn't have to read." I came home with *Alive,* the account of a plane crash in the Andes, and got hooked on nonfiction. Two subtypes had been my particular favorites. Long before I had even considered having a family, I was a marshmallow for narratives about special needs children. My other predilection was for true-crime accounts.

"But nobody teaches this stuff," I agonized. "It's, well, . . . it's popular. It's beach reading, night table reading. Do I dare take it seriously? And will anyone else?"

I decided to find out. In the spring of 1992, I offered The Literature of Family Crisis at our continuing education campus. The following fall, I offered it as a freshman honors course at our regular campus. We covered a wide variety of topics: poverty, homelessness, AIDS, substance abuse, eating disorders, suicide, unplanned pregnancy and its choices, mental illness, disabilities, chronic and terminal illness, domestic violence, rape, and growing up gay.

Reactions from colleagues have varied. The first group chides me with, "You're not a counselor or a social worker. Why do you want to teach this stuff?" And they are right. I'm not a counselor. And when students' writing has opened up areas of unresolved issues for them, I do not try to pass myself off as qualified to deal with those issues. Rather, I make the appropriate contact for them and allow the students to pursue the help they need. I am there for listening—I won't disappear from their lives—but I stress to them that I do not have the skills to lead them to recovery.

The second group of colleagues groans and accuses me of voyeurism when they hear my writing requirements for the course. "I don't want to know that much about my students. I'm here to teach a skill and try to impart some knowledge." Okay. But distancing and compartmentalizing is not me. I like the integration of my life with the students' lives and I like it when students discover the therapeutic power of turning raw emotion into a well-crafted manuscript.

Then, fortunately for me, the third group believes it has *always* been the province of English teachers to look at and discuss what it means to be a human being, with what it means to grapple with issues of morality and ethics and to emerge sweaty and bloody with no real answers. Their attitude is "So why *not* move into real life? Why *not* look at nonfiction narratives?"

The part that's scary for the first two groups of naysayers is not so much that we read "this stuff," but that my students have to produce their own narratives, which are, of course, about their own lives. And . . . they must be prepared to read portions of them aloud to the class. There was the spring two years ago when Jean, a forty-something woman with grown children, read the account of her college pregnancy and her decision to give the baby up for adoption. She concluded her narrative with a poem written by her mother and found by Jean only after her mother's death. The poem was called "I Miss Him, Too" and was filled with a grandmother's longing for her first grandchild, the child she had urged her daughter to forget, the child who had been the source of so much anger and resentment between mother and daughter. There were no dry eyes at the end of that class.

Is this group therapy? Well, yes, in a way. But then again, isn't good literature meant to wrench our emotions? My belief is that our own stories, well-told and well-crafted, are the most compelling texts of our lives.

"All right," you may say. "But besides a lot of used Kleenex, what do you have to show professionally for your changeover from business communications and technical writing to nonfiction narrative courses?" The first is that I make myself write along with the class. I share this manuscript on read-aloud days. So far, I have about thirty pages of what I hope will be a book about my son, our family, and the special education system. In addition, I have written two poems, using a genre I thought had been lost to me years ago.

Literature of Family Crisis is far from the only course I've developed since what I think of as my "coming out" to my department and my students. In True Crime Accounts, students formed research teams who presented their work to the class on topics related to the texts we read, topics like capital punishment, mental health issues, the sociopathic personality, and the mystique of cults. After reading ten chilling accounts of serial murder and other violent acts, we confessed one day that we were all bolting our doors and windows and sweltering through sticky summer nights. But it was a dream of a summer course to take and to teach in sheer interest level.

Reading and Writing in American Public Education I offered through the honors program. I included a unit on special education, so I was able to merge two interests of mine. In addition, both the students and I were enlightened by Jonathan Kozol's *Savage Inequalities,* his look into the horrifying conditions under which our inner-city children attend school.

As an English professor, I would not have the opportunity to read in such a variety of fields if I had not learned the trick of accessing special topics courses as well as looking for options to teach nontraditional courses. With budget cuts and faculty shortages nationwide, college committees look askance at new course proposals. However, if you've got a "wish course" languishing for want of an opening in your departmental curriculum, I encourage you to find temporary slots and look at your continuing education program as a place that welcomes innovation and a meshing of our private and public selves in course offerings.

Finally, I have offered Multicultural Autobiographies on both the graduate and undergraduate levels. We read about many cultures within American society and a few outside of it, and we write, of course, about ourselves, but in a very focused way. As always in my courses, the students present the texts they have chosen from the syllabus. In addition to presenting the texts to the class, students are encouraged to respond to works in a variety of ways: with parallel memoirs, with poetry, with original music, artwork, photography, or film. Of course, I include the autobiography of an autistic person on the reading list and this is the work I present. I am always a little nervous about taking time on "my issue," but the students' responses to the narrative of my son, to videos of him, and to the subject of autism itself has been so much more than I had ever expected or dreamed of. There are days when they have peppered me with frank questions, days when they have made connections with their lives and the handicaps that we all have, and days when they have approached me after class with "You know, I have a cousin (or a little brother or a friend) who is like your son." And there are nights when my phone rings and it's a student calling to let me know there's something on television about autism. There are times when I've arrived at class with unshed tears stinging my eyes and it's a tremendous relief to be able to say, "I had a hard time getting Andrew on the bus today. I need a minute." It's a relief to meet understanding eyes and to know the class will take over and initiate the day's discussion.

It is equally wonderful to mention to them (when appropriate) my daughter Katie or my husband Riley and to hear from them about their partners or siblings or parents or roommates. In short, it's just plain liberating to acknowledge to one another that we have lives, that we do not have to stay in our "student" or "professor" boxes. Quite honestly, on those occasionally down days we all have, I find my students infinitely more empathetic and supportive than many of my colleagues, some of whom would rather do a crab shuffle with downcast eyes at the mere mention of "family"—as though I had uttered a profanity in polite company.

None of which is to say I am of the professors-should-be-buddies school. But because my students and I share our writing and, by extension, our lives, I feel more like a senior colleague or a mentor than an authority figure. We work hard together; we read a book a week (even freshmen), breaking at midsemester for individual conferences and read-aloud workshops. We are invested in our writing and in each other.

How does all this add up for me professionally? The English department now offers its first course in nonfiction texts, an umbrella course whose topic can shift with the diverse interests of the faculty. I pioneered it as Narrative of the Differently Abled. In addition, I offer a graduate course in nonfiction workshop, a parallel at last to the creative writing workshop we offer at that level for poets and fiction writers.

I have come a long way from T-units, heuristics, and hermeneutics. My life, my teaching, and my research are finally complementary. Like all working parents, I still have times when job-related concerns take precedence over family matters. The children's school vacations in February and April are still sources of wracking guilt. My secretary schedules these weeks as part of her vacation; I cannot. But I can bring my daughter with me to the university. And all in all, the workplace is now a kinder, gentler part of my life.

Disabling Facts, Enabling Conditions: Motherhood and Teaching in India and the United States

Darshan Perusek

Given the contingencies of my personal biography, I could not have "fallen" into a more appropriate profession than teaching in the university. Fallen, I say, because I did not plan to enter this profession; the profession, as it were, came to me. I was the first student at Poona University, India, in fifteen years, to pass with distinction in English literature, both at the B.A. and the M.A. level. Notwithstanding my performance, however, my family members did not expect me to do any kind of paid work at all; in fact, my mother's fondest wish was to find a suitable match for me, her oldest daughter, by age sixteen. "Young brides look so pretty; girls lose their bloom by the time they are twenty," she said. Well, she still hadn't found the elusive groom by the time I had completed my M.A., and in the meantime, there were letters from two colleges inviting me to teach. "Teaching's a respectable profession," my mother now said; "you can teach till you get married. After that, it's up to your husband whether he wants you to work or not." That's how I became a teacher—without meaning to, by chance, by default, really, since a suitable groom failed to materialize till seven years later.

When he finally did I was twenty-four, he didn't mind that the "bloom" on my cheeks was gone, and we got married. A year later I had my daughter; a year and a half later, my son. By the time my son was born I knew that my daughter had cerebral palsy as a result of a long and protracted labor and, as the visiting Russian pediatrician at the

Darshan Perusek is a professor of English at the University of Wisconsin at Stout.

hospital in Delhi where I took her informed me bluntly, "She will never be like other children." My son was six weeks old when I was offered a job at the local college. I accepted it, and I have been teaching ever since. What I have to say in this essay about parenting and work is the outcome of my experiences related, directly and indirectly, to living with my daughter's disability. What I have learned is that the politics of family life and of domestic work cannot be separated from the politics of the workplace and of social and cultural institutions.

This is what the feminists of the sixties were saying, of course. But slogans are one thing, life something else. Furthermore, living with my daughter's disability also taught me, in a way no amount of theorizing could have, that the personal was the political in a much more immediate sense, in that the political on the personal front included, beyond the structure of family relations and the division of labor in the domestic sphere, the body itself, that "house" of bone and flesh and tissue with which we are each born and which we inhabit, with greater or lesser autonomy and freedom, to the end of our days. Feminist politics has been about dismantling barriers that constrain the autonomy of the female body and I subscribe to that politics. I have learned, though, living with my daughter, that we must also dismantle barriers that constrain the autonomy of the body that is injured and hurt, the body that is old and infirm, the body that cannot function as well in the world as that of the young and the physically intact. That this world is made by the able-bodied as if none of us will ever get hurt and none will never get old is all the more reason we must work on this front.

Something about Myself as a Feminist: A Tale of Two Daughters

When my daughter was six years old, she was hospitalized for corrective surgery on her legs. The hospital was a public hospital in Delhi, the ward a general ward for women, the patients, for the most part, peasants from surrounding villages and the urban poor. I had seen poverty before, of course. The women who came to work for my middle-class family were all poor—the charwoman, the laundry woman, the sweeper . . . I had, in fact, lived surrounded by poverty. But I hadn't really *seen* it: the poor lived in *their* world, I in *mine*. In the hospital, though, our worlds became one. We shared the same space; we experienced the same terror of the body in pain; we lived with the same desperate hope of someday returning to the blessed world of the well and the healthy. And in the hospital, I met Lajwanti, a twelve-year-old girl with rheumatoid arthritis whose parents had brought her six months ago from their home in a nearby village, where they farmed a few acres of land.

In the early days of Lajwanti's hospitalization, when their hope was high and their faith in the miracle-making powers of doctors bright, her parents came to see her often. But after all these months, they understood how matters stood with their daughter and stopped coming. They grieved, of course, but in the meantime, there were fields to be plowed and sown and other children to be taken care of. It would have been good if Lajwanti was cured and they could take her back, but that was not "God's will," they told her sadly; so it was better she stay where she was, out of the way.

"I'm no use to them," Lajwanti said matter of factly, explaining her abandonment, when we talked in the quiet hours of the night, the overworked and chronically angry nurses mercifully gone from the ward to their station at the end of the hall. "But a boy in your place—would he have been left here, too?" I asked, knowing well her answer even before she answered: "Yes, but a son's place is in his parents' home, a daughter's in the home of her husband. Who will marry a girl who can't walk?"

My daughter and I left the hospital a week later and I lost track of Lajwanti. My daughter lives with me in Wisconsin now; she has a motorized wheelchair, goes to college, and leads a fairly independent life. That is because, unlike Lajwanti, my daughter was not born poor, and unlike Lajwanti, my daughter was not subjected to the awful constraints of a feudal/patriarchal order where, for so many, to be born a woman is to live with the knowledge that you were never wanted in the first place ("It's a girl. May the gods be kinder next time.") and to be born a "defective" woman is to live with the even more bitter knowledge that you were indeed cursed by the gods above and by your fellow humans below, and that there was no place for you under the sky.

Lajwanti and the other women in the ward taught me my first lesson in the privileges of class. My class made the nurses come when I needed them; my class made the doctors answer my questions when I asked them; my class allowed me to get my own meals for myself and my daughter when my stomach revolted against the slop that was wheeled in huge clattering drums at lunch and dinner; my class got my daughter a bed in the overcrowded ward when other postoperative patients (moaning with pain that nurses wouldn't give painkillers for because it meant a trip down from their station to the ward) had to lie on thin mattresses on the floor. My class did all this for me. We all suffered, poor and well-off, but my daughter's and my suffering was visible; that of my illiterate, impoverished fellow patients was invisible, didn't matter. This was my introduction, in all its bleakness, to the dual burden of being born female *and* poor in a patriarchal society that was also a class society. Like so many women of my generation in my country, I did not, in other words, find feminism through my uniquely female experience, but through a broader class-related experience of injustice that helped me see injustice to all women.

Teaching in India: More Lessons in the Privileges of Class

I did not teach the first two years after I got married. When I started teaching again, my daughter was a year and a half, my son six weeks old. We lived in Mussoorie at the time, a minuscule town three hundred miles northwest of Delhi, in the foothills of the Himalayas. It was built by the British during the days of the Raj as a refuge from the merciless summer heat of the plains. The town had one main street called the Mall; for the rest, there were, aside from a few roads, mostly trails that led to houses with the most precarious hold on the side of a hill, often on the very edge of a bluff, like the one we lived in. You never walked on level ground in Mussoorie: the trail either dropped down precipitously to a house below or wound its way laboriously up to a house above; so you were always straining forward as you walked up or holding yourself back as you plunged down. When visiting friends at a house below the road, you made sure the inhabitants were in by raining a shower of pebbles on the roof. For a house above the road, tough luck; you just went all the way up, and if nobody was home, cursed your luck and the absent householders and hoped you would be more lucky next time.

I was able to accept the job I was offered, two infants notwithstanding, partly because my husband also taught in the same college and we could arrange our schedules so that one of us was home while the other was at work. Since the mornings involved more work with the children than evenings—bathing, nursing, feeding—we arranged it so I was in the home in the mornings. From our veranda, you could see the college a few hundred feet below, shrouded in mist. By noon, my morning chores done, I would get ready and step out on the veranda to see if my husband was on his way. And there he would be, unfailingly, making his way up the steep trail, straining forward, emerging out of the mist palely, disappearing, and appearing again. Sometimes, tired of too much infant company, I would meet him half-way up, give instructions for the rest of the day, and plunge downward on the trail with my head full of Shakespeare or Kafka.

Wonderful as this arrangement was, though, I could not have taken the job if it had not been for Laretiya. I met Laretiya, a young woman, like myself, in her twenties, as I walked back home from my interview at the college, wondering *how* I was going to manage everything. "I'm looking for a woman to work for me," I said to the quiet-looking, neatly dressed woman. "Do you know anyone who could?" "I'm looking for a job myself," she answered, "I'll do it." Laretiya, a widow, worked for me for three years. Her primary job was at a bank, where she did the cleaning and routine maintenance, but she had to supplement her earnings with domestic service to raise her five children. The oldest, Krishna, was about eleven years old and took care of the younger ones when her mother left for work; the youngest, about a year old, Laretiya would bring to the house, together with seven-year-old Kamala. Laretiya would take care of one of my children as I tended to the other, while Kamala would look after her little brother. After the children were put to bed, Laretiya would do the cleaning, washing, and cooking for the day. By the time I returned at five, Laretiya was ready to leave to take care of her own home.

I must add here that the domestic arrangements in my house were far from unique; in fact, without domestic help, no woman in India, to my knowledge, would be able to maintain a professional career. It is therefore not surprising that, like their Victorian middle-class sisters, the topic of servants, "good" and "bad," continues to be of more than casual interest to my Indian sisters, the grind of household work in middle-class Indian homes today being very much like that in nineteenth-century British and American homes before the advent of household technology. All domestic work—cleaning, cooking, washing—is time-consuming and labor-intensive in addition to being, like domestic work everywhere, monotonous and neverending, and middle-class families, even with a full-time housewife, depend on poor families like Laretiya's for relief from its drudgery. But for families like mine, with young children and with both parents working outside the home, servants are not just relief from drudgery; they are the very foundation of one's day-to-day existence. Without them, the whole edifice collapses, both of family and of work. Which explains the pity and horror you felt anytime you heard the panic-stricken announcement of a colleague: "My maid quit; do you know anyone you could send me?" This, too, was for me a lesson in the privileges, or the lack thereof, of class. This, too, was part of the broader experience of injustice that informed and shaped my understanding of injustice to women.

Teaching in the United States: On Your Own with the Nuclear Family

I left Delhi to go to Kent State in Ohio in 1971, the year after the May 4 shooting by the National Guard of four students. The reason, once again, was my daughter, who was now six years old and there was nothing more that Delhi could do for her. It was in talking about having and raising children with young women graduate students at Kent State that I understood for the first time the full meaning of the term "nuclear family" and its implications for women as parents. None of my peers, all single and all in their mid- to late twenties, were ready to get married any time soon, and none was even remotely ready to have children in the foreseeable future. "Are you crazy? Who do you think will take care of them?" Joan responded incredulously when I asked why not. At the time, none of our parents were old; so the question of who would take care of them when the time came did not arise. But each of us, myself included, thought it natural that women should be responsible for taking care of babies. Housework we could sit and negotiate with our men till the cows came home, because housework, even if unpaid dirty work, was still just regular work. But motherhood?

But although I, too, had been raised to see parenting as primarily a woman's function, I had never thought a mother was *solely* responsible for taking care of a child. Children in my world were more like communal property; everybody had a right to them. "Auntie, can I take Gogi for a while?" an older child would ask as she took my daughter from my arms. As for my son, I don't even remember him as a baby— my neighbor, who had no children of her own, would take him in the morning and wash him and feed him and sing to him all day until her husband got home. Then, when neighboring children would come home later in the afternoon, they would lead him away on one of those trails that, looking back now, I wonder how all those children survived into adulthood, so treacherous they seem.

Stephanie Coontz, historian, describes a similar communal attitude toward children in Lanai, where she was visiting Hawaiian-Filipino friends. The story is best told in her own words:

> My child was still in diapers, and I appreciated the fact that nearly every community function, from weddings to baptisms to New Year's Eve parties, was open to children. I could sit and socialize and keep an eye on my toddler, and I assumed that was what all the other parents were doing. Soon, however, I noticed that I was the only person jumping up to change a diaper, pick my son up when he fell, wipe his nose, dry his eyes. . . . Belatedly, I realized why: the other parents were *not* keeping an eye on their kids. Instead, each adult kept an eye on the *floor* around his or her chair. Any child who moved into that section of the floor and needed disciplining, feeding, comforting, or changing was promptly accommodated; no parent felt compelled to check that his or her *own* child was being similarly cared for. (210)

That's the communal attitude toward children I am talking about. In fact, I remember from my own experience that if a mother was overly anxious about her own kid, she was sharply reprimanded by a gray-haired matriarch with: "Do you think you are the only one to care about your child?"

What helped me as a student and, later, as a teacher in this country raising my children was that, for a brief shining moment, a similar communal attitude among young people existed here. My children grew up right in the very midst of passionate discussions over the war in Vietnam and the civil rights movement and Watergate and Wounded Knee. When my daughter would come home from school, whoever happened to notice the bus come in—Tom or Anne or Dave or Leonard—would lift her off the bus and bring her in. When my son, after Tiananmen Square, interviewed William Hinton of *Fanshen* fame for a radio show he and his friends do in Madison, Hinton expressed some surprise at his keen and deep understanding of events in China. "No surprise, Mr. Hinton," my son answered with some pride, "I was raised on *Fanshen*."

There were, however, *social* policies in place in this country that obviated the desperate need for familial help I knew in India. My daughter, for instance, found a place in school without my having to beg and weep, as I had to in Delhi, that she be admitted. That's because by now, the returning Vietnam soldiers, disabled in that monstrous war, had put disability on the national agenda, and the disabled, like all citizens, had a publicly mandated right to education. By the time my daughter was out of high school, dormitories, classrooms, and recreational buildings on all campuses had to be, by federal law, wheelchair accessible, and transportation for disabled students was in place on most, as well as personnel dealing specifically with other related services for them.

I did not see much sensitivity on the part of the university to the needs of mothers, because parenthood was seen then, and is seen today in large part, as a private matter, to be worked out between members of the family. I tested this sensitivity only once, when I asked the chair of the department for morning hours so I would be able to meet my daughter when she returned from school, and he answered, "I don't want to hear any Mickey Mouse stories." I learned my lesson fast: motherhood was a personal problem, and I must attend to its demands on my own time. The most pervasive insensitivity I saw, though, was to the needs of part-time faculty, who were for the most part former graduate students of the department and who taught all freshman composition sections at a fraction of what full-time faculty made, had no health insurance, had no say in anything having to do with their own or the larger life of the university, were picked and dropped at will, and when picked, often not told until the morning of the first teaching day that they had been "chosen." The university was, I must say, remarkably gender blind when it came to this: men and women suffered alike the indignities brought by a brutal freeze and retrenchment in faculty appointments from the late seventies into almost the mideighties. When in 1979 I had a miscarriage, I had to, out of my miserable part-time salary, come up with $1,100 for a night in the hospital. It took me three years to pay the bill. This was not because I was a woman; it was because I was not a full-fledged member of the academy.

Conclusion

My children are now grown and that should, theoretically, have put the issue of combining parenting and work behind me. But it hasn't, because my daughter's disability continues to keep it alive for me in a very real way. Her recent surgery, from which she is recuperating even as I write, reminds me once again of my debt to the collective struggles of those before me that allowed me to both work and tend to her physical and emotional needs. For instance, she could not have had surgery at the Mayo Clinic if medical assistance had not paid for it. Nor would I have been able to care for her at home had it not been for those household saints sent for my deliverance and succor by the county home care services: Linda, the supervisory nurse, who with the knowledge born of experience assured both me and my daughter that the horrible pain she was suffering would ease with time; Debbie, the young aide with a daughter of her own in a wheelchair, who understood so well what times like these do to both parents and child; and dear Lori, who has been my daughter's aide and therapist, and a friend and comrade to us both over the last year, even as she is torn with anguish over whether she is doing enough for her own young boy, also in a wheelchair. I think about these saints, and how little they are paid to do this work, and I wonder what ever happened to that brave feminist vision of putting a just price on the socially necessary task of nurturing and caring for the young, the old, and the sick. And I think of another parent I know, my dear friend Lorna, employed at my campus in custodial services, who helps me with housecleaning every two weeks. Lorna's teenage son has been charged with delinquency a number of times and her social worker accused her of being a "bad" mother: "You ought to supervise better his school work and make sure he doesn't get into trouble out of school," she said to Lorna, sternly. When Lorna reminded her that she left for work at 5:00 in the morning and did not return until 2:00 in the afternoon, after which she did various jobs in the day to make ends meet, the woman was not impressed. "Quit work if you have to. Your son is more important than your work."

The old ideology of motherhood is back these days, and back with a vengeance, to haunt with guilt married women with children who have chosen to combine parenting and paid work outside the home and single and married women with children who have no choice but to work for wages. The right to paid work, to economic independence, is a hard fought and a hard won right for women, and we cannot allow it to be compromised. But so is the right to have and raise children without being consumed with anxiety and guilt every day we leave them to go to work. The Chinese essayist and fiction writer Lu Xun cautioned readers in the 1930s against excessive optimism over Ibsen's Nora slamming the door behind her as she left to find and confront her own destiny. A decisive factor in that destiny, he pointed out, would be how she went about earning a living. I take it as a given that Nora's destiny must come to naught without a job, but for me, there has also always been the related question of how long Nora could have gone on without her children and, if her ailing father had still been alive, how she could have continued her life while he died alone, his daughter far away.

The need for economic independence is important, and the need to do emotionally fulfilling work is important too. But so is the need to love and be loved, the need to help those we love when they need us, and to expect help from them when we, in turn, are vulnerable; the need to welcome with a joyful heart children when they enter this world; the need to ease with gentle hands the pain of the old when they depart from it. In the midst of our productive work in factories and offices and schools and universities, this work of loving and caring must go on, else we will lose our humanity. Which means that, if women are not to perish from exhaustion, the feminist agenda must once again, with renewed force and vigor, take the personal—the family—into the political—the realm of state policy. A state policy that provides parents of both sexes space to raise the young and to take care of the old: paid maternity leave, paid parental leave, with choice for either parent to be with the child in its first year, paid family leave for emergencies, and paid home nursing for the elderly.

These policies are necessary if we want to make our homes hospitable to the young and the old without imposing an intolerable psychic and physical burden on women. But there's a harsh wind blowing across the land these days, and the chill is being felt by the most vulnerable sections of society. The "burden" that policymakers see and compute is financial, and this burden, they claim, is too heavy. There can be only three solutions under the circumstances. The first, that women return to their homes and pick up once again where they left off three decades ago, is unacceptable. The second, that we abandon our children, our parents, and our sick, is likewise unacceptable. The third is to pay the financial cost of the social policies that help us be human—and humane—and whole. That's the prize. Let us all, fathers and mothers, keep our eyes on this prize.

WORK CITED

Coontz, Stephanie. *The Way We Never Were: American Families and the Nostalgia Trap.* New York: Basic Books, 1992.

PART EIGHT

Eldercare

Care and Career in an Aging Society

Emily K. Abel

Although feminist scholars lavish attention on motherhood, they continue to slight other forms of caregiving. Numerous observers note, however, that child rearing occupies a much smaller place in women's lives today than in the past. Colonial women devoted most of their adult years to bearing and raising children. Today the typical mother has preschool children for slightly longer than a decade and can expect to live well into her seventies (Gerson, Alpert, and Richardson). But instead of reducing the period of caregiving, the demographic revolution may have shifted it to other parts of the life course. One recent study found that more than 60 percent of women care for elderly relatives at some point in their lives; the burdens typically fall on women between forty-five and sixty-five (Moen, Robinson, and Fields). Some women devote more years to caring for aging relatives than to raising children (House Subcommittee on Human Services).

The shape of women's caregiving responsibilities may change even more dramatically in the future. The elderly were just 4 percent of the population in 1900 (Feldblum), but they increased to 8 percent in 1950 (Siegel and Taeuber) and 13 percent in 1990 (Jessie Allen). It is projected that those sixty-five and over will constitute approximately 17 percent of the population by 2020 (Siegel and Taeuber). The rate of increase of the very old, who are most at risk of illness and disability, is especially great. The "old old" constitute the fastest growing segment of the population (Siegel and Taeuber).

Emily K. Abel is a professor of health services and women's studies at UCLA.

Women's growing involvement in eldercare is not only the result of inexorable demographic trends. Because the reigning view is that the United States cannot afford the high cost of institutional care for the burgeoning frail elderly population, public policies seek to reimpose the burden of long-term care on family members. Several states have attempted to limit the supply of nursing home beds and institute preadmission screening programs to control utilization of those that exist. Federally funded "channeling" demonstration projects have sought to divert disabled elderly people from nursing homes (Kane and Kane). Moreover, in 1983, the federal government introduced a prospective payment system under Medicare to reduce the high cost of hospital care. As a result, the average length of stay in hospitals has dropped (Kahn et al.). Health maintenance organizations also seek to shorten hospital stays. Many patients released from hospitals early return home to receive care from their families.

Few publicly funded services are available to relieve caregivers' burdens. A dominant concern of policymakers is that government-funded care not replace services now provided "free" by family members. Medicare thus emphasizes medically oriented home health care, not the social services family members provide. And the home health benefit under Medicare is extremely restrictive; recipients must be homebound, require skilled nursing care, and need services on an intermittent, rather than continuous, basis. Home health care thus consumes just a tiny fraction of total Medicare expenditures (Senate Special Committee on Aging).

Medicaid regulations do not require home and community-based care under this program to hew so closely to a medical model; nevertheless, the individual states are responsible for determining eligibility and coverage, and they differ dramatically in the extent to which they fund noninstitutional services (Rabin and Stockton). The two major programs that pay for social services for elderly people living at home are the Social Services Black Grant and Title III of the Older Americans Act. The level of funding devoted to both programs is meager (Estes, Swan, and Associates).

Like other forms of domestic labor, care for elderly people continues to be allocated on the basis of gender. Women constitute 77 percent of adult children caring for parents. Moreover, daughters are more likely than sons to live with dependent parents and to serve as the primary caregivers (Stone, Cafferata, and Sangl; Wolf and Soldo). Because elderly people turn first to their spouses when they become ill, we might expect spousal caregiving to be divided equally along gender lines. Partly because women tend both to marry older men and to live longer, however, a majority (64 percent) of the spouses providing care are women (Stone, Cafferata, and Sangl).

The gendered division of labor also extends to the particular tasks caregivers perform. Sons are more likely to assist parents with routine household maintenance and repairs while daughters are far more likely to help with indoor household chores and personal health care (Coward and Rathbone-McCuan; Stephens and Christianson). This gender difference may help to explain why caregiving has different consequences for men and women. Men take responsibility for tasks they typically can perform whenever they choose. Women, however, often assume tasks that keep them on call twenty-four hours a day. Moreover, the tasks performed largely by women are the ones researchers have correlated with high levels of stress (Horowitz "Family Caregiving").

Nevertheless, women receive less assistance. Daughters-in-law (but not sons-in-law) remain an important source of informal care. Sons caring for elderly parents thus obtain more material help and emotional support from their wives than daughters can expect from their husbands (Horowitz "Sons and Daughters"). Some evidence suggests that formal services also are distributed inequitably. Men who are caring for elderly spouses or parents receive more in-home services than their female counterparts (Susan M. Allen; Fitting et al.; Hooyman and Ryan).

The simultaneous increase of women's labor force participation and the aging of the population has sparked a new research industry devoted to examining the relationship between work and care. Various studies report that between 23 and 32 percent of employees care for elderly people (Neal et al.). Some researchers point out that caregiving often has little impact on waged work (Scharlach). One reason may be that women often assume that their primary goal should be to insulate their work lives from the intrusions of caregiving responsibilities; as a result, they sacrifice vacation, social activities, and time alone (Abel). In a study of adult daughters caring for elderly parents, I asked women whether caregiving interfered more with leisure or work. A respondent who lived with her disabled mother answered this way: "By cutting into the job, it cuts into the leisure, because the things I have to do for her take place Monday through Friday. So I take time off from the job to take care of her needs, and then I have to give up my leisure to take care of the job. It's a round robin." Researchers also note that paid employment sometimes has benefits for caregivers, muting the emotional consequences of tending the elderly and providing an alternative source of personal identity (Scharlach).

Nevertheless, care for the elderly, like child rearing, clashes with labor force participation in various ways. Waged work and family care confer different rewards, operate according to different clocks, and are guided by different value systems. Demands in one arena frequently are incompatible with those in the other. According to one study, 9 percent of caregivers quit their jobs, 21 percent reduce their hours of work, 29.4 percent rearrange their schedules, and 18.6 percent take time off without pay (Stone, Cafferata, and Sangl). Two researchers found that, of unemployed caregivers who had worked within the year prior to being interviewed, 35 percent had relinquished their jobs to render care, 21 percent had declined job offers for the same reason, and 28 percent found that caregiving obligations prevented them from looking for work (Stephens and Christianson). Still another study found that those caring for the disabled elderly have the same number of absences and take the same amount of time off work as parents of young children (Scharlach and Boyd).

Men and women tend to resolve the conflict between work and care in different ways. Daughters are more likely than sons to curtail labor force participation, while sons are more likely than daughters to reduce caregiving responsibilities. Government data collected in 1982 show that the proportion of caregiving daughters who relinquished paid employment was more than twice that of sons (11.6 and 5.0 percent). Of those who worked at some point during the caregiving experience, higher proportions of daughters than sons reduced their working hours as a result of caregiving obligations (22.8 versus 15 percent), rearranged their schedules (34.9 versus 27.7 percent), and took time off without pay (24.8 versus 14.1 percent) (Stone, Cafferata, and Sangl). Conversely, a 1983 study found that sons who held paid employment reduced the number of hours they helped their parents but that labor force participation had no significant impact on care by daughters (Stoller). Like child-rearing obligations, women's responsibilities for the care of elderly people may reinforce the notion that they are intermittent workers and thus serve as a rationale for employment practices that maintain their lower pay and status.

The conflict between work and care takes different forms for women situated differently in the campus job hierarchy. Higher status employees are most likely to have sufficient resources to pay for medical equipment and supplies, retrofit their homes, and "buy out" of their obligations by hiring less privileged women. Because few publicly funded services are available, elderly people and their families frequently purchase the assistance they need from either formal organizations or aides, attendants, and companions hired through ad hoc, informal arrangements. In cities with a large pool of immigrant domestic workers, middle- and upper-middle-class caregivers rely extensively on these workers to deliver care. Although very few caregivers pay a living wage or provide benefits, the expense of care is still prohibitive for most families.

In addition, most faculty and high-level administrators at colleges and universities have schedules that can be rearranged and leverage to demand special consideration. They thus are least likely to suffer sanctions when they receive phone calls from relatives during working hours or take time off to respond to their relatives' needs. But caregiving responsibilities may intrude on their careers in other ways. The women I interviewed who held professional and managerial jobs frequently complained that they could not work at their customary level of intensity or perform as well as they wished. A woman in a managerial position remarked:

> I'm just drained and run down and tired and just burned out by caring for my father, and I don't have that much left to give to my job. It's not my primary focus right now. It is not something that I'm directed towards right now. The job is really a very self-motivating position, and I'm not motivated. I would say that the quality and the motivation of the work have changed drastically. I don't think that the interest level is there. When I had no other responsibilities, my career was the motivating force for me. This is something that I feel very dissatisfied with. I have really lost interest in it.

A teacher reported a similar experience: "I don't have the same energy and the same enthusiasm for the class. I don't like constantly repeating the same curriculum year after year, but certain new activities I am not able to develop."

Faculty members who control the pace and rhythm of work may lack protection against relative's demands. A writer I interviewed described her experience after bringing her parents, both of whom were disabled, to live near her:

> The first couple of years my parents were here, I would work in fits and starts, because the interruptions were very, very difficult for me. It would be very hard for me to switch gears, and try to cope with calamities, to determine what really was a calamity. These tearful calls from

my mother are often over nothing, but sometimes they're about something. I had started working on a project, but there kept being ongoing demands on my time. I guess I stopped working, or I let it drag, but I never acknowledged it. I kept saying, "I've got to get back and get to work," and I'd go back and I'd do a page, and then I wouldn't do it for another week, and I kept fooling myself. I needed the crutch of saying, "I'm working," I guess, to able to give them an idea that I do something else. But at the end of six months' time, I noticed I hadn't done anything. And if I'd been working every day the way I thought I was, I would. I'd been fooling myself. I didn't have anything to show for the time.

Other family members also may assume that interruptions are insignificant to people who set their own hours. My family's experience offers an example. My mother's illness began just after my younger sister, a professor, had gone on leave to write a book. My other siblings also devoted enormous amounts of time and energy to my mother's care; however, because they had to make elaborate arrangements to be away from their offices, they assumed that this sister was on call for any emergencies.

Nevertheless, flexible work hours constitute an enormous advantage to faculty that is denied to other employees on campus. Women in staff and service positions frequently lose money when they take time off to engage in such activities as transporting relatives to doctors, investigating possible residential facilities, or rendering emergency care. Not surprisingly, among the various programs and benefits provided to employees with caregiving responsibilities at a major southern California employer, "flexible work schedules" and "family illness hours" were most frequently utilized (Scharlach and Boyd).

Although caregiving is predominantly women's work, care for the elderly is largely absent from the feminist agenda in the United States. To be sure, even if we drastically reoriented public policies, we could do little to remedy some of the problems caregivers encounter. They must confront human experiences that typically are considered taboo in our society—old age, progressive chronic disease, disability, and death. Most try to foster elderly relatives' dignity while asserting authority over them. Many are tending people who suffer from cognitive impairments that threaten to destroy their sense of self.

Public policies provide the framework within which the experience of caregiving unfolds. Because publicly funded services are not universally accessible, many women lack the power to determine when they begin to care for elderly relatives, the power to control the intrusions of caregiving in their lives, and the power to hand over responsibilities that have become overwhelming. An examination of the place of caregiving in women's lives also gives new urgency to two of the original goals of the women's movement—eradicating the gender division of labor and restructuring the world of work. When we campaign on campuses for specific reforms, we should ensure that they address the different and often conflicting needs of various groups of women workers.

WORKS CITED

Abel, Emily K. *Who Cares for the Elderly? Public Policy and the Experiences of Adult Daughters*. Philadelphia: Temple University Press, 1991.

Allen, Jessie. "The Front Lines." *Women on the Front Lines: Meeting the Challenge of an Aging America*. Ed. Jessie Allen and Alan Pifer. Washington, D.C.: Urban Institute Press, 1993. 1–10.

Allen, Susan M. "Gender Differences in Spousal Caregiving and Unmet Need for Care." *Journal of Gerontology: Social Sciences* 49.4 (1994): S187–S195.

Coward, R. T., and E. Rathbone-McCuan. "Illuminating the Relative Role of Adult Sons and Daughters in the Long-Term Care of Their Parents." Paper presented at the annual meeting of the National Association of Social Workers, Chicago, Nov. 1985.

Estes, Carroll L., James H. Swan, and Associates. *The Long Term Care Crisis: Elders Trapped in the No-Care Zone*. Newbury Park, Calif.: Sage Publications, 1993.

Feldblum, C. R. "Home Health Care for the Elderly: Programs, Problems, and Potentials." *Harvard Journal on Legislation* 22.1 (1985): 193–254.

Fitting, M., P. Rabins, M. J. Lucas, and J. Eastham. "Caregivers for Dementia Patients: A Comparison of Husbands and Wives." *The Gerontologist* 26.3 (1986): 248–52.

Gerson, M. J., J. L. Alpert, and M. S. Richardson. "Mothering: The View from Psychological Research." *Signs: Journal of Women in Culture and Society* 9.3 (1984): 434–53.

Hooyman, N. R., and R. Ryan. "Women as Caregivers of the Elderly: Catch 22 Dilemmas." Ms. 1985. Author's possession.

Horowitz, Amy. "Family Caregiving to the Frail Elderly." *Annual Review of Gerontology and Geriatrics* 5 (1985): 194–246.

———. "Sons and Daughters to Older Parents: Differences in Role Performance and Consequences." *The Gerontologist* 25.6 (1985): 612–27.

House Subcommittee on Human Services, Select Committee on Aging. *Exploding the Myths: Caregiving in America*. 100th Cong., 1st sess., Comm. Pub. No. 99–611.

Kahn, Katherine L., Emmett Keeler, Marjorie J. Sherwood, William H. Rogers, David Draper, Stanley S. Bentow, Ellen J. Reinisch, Lisa V. Rubenstein, Jacqueline Kosecoff, and Robert H. Brook. "Comparing Outcomes of Care before and after Implementation of the DRG-Based Prospective Payment System." *JAMA* 264.15 (1990): 1984–88.

Kane, R. A., and R. L. Kane. *Long-Term Care: Principles, Programs, and Policies.* New York: Springer, 1987.

Moen, Phyllis, Julie Robinson, and Vivian Fields. "Women's Work and Caregiving Roles: A Life Course Approach." *Journal of Gerontology: Social Sciences* 49.4 (1994): S176–S186.

Neal, Margaret B., Nancy J. Chapman, Berit Ingersoll-Dayton, and Arthur C. Emlen. *Balancing Work and Caregiving for Children, Adults, and Elders.* Newbury Park, Calif.: Sage Publications, 1993.

Rabin, D. L., and P. Stockton. *Long-Term Care for the Elderly: A Factbook.* New York: Oxford University Press, 1987.

Scharlach, Andrew E. "Caregiving and Employment: Competing or Complementary Roles?" *The Gerontologist* 34.3 (1994): 378–85.

Scharlach, Andrew E., and Sandra Boyd. "Caregiving and Employment: Results of an Employee Survey." *The Gerontologist* 29.3 (1989): 382–87.

Senate Special Committee on Aging. *Home Health Care at the Crossroads: An Information Paper.* Washington, D.C.: GPO, 1988.

Siegel, J. S., and C. M. Taeuber. "Demographic Perspectives on the Long-Lived Society." *Daedalus* 115.1 (1986): 77–118.

Stephens, S. A., and J. B. Christianson. *Informal Care of the Elderly.* Lexington, Mass.: Lexington Books, 1986.

Stoller, Eleanor P. "Parental Caregiving by Adult Children." *Journal of Marriage and the Family* 55.4 (1983): 851–58.

Stone, R. I., L. Cafferata, and J. Sangl. "Caregivers of the Frail Elderly: A National Profile." *The Gerontologist* 27.5 (1987): 616–26.

Wolf, D. A., and B. J. Soldo. "The Household Older Unmarried Women: Micro-Decision Models of Shared Living Arrangements." Paper presented at the annual meeting of the Popular Association of America, San Francisco, 1986.

Eldercare and Multicultural Values

Gretchen Holbrook Gerzina

Several years ago my husband and I dropped our children off with my parents and set off on an extremely rare weekend alone. I hadn't driven more than three blocks when, out of the corner of my eye, I saw a man go down on the opposite side of the street. Without thinking I made an immediate U-turn and jumped out of the car. There on the sidewalk, next to a hedge, wearing bedroom slippers, lay an old man, bleeding from both elbows. As we helped him up we asked the expected questions: Was he all right? Was this his house? Where did he live?

He lived, he told us, about eight blocks away, in a nursing home. He had left without permission to try to navigate his way to the neighborhood convenience store where they were selling cookies at two packages for a dollar, today only. He gave me his dollar and my husband dusted him off while I ran to the store. When I returned and handed him his bag I asked, "Do you do this often?" He laughed and answered in a shaky voice, "Not any more."

"We'd better give you a ride back," I said, but at this he began to panic.

"Please don't take me back," he begged. "I don't want to go back there."

But there was nowhere else to take him, so we bundled him into the car and drove him back. On the way, he told us about the business he'd started and run for over forty years, how his wife had died and his

Gretchen Holbrook Gerzina is a professor of English and associate dean of the faculty at Vassar College.

health had slowly failed. He told us how badly he missed his independence. On the porch of the nursing home were several old men, distinctly unalert, whom he greeted loudly as friends. They stared.

"You don't have to go in," he assured us, but his legs wobbled and
his hands shook, and his elbows had bled all over the armrests of the
car.

"Someone just needs to clean up those cuts for you," I said. "Everything will be fine."

But it wasn't. The place was a pig sty. A dozen seemingly senile
people dozed and stared in front of a television. There was no desk, no
nurse, no one in command. My ward was extremely agitated as I asked
person after person who was in charge. They just stared at me. When
I called up the stairs several times a nurse appeared, and when I tried
to explain what had happened she brushed right past me and grabbed
my ward's arm.

"There you are!" she barked. "Run off again?" And then, turning to
me, "It's the third time this month he's done that; he's really in trouble
now." Without a thank-you or a good-bye she dragged him off, leaving
me in the lobby. When I got back into the car I felt angry, guilty, depressed, and the lightness of a weekend away from my children had
turned into the weight of multiple abandonments.

When I began graduate school my children were two and five, and my
academic experience was framed by child care. By the time I got tenure they were sixteen and nineteen, and my academic experience had
been framed for several years by eldercare. In my graduate program
there was one other person of color—a black woman who dropped out
and moved away at the end of the year—and one other married woman. A year or two later another black woman, also a mother, entered
the program, as did two black men, one of whom was married with
children. I refused to believe that having a family in any way imped-
ed my ability to succeed; I took only one incomplete, which I made up
in a week. It wasn't until after I was done that I began to realize how
different my experience had been from that of my classmates. Much of
it was positive: I felt grounded and loved instead of lonely and confused. By the time the boys were in bed my head was incapable of
work, so I generally got a good night's sleep. But there were lots of other difficulties. All the required seminars took place outside of the hours
when I could find affordable child care. When my classmates were
meeting for coffee and conversation, often with professors, I was toi-

let training a small boy. I had not only my illnesses to consider (including two operations in four years) but also an unending string of my children's illnesses. I was expected to teach freshman English, take three courses, and volunteer in kindergarten at the same time.

But these were choices I had made in coming to graduate school as a mother. Subtler things were more insidious, like a very old-guard faculty unaccustomed to graduate students of color, let alone women with children; there were only two full-time female professors there at the time, as I recall. There was an academic and experiential language I didn't speak at first. I had some traumas but landed on my feet, winning a lucrative grant in my dissertation year and finishing my degree in five years, ahead of nearly everyone with whom I entered.

Several years later, during the week in which I entered my current job, four things happened: my sister remarried from my house; I began the two-hour-each-way drive between my home and my job; I turned forty; and my father went into congestive heart failure in my home. These set off a series of difficult choices. I couldn't cancel more than a day of classes; I was too new. I tore up the road between Poughkeepsie, New York, and Saratoga Springs every other day to see him in intensive care and later to take care of him in my home. For the past several years something like this has been my life. The semester I came up for tenure, I was living in my home two hours away, in and out of the hospitals where he had two cancer operations, a colostomy, and four heart failures. Even when he's well and in his home he requires a special diet, and my mother can neither drive nor cook. We stay on top of his food, shopping, visiting nurses, and medications. I fight with the doctors and bless them alternately. My children, teenagers during this period, developed problems in school and when I had to be away my husband covered all the fronts.

Somewhere in all this I wrote two books and began a third, yet it wasn't until I was asked to speak on the subject of family care issues in the academy that I began to think about my dual careers as worthy of discussion in an academic setting. Before I do, I'd like to recount another person's more difficult story with, I should say, her whole-hearted permission.

A friend and colleague of mine, also a black woman, lost her mother the year before we met. Her father became ill and moved in with her brother in South Carolina the next year, and she had to fly back and forth continually. She was on leave the third year, when her father died, and spent most of it flying back and forth to the South embroiled in family disputes about inheritance. During this same year she dis-

covered that the man she had lived with for fifteen years was seriously ill. In the fourth year of our friendship, he required round-the-clock
nursing care before he died. In the short time we've known each other she lost literally every family member she loved and has, as she puts
it, "no name to fill in to notify in case of an emergency" on her insurance forms.

When she took him to a concert at St. Paul's Cathedral, to what she
knew would be their last outing together, she realized from looks and
comments that people in the audience thought the black woman with
the extremely frail and sick white man was his nurse, his "caregiver." At
work, to which she also commutes two hours each way, she has felt
the subtle insidiousness of institutional racism and the panic of trying
to get her "work" done while caring for and watching her family get
sick and die. Once, when we were comparing notes over a rare dinner
out and I said that few of our colleagues seemed to have the same
problems we faced, she commented, "Black folks don't put their people out."

As sweepingly general as this comment was, it got me thinking
about the unquestioning clinging to a cultural and familial base that
many of my friends struggle to balance with an increasingly far-flung
academic job market. We're all familiar with the issues of commuter
marriages, single parenthood, and child care, particularly as they affect junior faculty desperate to keep hard-earned and exhausting jobs.
Add to this mix the necessary loosening of cultural, communal, and
familial ties and the problems of coordination become far greater. Take
one step farther and add feelings about family and culture and community and the mix is overwhelming. My father, a black man, never
finished high school but worked in a factory, in a gas station, and in a
liquor store so that I could go to college. He will never fall on the street
trying to escape from a nursing home, be mistreated by a nurse, or, in
my friend's words, be put out.

The real question is how the academy can help us all to deal with
this mix. I have no answers, for in large part these are issues facing
society in general. But there are several things we can do.

1. Recognize that in an increasingly multicultural society, faculty
will arrive with and continually reflect their cultures' norms and values. Faculty of color have more responsibilities as mentors, advisors,
and guides that are crucial but also extremely time-consuming.

2. Move away from the concentration on early child care that has
turned off so many of us to discussions of women in the academy. I
have spent my entire career in family care, and for only five or six of

those years has day care for preschool children been an issue. In fact, I would like to see a system of day care for elderly people established in institutions for higher learning and not so far down the road supportive retirement homes for academics, connected to the very institutions to which we devoted our careers.

3. Practice what we preach. Too many of us speak and write glibly about the triumvirate of race, class, and gender without realizing just how much it directly affects the people sitting next to us in the room. At one point I found myself in an emergency room cubicle, my father hooked up to three monitors, my children home alone, and a man literally having a heart attack behind the curtain next to me, as I tried to grade papers for my women's studies class. Something, I finally decided, was *very* wrong with this picture. (And I might add here that I don't have a single black or Hispanic friend in academia, male or female, who is not or has not recently taken care of a family member.)

4. Think of establishing new ways of allotting course loads so that long-term caregiving can coexist with an academic career.

5. Think about ways of altering the movement of the tenure clock. Is it always necessary that six or seven years inexorably tick on at the same pace for all people? This goes for men as well as women, for men are also likely to be single parents and caregivers for the elderly.

In sum, we need to broaden the imperatives of caregiving and recognize that our moments between caring for young ones and caring for loved ones and old ones, like the moments between leaving my children and picking up someone else's father, are brief.

The Nurture Sandwich: Between Child Care and Eldercare

Diana Hume George

Women do most of the nation's elder-care, in addition to child care; the largest source of conflict between female and male adult siblings is care of aging parents. For women in the "sandwich generation," whose children ostensibly grow more independent as aging parents become newly dependent, the resulting conflicts can become acute, especially given the economically driven demographics showing that many adult children now return to the parental home for a period of time. Women facing this worldwide glut of nurture expectations are also, in industrialized nations, the first generation attempting to advance in the workplace. Most professions, including academe, demand increasing time on the job, where in addition to legitimate expectations women also perform unpaid, unrecognized, invisible work that is the source of many stories in this book.

Naomi Wolf says something about the "beauty myth" that fits the ungorgeous among us, too: "As the century draws to an end, working women are exhausted: bone tired in a way their male colleagues may not be able to imagine" (53). The untenable situations in which so many working women find themselves are surely in part responsible for the glass ceiling. Female lawyers, for instance, become associates but seldom partners; female professors are concentrated at the lower and middle ranks, with only 5 percent achieving full professor status. Inequities now forbidden by law are thus ensured by love. We can't do it all, not all the time. Sometimes we take ourselves out of the running.

Diana Hume George is a professor of English and women's studies at Pennsylvania State University at Erie, the Behrend College.

I am firmly sandwiched—mother of two, grandmother of three, primary caregiver for one parent, with two other parental figures whom I needed to visit regularly in varying stages of their decline. I am among the few female faculty in the country lucky enough to achieve high rank. I don't sleep much. Caffeine and irony are my drugs of choice. With grown children who still need my time and love and their children, who would like to see their grandmother occasionally, the quality time issue I thought was done when the kids grew up has extended forward and backward into what is now a four-generation web. It seems as if I woke up one day and found myself a matriarch. When the family matriarch works an eighty-hour week, the question isn't quality time, it's any time at all. When I look at the tiny members of my family's new generation, I know how rapidly their first years will pass. If I don't see my newly born grandson for weeks on end, I'm missing the construction of all those cities of neurons in his brain. I can't ever go back.

With parents, the problem is mortally serious. When they die, I will never again see them in this life, as my mother frequently reminds me. And this life, right here and right now, is also the only one I know for sure that I will live. Will I just keep hurtling from one humanly rich, exhausting call of love and duty to the next, year in, year out, until I drop in the hall? Am I ever going to read a book instead of just scan it? If there's such a thing as reincarnation, could I return as a hermit?

More and more I see myself, and women with whom I speak of this, as a cliché from the heart of this book, a textbook preview of what's coming for the first generation of superwomen, those of us who were our own guinea pigs in a badly designed experiment. It's happening to me a little sooner because I started the cycle young, at seventeen, which is not characteristic of most professional women in my socioeconomic group. (Just dumb, I guess.) When I finished raising kids and commuting on the tenure track, the engineer switched the train onto the daughter track. There's still plenty of parenting too, but now I don't know who to do first. Do I grab an hour with the granddaughter who has taken to automatic crying when she lays eyes on me because "I never see you, Nana?" (Automatic crying is a lot like automatic writing, except the medium is guilt.) Or do I drive across the state line to help my mother with her storm windows because she has pointed out that, after all, I'll be able to see the little one for years but, well, when she's dead, that's that. Why not do both so I won't feel too guilty? While I'm at it, I could stop at the nursing home to see Dad and write a seminal article or two while he's napping.

If this time of life coincided with a slowdown in professional terms, sleep would be part of life. But with speedup as evident in academe as anywhere else, we all have more work. For the years I've been the filling in this sandwich, I've also been at the peak of my career duties as a senior faculty both locally and nationally. After tenure, you do more of everything—more reference letters, theses, leadership roles, mentoring. And if you don't, there is a circle of hell in which you pay. It is nowhere near Paolo and Francesca's, who got a lot of orgasms for their trouble. But then, you're not having a midlife affair, and you don't have time for that nonsense. There are diapers to change. Your grandson's. Or your dad's.

But I recognize that my life's intensity represents a series of choices for which I must take responsibility. I have been complicit in creating this scenario. I can claim a certain kind of innocence, and oh, I do, at every turn. But what on earth did we think we were doing when we set out to Have It All? To do that, there will be times of life in which you'll have to Be It All.

While my narrative strategy in writing about metaphorical mothering on the job counsels something very close to despair, I have brighter ideas to offer about the nurture sandwich. First, and I mean this, it's a matter of attitude. Those of us in the sandwich generation must refuse unreasonable workloads, and with the help of an extremely understanding administration, indeed I recently have. But when that's done, I've found it deeply useful to recognize that my life is chosen. All I have to do is be willing to live rather lovelessly, or be unresponsive to my elders or kids, and this would all change—that's always an option. We can choose to say, Me first, and for those who want to, there are undoubtedly advantages. I remind myself of that in order to remain clear on choosing an ethic of care—and to know that I choose it again and again.

Membership in the sandwich generation is finite, probably more finite than either your life or your career. In the normal course of things, the older generation does leave us. My recent history supports my point. When I began this essay, I had three elders in my life. Now I have two. My former partner's mother was elderly but healthy when I left her son. I promised to remain in her life until her death. For the first couple of years after her stroke, I drove to her nursing home in another city once a month. The last two years it could not be as often, but despite advice to let her go, to cut back on my emotional overload by writing her off, I did not. When she died I held a memorial ritual for her and accompanied her body to be cremated. If I had not done this, I would not have been at peace.

My stepfather is primarily cared for by others. After his stroke ten years ago, I was one of his primary helpers for two years. He has been seriously ill and near death so many times the past year that our death watches have become nearly casual—he's the bionic man, he never dies, he always comes back surprisingly strong. Yet in his eighties, stroke-ridden, mostly paralyzed, on dialysis, he is certainly near the end. At this point, I want that for him unabashedly. May his body let him go, and may we let him go, too.

And when he dies, that will leave only one person among my family elders. My mother is healthy and lively, and I hope I long have her fine company. Sometimes I fail to see her because of another family member, sometimes because of work, but usually I will be there for her when she needs me. If a book review gets written late, or not at all, okay. She's my mother.

My grandmother role is more problematic. My generation knew who a grandmother was. She was old and at home and cooked great meals and wore an apron and sewed. We have this idea of The Ur-Grandmother, whether or not we had one. But I became a grandmother at thirty-eight, I'm never home, I have no time to cook, I don't own an apron, and I can't sew. I make books, not pies. My grandchildren are in the first generation facing this role redefinition because the baby boomers are their grandparents. We're not big on white flour. But maybe there will be no trauma here, because the kids don't have our expectations of what a grandparent is; the only conflict is likely to be the disjunction between our own mental image and the real grandparents we are, or will be. Our children learned to redefine who a mother is and what kind of work is appropriate to that role. Their kids find in us new models for grandmothers. With my granddaughters, now eight and ten years old, I do lunch. Out.

I speak here of eldercare, but we should broaden this, in policy formation, to include care for any family member, with family broadly defined to include unmarried heterosexual and same-sex partners. Academics should be able to be with their seriously ill or dying parents—or mates or any beloved—without feeling that they must leave bedsides to teach. Family-friendly institutions need to make provisions as concrete for this as for childbirth care. The beginning and the end of life are equally vital. We always tell people that they can take whatever time they need in such circumstances, but it's not really true. With overworked colleagues covering classes, faculty always feel responsible to take less leave than they should. While it may sometimes be true that work forms the core of sanity at such times—and is actually a helpful diversion—that's a decision each person should make for him or herself, not one that we should assume or assign. Colleges need to hire substitutes to cover faculty facing extremities, whether they are created by joy or sorrow, by coming into the world or by leaving it.

When a colleague's mother died, he spent a lot of time with her and did not regret it. I saw this again with another colleague's father— and it was not lost on me that both caregivers are men. In our privileged corner of the world, perhaps eldercare will become more equitably shared in this generation. It is crucial that men take on more of this human work so that working women are not emulating an outmoded model of detachment. Many people die regretting that they did not spend more time with those they love. You never hear of someone lying on his or her deathbed saying, I should have spent more time at the office.

WORK CITED

Wolf, Naomi. *The Beauty Myth: How Images of Beauty Are Used against Women.* New York: Anchor Doubleday, 1992.

PART NINE

Valuing Family

Faculty Wives: Lesbian Family Values

Carolyn Leste Law

My partner Diana is at work. She's "at work" though she's sitting perhaps twenty feet from me, at the breakfast table on the other side of our small apartment. As I write that sentence I realize that I too am "at work"; isn't writing that sentence my work? Writing this one? We've always struggled to distinguish "work" from "not-work." The distinction is growing even more blurry now that we are actually living together, after two years of ridiculously stressful separation and stunning long distance bills. While I hustle from term to term for part-time teaching positions, Diana's tenure review looms before her (I nearly wrote "us"), and I am bracing for dissolution altogether of the category "not-work."

I am finishing my dissertation, a euphemism for floundering among notes and books and guilt and fear for the past year or so. About that fear, I don't know if it is of failure or of success. Both seem equally fearsome and threatening. On the one hand, of course I fear failure, coming so far—a blue-collar kid writing an esoteric dissertation on avant-garde manifestos—only to admit that indeed the odds are too greatly stacked against me, to admit that after all I don't have enough . . . resources? desire? time? discipline? smarts? On the other hand, I fear success, too, and the inevitable decisions we would surely face were I to have "Ph.D. in hand," as the job ads say. Is either one of us up to saying, "Oh yes, and can you find a tenure line for my lesbian lover, too?"

Carolyn Leste Law is a doctoral candidate in English at the University of Minnesota.

Our case is not unique, really, nor even unusual, I know. Heterosexual academic couples confront many of the same pressures and uncertainties same-sex academic couples confront, and happily we enjoy many of the same rewards. Well-educated, middle-class gay men and lesbians in the 1990s, especially on American university campuses, are freer than ever to be out at work, to live where they choose, to bring sexual orientation into political debates. Among the liberal professoriat, certainly among our friends, to be homophobic is as gauche as to be racist or sexist. I appreciate our straight friends' respect for our relationship, and I feel we are genuinely accepted and acknowledged as a couple in the university community (albeit sometimes clumsily). Yet the liberal "we're just like all of you" public relations campaign of many gay and lesbian faculty, ourselves included, obscures some vitally important ways in which our committed same-sex relationship is *not* like those of our straight colleagues and friends. For one thing, the freedom I feel to be out, visible, and activist is tenuous at best; in most places, I have no protected civil rights to enforce my "freedom." For another, why should I feel *appreciative* of respect, acceptance, and acknowledgment of my family? Do my straight friends feel appreciative of those basic dignities? I doubt it; they expect nothing less.

One dramatic difference between my family and similarly situated married couples is in benefits extended to spouses and families of full-time faculty/employees at almost every college and university in the country. For instance, this morning I had a tickle in my throat. This afternoon my nose was a little runny. I have no health insurance and every twinge, sniffle, or cough brings dread. I'm sick with worry. When I saw a doctor a few weeks ago and explained to him my awkward insurance situation—racing the clock to squeak in under my student coverage expiration—he said sympathetically, "You're exposed." There was a time when doctors spoke of exposure as a risk of disease, now they speak of it as a risk of bankruptcy. I am exposed because I am no longer a full-time student, not fully employed (the "exposure" of part-timers like me is another essay altogether), and I am not—nor can I even choose to be—married to my partner.

It is hard for me not to sound bitter. From my point of view, unmarried faculty at most U.S. colleges and universities experience blatant discrimination in compensation based on marital status. While this discrimination is suffered by all unmarried staff, the value of spousal and other family benefits is an area of compensation from which same-sex partners are *categorically* excluded. Unlike unmarried heterosexual couples, that exclusion is based solely on the gender of the employee's partner. I'm left in the odd position of arguing for antiquated academic "family values": I want to be a faculty wife. The radical part, of course, is that I want to make my lover one, too.

What a term, eh? "Faculty wife" hardly trips off the tongue of a lesbian feminist like me. Understand, I'm not calling here for legal marriage for same-sex couples, though that is the obvious answer, ironically, to the conservative hysteria domestic partner benefits inspire, nor am I arguing only for a broadening of benefits policies to encompass unmarried persons. These are at base legal matters and, though not insignificant, represent only half of the larger issue. Rather, I invoke the faculty wife to better plot the dilemma peculiar to lesbian academic couples that is both legal and social: on the legal axis, the faculty wife subverts a discriminatory practice; on the social axis, the faculty wife entrenches a sexist domestic role.

The faculty wife of legend—surely she lives in very few homes of junior faculty these days—followed her husband to fellowships and research residencies all over the globe; she raised charming children; she entertained deans and senior faculty with grace and aplomb; she channeled her own superb education fully into the service of her mate's scholarship and career, working outside academia only in the most dire financial necessity or teaching an odd course now and again; most important, she maintained domestic calm, quiet, and orderliness in which his first book could blossom in year five, or four, or three. I'm torn between trying to be such a person to my partner and squashing my resentment at not having one for myself. That we all should have a wife is an old, old feminist joke, after all, but the *faculty* wife is a particularly enduring species of the genus because the academic workplace so stubbornly continues to believe in her existence and remains maddeningly unresponsive to the changing real lives of its employees.

The "angel in the house" is a figment of the patriarchal imagination that has thoroughly been revealed, but watching Diana's tenure review unfold, watching my dissertation stall, it becomes clear that the "angel in the academic house" and the narrowly defined lifestyle she epitomizes are even today presumed in the very structure and expectations of academic work.

As universities and colleges of every stripe grow more and more obsessed with publication as the only signifier of performance (though most try to deny it), the expectations for junior faculty simply expand, often in extremely ambiguous ways, rather than adjust to new work conditions. The expanding expectations are partly explained by explosive performance inflation all down the line: new graduates are being thrown out of vita piles for too few publications—a criterion that some of the search committee members would not be able to meet; the notoriously tight job market in higher education in the past couple of decades (which shows no signs of loosening) has Yale and Stanford Ph.D.'s accepting tenure-track jobs in third-tier state universities; the backlog of Ph.D.'s taking one-year positions and serial postdocs has created a glut of extraordinarily experienced teachers and researchers in lines hundreds deep for a shrinking number of tenure tracks. The result is an atmosphere of desperation that makes tenure review synonymous with mind-numbing, hair-graying, health-compromising, relationship-straining stress. Under such conditions, can one really be asked to run the vacuum, too? To arrange a short weekend away? To speak to one's partner over dinner, much less make it? Under such conditions, so desperate in the history of our genteel profession, the faculty wife of yore mocks us and guilts us. More than ever does the assistant professor interested in promotion need a dedicated support system, a faculty wife, to create the atmosphere conducive to the development of book manuscripts, articles, conference papers; the management of teaching loads, committee work, student advising, colleague favors, community involvement, and, of course, politicking.

Try as I might, I just can't get the gender issue completely out of this scenario. The "trailing spouse" phenomenon of the dual academic couple is overwhelmingly more often a woman. This new, dubious term is the nineties version of the old faculty wife of which I speak, though "trailing" suggests she's much more a burden than a help. While more and more women are taking graduate degrees, the immediate result is not necessarily a commensurate increase in women faculty. More women in graduate school means more dual-career academic couples, for obvious reasons, often in the same or similar disciplines. So gains made toward gender parity in the total Ph.D. pool run headlong into the gender disparity of existing university faculties. When the hard decisions arise—live apart? commute hours per day? forget the baby?—it is far more likely that the woman's career will "give." The peculiar dilemma for the same-sex couple, especially the lesbian couple with lifetimes squared of sexist socialization behind them, should be apparent. What is there to be done when we're both faculty wives trying as well to be academics? Or is it the other way around?

As it is, Diana and I are unceremonious DPs, domestic partners— a status that carries genuine status in only a handful of cities in this country. Even in those few progressive places, like Minneapolis and the University of Minnesota, the designation is so hotly contested that it is often reduced to nothing more than an administrative gesture of good will, conferring few if any real or enforceable benefits. When Diana and I tried to register our partnership in the city of Minneapolis, our application was denied because we maintained two residences. When we pleaded with the powerless staff in the city attorney's office that academic couples very commonly live in separate states and yet their marriages are no less recognized, we were met with a little sympathy but no encouragement. What they failed to understand through their fear of permissiveness unchecked was that DP registration is genuinely important to us when one of us is hospitalized and "relatives only" may see the patient. It is important to us in the event that employee benefits become available to couples "committed to the same degree as married persons." It is important to us in the event that some college administrator is not hostile in principle to a same-sex spousal hire.

My dilemma as a lesbian faculty wife isn't really so difficult a concept to grasp, though the problems it reveals are complex. I wish to be acknowledged for the work I contribute to the university that employs my partner. And to be sure, the support I offer her, emotional and logistical, is as real a contribution as hers, though indirect and of a different sort. I want her support of me, likewise, to be worthy in the academic economy to the same degree as the support of spouses of employees. Yet I wish, also, to refigure the academic workplace to be more responsive to changing lifestyles and work conditions of all academic couples. As long as the academic workplace presumes the secondary service industry of the faculty wife, women, gays and lesbians, and, I suspect, single persons will continue to leave the profession in disproportionate numbers, linger longer at lower ranks, and occupy the least prestigious positions at the least prestigious institutions: service courses, support units, community colleges. Suffice it to say, I'm conflicted. What I argue for on the legal axis, I argue against on the social.

Not long ago, the Department of Human and Family Resources and the Employee Wellness and Assistance Program surveyed faculty perspectives on family policies at the university where Diana works. Its instrument shows an encouraging awareness of the variety of circumstances that affect faculty performance, as employees *and* as human beings: child care, eldercare, relocation and separation, and dual academic careers, among others. And notably they do so without heterosexist biases; though the terms *gay, lesbian,* and *same-sex couple* do not appear anywhere in the booklet, neither do *husband, wife,* and gendered pronouns. But this is the survey, not the responses. We have yet to learn the actual faculty perspectives on whether the university's "family-friendly practices" should "include partners without legal marital status."

While I am heartened by this survey, I'm wary of hoping too much for it to result in workable alliances or practical strategies for confronting higher education on these issues, much less for changing it, because the challenges are both legislative and sociological. It is a comparatively simple task to recognize domestic partners and to provide domestic partner benefits equal to those of spouses. It is quite another to dismantle a powerful myth of higher education and erect in its place a new vision of academic work, academic life.

Be Fruitful, but Don't Multiply: Institutional Denial of Gay and Lesbian Families

Jeffrey J. Lockman

In many academic quarters these days, queer theory is all the rage. Journals, conferences, and even undergraduate courses routinely contain openly acknowledged gay and lesbian material. Where homocentric content in the academy was in the past difficult to find, it is now hard not to notice. Regarding the explosion of gay and lesbian studies across disciplines and journals, one high-ranking university official at Tulane, my academic home, recently exclaimed, "Isn't it great?"

This expression of support is certainly a far cry from the real and perceived homophobia that many academics still encounter in their professional lives. Yet even where support for gay and lesbian academic pursuits is strong, there is denial that gay and lesbian faculty can have families and raise children.

In the academy, queer theory does not translate into practice. University officials take the prestige that comes from their faculties' gay and lesbian research. They even use such work to demonstrate how they, as administrative officers, champion diversity. Yet through institutional benefit policies that deny the existence of children of gay and lesbian faculty, the very same officials disavow the possibility of gay and lesbian faculty as parents. In effect, the message to gay and lesbian faculty is, "Be fruitful, but don't multiply."

I have had the opportunity to reflect on the impact of this message as a gay father and professor at Tulane University. I recognize that I am strong enough to withstand this challenge to my self-worth. I realize

---

Jeffrey J. Lockman is an associate professor of psychology at Tulane University.

that I can carry out my responsibilities as professor and parent without this message getting in the way. But at the same time, the message is hard to ignore. Institutional validation for being a gay professor and a gay parent is absent at Tulane and many other institutions like it.

I confront this issue during my late afternoon walks on campus with my son, Benjamin. During these jaunts, I come across some of my students, who walk up to us and ask, "Is that your baby, Dr. Lockman?" The question is understandable and innocuous. The reason for it is not so much that I'm gay and am viewed as a surprising candidate for fatherhood. My undergraduate students may or may not know about my sexual orientation. More likely, they ask the question because they know that I am a developmental psychologist and that I study infant development. The students are wondering whether Benjamin is research subject or son, whether they are witnessing me as professor or parent.

To their question, I simply want to reply "yes," and as the Oscar Hammerstein II lyric in *Carousel* goes, ". . . and that's all there is to that." But the answer is more complex. I really should explain to them that the answer depends on whose perspective you adopt. On the Tulane University campus, where I stand with Benjamin in the shadow of the administration building, our little gay family is not necessarily considered a family at all. Family at Tulane, after all, is a heterosexual privilege.

Many would hastily label us a nontraditional family; sometimes we call ourselves a family of the nineties. To behold our family, don't think of *Heather Has Two Mommies* but instead, our work in progress, *Benjamin Has One Mommy and Two Daddies*. These are the facts. Rebecca (also a professor at Tulane), Mark (my partner), and I are jointly parenting our son, Benjamin. All the adults are homosexual. We own a house together in which Benjamin is being raised. Rebecca and Mark are Benjamin's genetic parents, but I am Benjamin's father as well. We have a legal agreement in which we codified our roles as parents before Benjamin's birth. I have been with Benjamin since he was born and contribute to his child care, both in terms of time and finances. In terms of our love, devotion, and wishes for Benjamin, we are anything but nontraditional.

Indeed, given these facts, many would consider us a nuclear family, perhaps a postmodern one. Yet for gay and lesbian families on campus, including our particular variation, institutional recognition is absent. We have confronted this reality in our repeated attempts and failure thus far to obtain a significant child health care benefit that is available only to certain types of employee families at Tulane. The benefit is conditioned on heterosexual marriage. But the problem goes beyond this particular benefit and extends to all institutional benefits in which dependents are defined in terms of heterosexual marriage.

The so-called married employee benefit at Tulane enables any two employees of Tulane who are married and are raising a child together to purchase dependent health care coverage at a significantly reduced rate. In the case of such dual-employee families, the benefits policy allows one employee to declare his/her employee spouse *and* children, dependents. The amount that the university would have contributed automatically for individual coverage for the other employee is then credited toward the purchase of dependent coverage for that entire family unit. In consequence, that family pays only $20 a month out of pocket for dependent coverage in contrast to the typical $200 monthly sum. And as a result, because the benefit is predicated on heterosexual marriage, there is a tenfold difference between the cost of insurance for homosexual dual-employee families and married ones.

The benefit is a significant one. Projected over roughly twenty-five years, the time frame of dependent coverage, the benefit totals more than $50,000. In a *New York Times* story about our challenge to this benefits policy, the general counsel and senior vice president of Tulane, Ronald Mason Jr., declared that "this is a single-mother-with-a-child issue." In short, homosexual parenting is not just silent on the Tulane campus, it is denied.

The present exclusionary benefit exists even though Tulane states that it does not discriminate in employment or in the provision of employee benefits on the basis of either marital status or sexual orientation. When we have met with university officials about this contradiction, we have repeatedly been asked why can't we get married—even though these officials have known about our sexual orientation. Besides the fact that a university should not be in the business of playing matchmaker, this line of questioning shows little respect for the groups and classes of people that Tulane's nondiscrimination policies purport to protect.

Tulane, like other universities that define important benefits in terms of heterosexual marriage but nevertheless possess marital status and sexual orientation nondiscrimination policies, is receiving credit for providing protections that it does not fully deserve. Regrettably, the courts have sent mixed messages on the extent to which these nondiscrimination policies must be honored. Because many such policies contain language that goes beyond that which is required by federal and state laws, a university may not be under legal obligation to adhere fully to certain of its claims. Thus, in the very setting where students are taught about the meaning and power of words, the speech acts of a university administration hold uncertain meaning.

Beyond the impact on our particular family, the present policy, including the defense of it by university officials, creates a hostile atmosphere for other gay and lesbian employee families. It dissuades such families from disclosing their identities because of the potential for real forms of discrimination. It discourages such families from having children because of the financial and psychological costs that are involved. And it reduces the likelihood that there will be other gay and lesbian families with children on campus from which similar families—parents as well as children—can draw much needed support.

Further, the present policy sends a message to the prospective parents in our university community, especially our homosexual and heterosexual students, about the types of families that will be affirmed in our society and those that will not. For our homosexual students, the lack of institutional validation of the gay family is but one more example of the homophobia that surrounds them. It says to them that they should not be parents, that a dream that many of these students might entertain for themselves is one that is not supported by their university. For our heterosexual students, the current policy only validates what they hear from their more unenlightened peers and many of the societal institutions around them. Instead of mirroring current societal attitudes and practices, universities, as institutions of higher learning, should formulate and effect policies that acknowledge the diverse forms of families on campus and in our culture.

WORK CITED

Noble, B. P. "A 'Married, with Children' Bias?" *New York Times*, Mar. 12, 1995: sec. 3, p. 25.

The Arrogant Academy, Activism, and the Transracial Family

Sondra Hale

As a parent of two grown adopted Eritrean (African-born) daughters and the spouse of an academic, I have many misgivings about my profession in terms not only of the academy's impact on family life and personal politics but also on race politics. I am a Euroamerican woman from a midwestern working-class populist farming and mining background. As a poor "illegitimate child," raised in an "integrated" urban slum, who mainly socialized with black children, I got used to being called "white trash" and "nigger lover." My mother raised me as an egalitarian/populist/cultural relativist liberal; the words *tolerance, integration,* and *understanding* were offered as solutions to racial/ethnic (and probably class) conflict.

I was the first person in my extended family to graduate even from high school. My rebellious mother, who thought her only child could "be a contendah," caused me to believe that going to college was a career (little did I know that it *would* be). When people asked what I was going to do when I grew up, I would answer proudly, "I'm going to college."

I graduated from UCLA in 1960 with a B.A. in English and got married to my former geography teaching assistant. Gerry Hale and I went to Sudan for his Ph.D. fieldwork, stayed three years the first time, and returned many times thereafter. During the first sojourn I became radicalized and was reluctant to leave. I had identity problems about "being Sudanese," just as I had thought of myself as black when I was growing up in Des Moines. Perhaps because I had not fully internal-

Sondra Hale teaches anthropology and women's studies at UCLA.

ized that I was "white," nor the meanings attached to that positionality, I initiated our unconventional decision about parenting some years later.

Returning to graduate school in the radical sixties for a degree in African studies and then anthropology, I cofounded the African Activist Association and its radical journal and participated fully in New Left, civil rights, and antiwar activities on and off campus. Gerry and I balked at the idea of being parents, viewing me as chronically on the verge of finishing something: a B.A., then an M.A., another M.A., Ph.D. fieldwork, and then the protracted process of writing a dissertation. We considered adoption, not because we were keen to have children, but for a combination of personal and political reasons. We thought of adoption as expedient and noble, being propagandized to think of the world as overpopulated. Moreover, popular media informed us of the available and forlorn mixed kids who could not get adopted. We felt it was our duty to adopt an "unwanted child."

Because so many of my friends were African or African American, I thought we had a conducive environment for raising a kid of color. However, many of these friends strongly advised against it. Being the good politico that I thought I was and anxious to be thought of as nonracist and wanting nothing to impede my campus activism in the African, black, and diasporan movements, I dropped the idea. By the midseventies and three trips to Sudan later, we departed for another two years in Khartoum. It was a depressing time to be in most of Africa. Famine and civil war were ravaging Sudan and its next-door neighbor, Ethiopia (and Eritrea). We were agitated about the situation of the Eritrean People's Liberation Front (EPLF) and its difficult, ultimately thirty-year struggle for liberation from Ethiopia. We learned of an orphanage in Asmara, Eritrea, that was flooded with hundreds of malnourished children, many of whom were orphaned by the war. The government could not accommodate all of the orphans, and we were informed that things would get worse; the children were endangered. Not just the war but famine was at the doors of the city. Gerry and I put some of our concerns together (and others behind us) and made a spontaneous decision to go to Asmara in the midst of a war to adopt a child. We saw it as a life and death decision, and I flung my race politics aside.

The process of the adoption involved rushing into Asmara for two weeks in 1974–75, with the EPLF on the outskirts of the city, the Ethiopian troops building up, and anti-Americanism rising. Instead of one baby, we adopted two children, ages two and seven. While we were preparing the papers to leave for Sudan with our legally adopted children, the Ethiopian government passed a decree prohibiting any Ethiopian citizen from leaving the country. With the EPLF ringing the city, which meant among other things that the airport would be closed and the city cut off, it was necessary for us to get the first flight out. The children were officially ours, but without papers, we could not get them out. With only twenty minutes left before boarding, our lawyer arrived with papers for the children. He had somehow had them declared "stateless," and they were able to travel with *laissez-passer* documents.

The nature of "the academy" had a great deal to do with our decision to participate in what is now referred to as a "transracial adoption." Although I had been one of those sixties anti-establishment campus radicals, I still must have internalized the notion that the academy was a liberal, genteel, and benevolent institution and, more importantly, that it was a place where we had acquired the knowledge and politics needed to raise our kids as "black." We knew a great deal about Ethiopian/Eritrean culture and thought of ourselves as instrumentally respectful. Furthermore, we saw academic life as a positive environment for a biracial family, not recognizing that one factor had drastically changed. When we had left UCLA for Sudan in the midseventies, there were increasing numbers of students and faculty of color, a vibrant African studies milieu, a healthy new black studies program, a number of "mixed partners." There seemed every reason to believe that this academic environment would be ideal for our family experiment. Los Angeles itself was increasingly cosmopolitan, and UCLA made claims that the university would soon reflect that diversity.

White arrogance comes into play in a number of other ways: I had always seen myself as marginal and therefore as having a profound understanding of marginality, meaning that I saw myself able to deal with the questions of cultural imperialism at the forefront of any progressive parent's formation of a transracial family. Moreover, I rationalized, I was different in the way I would approach our situation because of my respect for and knowledge of Africa. We saw ourselves, therefore, suited to raise children biculturally in the same way we felt competent to impart those attitudes to our students.

Our concerns translated into a twofold strategy: protect the kids from racism (partially by raising them to recognize it) and give them respect for and pride in their past. We would do this by living some kind of "African life" (books, material objects, sprinkled with some "Afrocentrism," hopefully without romanticism), by maintaining the

Tigrinya language, by being appreciative of African societies while maintaining a critical stance about corrupt governments, and trying not to be nationalistic or romantic, which I saw as another form of racism. We also thought our daughters would be surrounded by African and African-American friends and colleagues.

Dreams of biculturality dissipated the first minute. Our older daughter, Alexa, then seven years old, had other ideas. She immediately refused to speak Tigrinya with our Eritrean baby-sitter in Khartoum. Alexa did this despite not speaking any English and our not speaking Tigrinya. She pretended that she had forgotten the language entirely. We later assumed that Alexa rejected the baby-sitter because Atsede was a reminder of her poverty-ridden past, but the effect was a rejection of her native language and culture. When Adrienne, our younger child, rejected contact with her Eritrean family (with whom we had kept in touch), it cemented our failure—or underscored our naivete.

We returned to an academy that was changing. Reagan had left his mark on our university, and the social forces that put him in power were in place. Many of the social gains of the sixties had already been subverted or eliminated. This whitening of the university community embittered a number of African-American academics. Black intellectuals saw cultural imperialism prevailing in its many forms. The campus had grown increasingly segregated. Our presence as a transracial family has not been a welcome one. To do my political work, I have rarely revealed to African-American faculty or faculty of color that we have adopted black daughters. Considering my active academic life in the sixties and the social composition of that life, this situation is very different from anything I could have anticipated.

Nothing is what it should have been. When we were able to buy a house, we carefully selected a diverse community with cosmopolitan schools. Yet our block remained white for most of our daughters' childhood. The school, as well as the community, reflecting Los Angeles in general, remained segregated. Meanwhile, the academic environment offered us the obstacles to parenting that it offered everyone else: no job/promotion accommodation for time spent parenting severely affected Gerry, who did most of the child care. The only situation more difficult than a woman trying to parent and make it through a fast-track academic career is a man trying to do the same. For some years Gerry was practically a single parent and I was the absent wife trying to survive as an itinerant academic. He was expected to have a partner doing most of the social reproduction, making it possible for him to put his career first.

Moreover, our kids needed more than some other kids. When we returned to the States, they were still recovering from their years of malnutrition, especially our younger daughter, who was sick a great deal. We spent much time in doctors' offices. Even when they were both well, we had to pay very close attention to health and nutrition. Our older daughter was behind in school and needed extra help. There were also the social adjustment needs of immigrant children—the promotion of lots of "enrichment" (read: "white") activities.

I had speculated that becoming a parent would not mean giving up anything. My agenda, not to be deterred, included finishing the Ph.D., holding a good job at a research institution, publishing books as well as articles and poetry, curating art exhibits, indulging myself in an active social life, being a damned good parent, and, most importantly, continuing my life as a socialist feminist activist and community organizer, all with a smile and good health.

I engaged in both "political feminism" and "academic feminism." I developed a consciousness about domestic labor divided equally between Gerry and me; the forces of socialization that could turn our daughters into Barbie dolls ("white"); my need for validation of my experiences as a woman, a mother, and a worker; and gender discrimination and sexual harassment in the workplace.

Unfortunately, feminism consumed me, drew me away from my parenting, and for some years dominated my life in ways that were not always healthy or productive. I became the first full-time director of women's studies at California State University at Long Beach, one of the more radical grass-roots programs in the country. Commuting daily from Los Angeles, staying overnight to live out my job "in the community," taking the job to the streets, and eventually taking it to the courts were the essence of my life for more than a decade. When university authorities, goaded by the Christian Right, took action against an activist feminist faculty, they sacked me first because I refused to fire the lesbian faculty when they ordered me to. The ACLU took our case and we struggled in the courts for nine years. That is a long time to think about women, feminists, lesbians, mothers, family, and work in the academy. It is also a long time to neglect one's kids.

Parenting in the intense years of feminist struggle with the academy was difficult enough, but there were also elements of feminism that made raising African-American daughters even more problematic. The association of my name with lesbian issues led to their rejection, for a time, of a great deal of my life. Their homophobic African-American friends were rather appalled. It was one more "white thing" that Alexa and Adrienne had to endure in their transracial family. That the academy often withheld validation of feminist agendas only exacerbated the situation. Later, when both daughters took women's studies classes at universities, their realization of racism within feminism caused some doubts about mom's projects. They have since come to see me as a renegade.

In general, my activism made both parenting and life in the academy more difficult, although I am not sure of the intersection of these. Our children resented the absent mother, the high-profile politico whose intensity too often spilled over into family life: not letting one daughter audition for the role of a maid in a young people's theater production, boycotting products dear to both of them, appearing on the news. There were also the frightening aspects of my political life: counterdemonstrators shouting hateful things, men's angry voices amplified through battery-powered megaphones, fists shaking in the air, emotional language. My dream of packing the kids off to demos was dashed when I saw how frightened they became. Once someone shouted a racial slur; at a reproductive rights rally a "right-to-lifer" saw Adrienne with me and shouted, "What if your birth mother had aborted you!" They also had to endure other insults: that what I was doing was not dignified or feminine, that I am a "baby-killer," that I support immoral conduct, that the people I support are "terrorists."

In the academy such ideology is coded. Since graduate studies I have received messages that I should "pay more attention to my scholarship and less attention to politics." Or that my scholarship would be "better if I could contain my political agenda." Or that I "lack focus" (read: "dilettante") when I engaged in curating art shows or writing art criticism. With regard to defending the rights, through unions or otherwise, of women or faculty of color, I heard, "She would serve herself better if she took care of her *own* career." For certain, my marginality in the academy, partially a result of activism, has greatly affected my family's economic stability and, therefore, our family life.

The academy encourages us to intellectualize everything. When I bring that process home, the academic language translates to my offspring as a certain detachment, a distancing from *their* real experience of racism.

The political nature of knowledge meant that we were trained to think of ourselves as enlightened scholars capable of "transcending" race, class, and gender. It took me many years to figure out what the concept of "transcending" really meant: covering, hiding, coding, putting a gloss on, ignoring, obscuring, and remaining silent about. One thing I can say for our family is that we were always, by our mere presence, visibly rubbing against that grain.

Having two activist parents has not been easy on our daughters. They spent years rejecting our politics and putting their energies into becoming engaging on a personal level. As one might expect from two people raised in the same family, they do share some values and have developed some positive traits as a result of living in a bicultural/biracial family. Now in their twenties, they both seem wonderfully accepting of "difference."

Possibly, some of the differences we see between our two daughters result from the ages they were when adopted. Our older daughter seems very much in touch with her heritage. She progressed from being a groupie of Reggae music to Rasta-spirited activities, which led to a trip to Jamaica. It is not far to move from Rasta to Ethiopia and then to Eritrea—if indirect. In the summer of 1994, after she had graduated from the University of California at Santa Cruz in sociology and ethnic studies, she returned to Eritrea for a year to teach EPLF women fighters. Alexa had always been a bit intolerant and judgmental of her younger sister's avoidance of her Eritrean roots. Ironically, her heritage trip to Eritrea made Alexa more open to people's different choices in life, including her sister's.

Adrienne, while still haunted by identity issues, has made her odyssey to Eritrea, reuniting with her birth family. She wishes the world would stop looking upon our family as having "lived our lives wrong" and hounding us for who and what we are. She now has a graduate psychology degree and is looking toward more graduate studies. She is very person-oriented, giving, and tolerant of human frailty. She says we are the only family she has ever known and that she considers herself an African American and that's that.

Mommy and Me

Brian Rosenberg

I chair both a fifteen-person English department and our tenure and promotion committee. I teach four courses each year and direct eight or ten senior theses. I have two young sons—five and one—and generally need to be home no later than 4:30 to take over for the caregiver in our employ. On Tuesdays I stay home all day with the boys. My round-trip commute is just short of eighty miles, a relatively easy trip when the weather cooperates but often treacherous and twice as long in winter. I write books and essays, because of the requirements of my profession and my own pleasure in doing so. And I have the second most demanding schedule in my family, hands down.

My wife is a physician in private practice, which explains, among other things, my commute: her office and my college are in separate counties, and her need to be always within hailing distance is far greater than mine. This seems only fair, since our reason for being in this not wholly desirable region, rather than somewhere with better weather and better restaurants, is my job: it's far easier to find work as a doctor than as an English professor, so she went where I found a suitable position. (I often wonder if, a dozen years ago, I would have been so obliging had I been similarly tested. I suspect not.) I skip the occasional meeting and most college social events to accommodate her schedule; she crowds dozens of errands into her afternoon off to accommodate mine.

Brian Rosenberg is a professor of English at Allegheny College.

Certainly I expect neither admiration nor pity: there's no great obstacle I must heroically overcome, no absence of pleasures in my day. Mostly there's routine and the need always to be somewhere on time—and I feel tired. Sometimes there's puzzlement: I love my family and like my job and can't wholly understand why the interweaving of the two creates so much I neither love nor like.

Because I spend more time as primary caregiver to my children than do most men, I regularly confront the subtle and not-so-subtle gender biases embedded in our culture. When I accompanied my then-two-year-old son to a preschool program entitled "Mommy and Me," I was the first "Daddy" in fifteen years to do so. Many of the mommies seemed to view my participation as either superhuman or mildly funny. My ability successfully to navigate a supermarket or bookstore with two children in tow tends to be viewed as remarkable, often by mothers who daily and without much self-congratulation do the same things. To some women there seems something adorable about a man alone with children and laundry. To some men there seems something pathetic.

One would expect the academy to be among the few places where the simplest parental stereotypes are not in force, since much time is devoted to undermining thoughtless assumptions about gender. And to an extent this is true. However, my experience tells me that the academy is far less enlightened on these issues and far more like the rest of the world than one might expect, and that men who regularly and with great conviction teach feminist readings of *David Copperfield* are quite capable of stepping out of the classroom and acting like better educated, more benign versions of Mr. Murdstone.

Let me be careful not to overstate: many of my male colleagues spend lots of time with their kids. But by and large the pattern across the institution is the familiar one, with faculty mothers expected somehow to juggle career and children and faculty fathers married to women who stay at home, work part-time, or hold full-time positions clearly secondary in importance (and usually income) to their husbands'. Since academic men appear to be drawn to educated women, a remarkably high percentage of these wives have aborted their training or careers to come to a small town in a depressed region with few white-collar jobs. A good number of my married male colleagues, including some with lots of children, take obvious pride in spending as many hours in their offices as possible, even though they don't *really* have to; some arrive before most ordinary human beings eat breakfast and depart, reluctantly, for dinner. Often, during my hurrying and commuting, I wonder whether I'm spectacularly efficient or they're wasting piles of time, because they don't seem to be getting very much more accomplished than I am.

Contradicting expectations about child-care responsibilities, I've found, has advantages and disadvantages. In terms of formal institutional policy, paternal caregivers don't exist: my place of employment is pretty typical, I imagine, in having a maternal leave policy, yet no paternal leave policy. Fathers are not expected to need or want time off after the birth of a child, regardless of the mother's personal or professional situation. On the other hand, my conflicts seem to be viewed with a tolerance not typically afforded working mothers. The adorable factor again. Occasionally my schedule demands that I bring the boys to my office, where they wander the halls being intrusive and noisy and generally disruptive. I think this is widely (maybe not universally) seen as endearing. I suspect—not on the basis of tangible evidence but confidently nonetheless—that a woman who did the same thing would be viewed with raised eyebrows. Or maybe not. Maybe she'd simply *worry* about being viewed with raised eyebrows more intensely than I do.

Then again, maybe she'd be, like me, too tired and busy to think much about it at all.

The Fourth Generation of Women Facing the Question

Ursula Broschke Davis

She was invited to write about her experiences as a professional woman and mother in academia. She had not decided how to define herself: as a professional mother or a professional woman. It seemed to her that she had failed at both and maybe had done all right at both. She felt that she had excelled at nothing, and there was the dark suspicion that she was in a no-win situation and all the written-up supermoms were just an invention of some clever media consultant. How was she supposed to start writing? Who was she really? How could she find out?

The image that looked back out of the mirror was strange. "Should I cut my hair and look more dignified, or should I leave it longer the way I like it?" she asked her mirror image. The image looking back at her was that of her mother telling her to do whatever she thought was right. "Stop." She was not supposed to resemble her mother's image; her image was supposed to resemble the images of her aunt and her grandmother. Yet now her mother was staring at her. There was a mistake, a terrible mistake. She did not resemble her mother, neither in looks, nor character, nor being. Why was her mother there staring at her; why was she taking over her own image? Where was her grandmother, the woman she had always adored? She used to go to sleep with her grandmother's autobiography as she tried to unlock the key to her past. She looked at her grandmother's photo next to the mirror. "Grandma, help. Who am I? Have I become Mom?" She realized for the

Ursula Broschke Davis is a tenured assistant professor of communications at Pennsylvania State University at Erie, the Behrend College.

first time that her grandmother's look had never been directed at her (the camera lens) as she had assumed in the past. It went straight into the far distance. She rushed over to her mother's photo. Her mother did not even pretend to look into the camera, but far away, searching for people somewhere that understood her.

She felt trapped between her grandmother's and her mother's photos, trapped in her mirror image that turned her life upside down. Who had she been all her life, the career woman—the career climber and success story—or the pathetic mother who tried to control her children's life? Could she be both? Maybe finally she had to face her mother's image and her mother's obsession with children, while admitting to herself that even her career-oriented grandmother had made several decisions that did not fit a career-obsessed woman. She went over to her desk and started to recollect her world and slowly to write:

> The most important influences in my life were: my mother, my brother, my aunt, my mother's best friend, my fifth grade teacher . . . most of all my grandmother. When my grandmother died she left behind a diary that my uncle published, for me every sentence is full of her laughter. My memories of her stem from the chaos after World War II—typhus, diphtheria, hunger, cold—yet my memories of her are the brightest of my life. When I think of her, I can feel her laughter, her soft big body, her bright shiny eyes, her snow white hair. She lived to be sixty-nine years old, a full life, no complaint is in her diary, although she lived through Germany's darkest history, two world wars, and the hours and days when her husband and son were imprisoned by the Nazis.
>
> She was a woman prominent in political life, a parliamentarian, a woman in control of the men in her life. She was a charismatic leader— had she been a man, this would have been the appropriate adjective for her. I have only feelings, but these feelings tell me that she was the woman who was the most comfortable with her femininity and sexuality that I have ever met. To me, she was also the most liberated woman I ever met. As a professional, she was 100 percent woman, and as a private person she was so free that she did not have to make it a point. She raised three children, worked all her life professionally, built up her career parallel with her husbands'.

The image that looked out of the mirror at her was not her grandmother's. It was her own. She went to the bookshelf, picked up the diary, and began to read what her grandmother had written:

> I was born in 1881 in Berlin, the sixth and youngest child. The ancestors of my father came from Switzerland. He was a sculptor and furni-

ture builder who had his own factory. My mother's aim was to bring up her daughters to become good wives. However, this maternal goal did not succeed with me. I decided to go out into the world and work. I started out in the garment industry. When I realized that women were exploited in this business, I started my own business. I had four children, never quit my job. Housekeepers and a governess took care of the household.

In 1903, I became a member of the board of directors of the association of professional women. In 1910, when a new law allowed women to join political parties, I did. I was elected to the Presidium of the Socialist Party in Berlin. I was reelected fifteen times, but I did not neglect my duties toward my family because the time I dedicated to work in the party Presidium was during the evening hours.

In 1919, I was a candidate for the German National Assembly. I was elected to the Presidium of the Berlin House of Representatives. Berlin at the time was the third largest city in the world with 4.5 million inhabitants. During the Weimar Republic, I lived in the limelight of Berlin's social life, which was followed by persecution during the Third Reich. After World War II, I was voted into the first city parliament.

She closed the book trying to visualize her grandmother's image again. Her uncle had written the introduction to the autobiography of her grandmother:

Our mother devoted decades of her life to the common good of the people in Berlin, not only in her duties in parliament but also in different charitable organizations. Throughout our youth we were often bitter that our mother as well as our father seemed to care more about their duties to humankind in general than to their children. The very same fact made us very proud once we were grown.

In the introduction to her memoirs, her grandmother had written:

My memoirs are not supposed to be a guide for my grandchildren, but I hope they will be able to recognize how interwined my personal struggle was with the struggle of all working women. As a young person, I was searching for an ideal, for a higher purpose in life, and I found it in the effort to help better the conditions of the working class. This goal helped me to become part of the House of Representatives in Berlin and helped me to look beyond the limits of the goals of my personal life.

Now she understood why she had not seen her grandmother's image in the mirror. There was no way she could reach her. Her grandmother had attempted to better the conditions for humankind while she was in the middle of writing a selfish essay on the overworked tired female professor. How had she become a self-indulgent complainer? What was wrong with being tired? As her uncle had pointed out, her grandmother's children could not appreciate her dedication to a larger cause until they were adults. The two older ones, her uncle and her aunt, became involved in public life as journalists and politicians. However, her mother—the youngest—had missed a family life. Her dolls had been her only companions when she would spend her dinners night after night with a succession of housekeepers. That might have been the reason why her mother was determined to dedicate her life to children. Her mother had adopted and taken in a number of children in addition to her own three. She remembered the warmth of the house when she came home from school. Her mother gave her children the security to be courageous and to brave the world.

But how little did she really understand about her mother's childhood. She saw only the glamor her aunt and uncle were surrounded by, those in the limelight of post–World War II Germany. She saw heads of government and the generals of the Allied Forces in Berlin populating her uncle's house, while her own house was filled with dolls and children. She wanted out. Her mother knew this and encouraged her to read and study and prepare herself for excellence in the world of books and thoughts. She remembered:

Somehow I missed my dolls in the process. But I was proud and happy to excel and find the acclaim not only of my parents but of the whole family clan. I was groomed for a life in the world of words and thoughts. I loved it—I could not wait to join my uncle, my aunt, my brother and leave my mother and her children and dolls behind. I was ambitious and reckless. I could not perceive my mother's world. I could not give the love back that she needed. I was so busy leaving, I could not look back. My mother was lonely because her children succeeded in leaving her and forgetting her. There I was at the age of twenty-one, one of the few women who studied economics at the University of Berlin, a freshly baked economics editor of a daily newspaper. I worked sixteen hours a day and slept only on the weekend. I was driven; the success and the admiration of older people was sweet. I knew I could write, and I wrote. I knew I could formulate thought, and I formulated thought. All the reading I had done throughout my school years paid off. I was a success. I was on my way. I was a woman—but my success was like my grandmother's in the world of men. I did not write about house and garden or fashion, not even the theater and literature. I wrote about economics and business and political economy. I judged the policies of the men in our country, wrote critiques about their decisions in financial and business matters and economic policies. Who needed sleep if one was one of only two women among three hundred men at a briefing of the foreign press corps concerning European Community policies in Brussels, Luxembourg, or Paris? Who needed anything else? Of course there were men in my life, but they were at the periphery, only there if they did not interfere with my work.

I even managed to fit my husband and my first child into the scheme of things. It was kind of fun to be pregnant and to be pampered and to wobble around Paris with a huge excuse: "She is pregnant . . . she just had a baby." But soon I felt restless and had the compulsion to go back into the "real" world—walking to and from the Jardin Luxembourg and concentrating on the intelligence of the baby genius only lasted so long. Back it was, but now, of course, the schedule around the baby made things worse. If the job consisted of sixteen hours a day before, now the additional "quality time" for my daughter made it nearly impossible. I used to faint in the office. Often I forgot to eat and never slept enough. Every fainting spell on the job guaranteed my body at least two or three days of rest.

Did I care for my daughter and her well-being? Yes, I think very much. But could I give up my life for her? I felt trapped; I did not want to risk losing my job, but more so my networking connections. Without those a journalist is worthless, and I was not bred to feel worthless—the clan had made it a point to illuminate the importance of my dedication to a career. That's why my mother did not permit me to enter the kitchen but sent me to study. I owed it to her to make the best of my career.

I do not know what caused the change, but I must have wanted it. I was pregnant again. This one was a baby boy. With my little girl and her dolls and myself with this new live baby doll, I felt terribly trapped. There was no longer light at the end of the tunnel. Why didn't I give up? What was my obsession all about? I did not have to succeed. I had the right to fail. I dug myself into a mental depression. Nobody knew it but I myself. I had nightmares every night. I no longer wanted to return to work. I wanted people to forget about me. I wanted to die. But what would happen to my children if I died? Who would be hurting them, not understanding their innermost feelings? I could not die. I had to struggle. But I did not know how. I tried to write, but the pages stayed empty. I still have boxes unopened with manuscripts, but I know the pain was too great—the writing was in invisible ink. I decided that since I would die soon, why not enjoy my last years on earth and go back to school? So I enrolled in a Ph.D. program.

I slowly rediscovered life. Too long had I lived in the fast lane to enjoy all the great opportunities I had had. When we studied one famous writer in one of my history classes, everyone was speechless when I mentioned that I knew this writer and had known others in Paris. When famous politicians were discussed, I could honestly say that I had met some of them, interviewed them.

I did not want to leave, but graduation came and the Ph.D. was handed to me. I was now heading back to the corporate world. I went on corporate interviews, but I did not want to succeed in that world. And here I am, a professor at a university who writes articles and reads books and teaches classes—and tries to write books, too. All my life I had written articles, but never did I feel I had the time to develop a book. Now I was able to publish books. I have reached a point in my life where I feel I did what my grandmother and my mother had wanted me to do. I am a professional woman, I raised two children, and I am thrilled with my life.

She looked up into the mirror. She was back at the beginning. She was supposed to write about being overworked and underpaid. True, if writing articles and books, reading and teaching is work, then she felt overworked and underpaid—but what was she comparing her tiredness with? The professional journalist, the lawyer, the corporate executive, the waitress, the factory worker? There are millions of women working on the global assembly line losing their eyesight at age twenty-one and being replaced by younger workers.

She felt her profession gave her the great leisure to find her own interests. Of course there were not enough days in a week to write it all and edit it all and prepare the teaching for all these lessons, but she was able to use her mind and to reflect on things as they are and as they should be. She treasured that she was being paid to think and rethink life. She felt that she was asked to shape and to reshape society and to spread the gospel of critical thinking among the young. She was part of a profession that demands reflection on one's own needs as well as those of the society at large. There was no room for self-pity. She turned off the computer and with a smile looked at her grandma, who miraculously seemed to look at her again.

And Now the Fifth

Joyce-Nathalie Davis Florida

I'm the fifth generation of women in my family struggling with career and mothering decisions. But I'm not a mother. And I loathe the word *career*. So I hesitate to pontificate on this issue or to succumb to the tendency of the young(er) to think they can fulfill high-falutin' prophecies of becoming the long-anticipated generation that will finally get it all right. I would much rather think about my mother writing her essay. My mother. I can almost predict what she will write. That she tried to do both—career and motherhood—and fears that she has failed at both. Other people's successes are her failures. Women write about how brilliant their careers are—having deserted their kids in day care—and they're impressed with themselves. Others can't get over how perfect they are at being full-time mothers—ignoring their kids as they bake the perfect bread, grind the perfect baby food, or decorate the perfect house. Others are busy creating the perfect progeny—molding her into everything they wish they could have been. Not my mother. She has always marched to the beat of no drum at all.

My mother. I like to call her "the thinking-mother" model. She talked to me as an equal from the very beginning. When other mothers recited Mother Goose horror tales, she recited Sartre. She taught me more about literature, art, history, and philosophy than I ever learned through graduate school. I can remember strolling along the tree-lined streets of our various neighborhoods, in various countries, with my little brother in his *voiture d'enfant*. As we walked and picked flowers, I

Joyce-Nathalie Davis Florida is a Ph.D. student in sociology at Harvard University.

would recite the multiplication tables for her, or we would recite a passage from Sartre or Camus in unison, like a chansonnette. I can remember when she would drive me the thirty minutes each way to my ballet class while she was doing her Ph.D.; and she would give me a lesson on art or history, always starting with, "When man first began . . ." Pierre and I used to laugh and cry out in unison, "Art 101." or "History 101." But we secretly loved it. And we always remembered it.

Although she may say she was an at-home mother, she was a thinking mom, writing, traveling, studying, always sharing with us. When we were kids, she would ask us to "check" her articles or research papers (for grammar, she used to say) and in the process she would expose us to something new. I remember when I was in my preteen years of hell and she wanted to introduce the world of African-American literature to me, but I resisted. One day, she quietly placed Baldwin's "If Beale Street Could Talk" in my lap. "It's a love story," she told my pubescent self. I eagerly finished the story that very afternoon. That is how I was introduced to the world of James Baldwin, Chester Himes, Richard Wright. But she wasn't one of these autocratic, self-titled "thinking moms." She didn't educate her children to impress her friends. She educated them to dare to ask "Why?" and then enjoy discovering the answers all by themselves, for themselves.

She also knew when to draw the line. She didn't believe in overexposure. I remember when we went with Daddy to the Caribbean as he studied native folk music. We would be driven high up into the mountains to watch private voodoo ceremonies, held by the natives only. We were there—saw them in the flesh—not those made-for-tourist ceremonies, but the authentic ones. Mom could always sense when it would be too much and she would sneak us down the hill to a house "to rest," she would say. She knew what her children could handle and what they couldn't.

Bad memories. The most vivid bad memories Pierre and I have of our childhoods, Mom told us herself when we grew up. She constantly tells me how miserable I was when she worked in Brussels full-time, but all I can remember are the two weeks she was in the hospital for surgery. She's constantly telling the story about Pierre knocking at her door when she was writing her dissertation. "Are you finished yet?" he would ask. I remember that. But he swears he doesn't. I guess we don't remember because these were anomalies. She had given us—her children—herself. And we knew it. She educated us, cultivated us, created two people for this world that she hoped would make it a better place. She gave herself to us. And we talk about it often now as adults,

Pierre and I. We feel her there, with us, wherever we go, whatever we're doing. She's deep in our core; we are never alone.

Did she give of herself completely because she's a good mother? Well, yes and no. That's just the way she is. Now I see her giving herself completely to being a professor, a writer. She gets involved with educating the next generation—she cares. Sometimes I hear the same concern in her voice when she tells me about one of her students as I used to hear when she talked about us. Everything gets 100 percent. "She gave up her career," many of her fellow feminists would shriek. She hurt her career? Well, I guess she could have been a professor for twenty more years than she will have been. I'm not sure what difference that would make for her, what that would have gained her. She'll still arrive at the same place. But she got to experience life, not just the artificial constructions created in ivory towers, corporate headquarters, or government bureaucracies. Many say my mother was torn between motherhood and her career. And she would be the first to agree—she always nods her head silently and agrees when she hears someone saying something stupid. But I don't believe it. I think she knew exactly what she was doing.

They say a good mother makes you feel completely safe in her bosom, makes your home a haven from the big, bad world. Not my mother. She opened the door and all the windows and let the world in. Then she pushed us out the door and made us see it—traveling to developing countries where she had no idea what to expect, marching down the streets with angry protestors, fighting to right the injustices of a racist world, interviewing poor uneducated folk, dragging us to nightclubs to hear sad black men wail in their horns, knowing one day we would say with pride that we had heard Louis Armstrong or Dizzy Gillespie play. No shielding us from the world, she forced us to see it, to ask questions, to make us feel at home in it. Sometimes we used to get tired and complain. "Why can't you be an *ordinary* mom?" we would accuse her. "Because then you would be *ordinary* kids," she would yell back, just as loudly.

Mom was one of the few women at the time to study economics at the University of Berlin. She was an economic editor before most women (or men) studied microeconomics in college. She moved to a country whose language she did not know, got a Ph.D., became a professor, and published books and articles on a world of people and experiences that would probably never have touched the family otherwise. She brought a whole new existence into the German collective of her family. I think she sensed her children needed something different than her mother had given her. A healthy dose of reality. With no war, no hunger, no disease to scare them, I suspect she decided to educate them, to make them become better than the people who had destroyed the world when she was a little girl. She taught them everything they could stuff in their heads. She demanded cultivated behavior, elegance, open-mindedness, racelessness, freedom from religious and intellectual oppression. She demanded that their horizons grow and grow. She refused to let them compartmentalize themselves. She refused to let them take it easy. She didn't encourage them to simply take the fastest, easiest career path, mapped out by college boards and ignorant high school counselors. She wanted them to be explorers of life, of humankind. Just like herself.

"Career versus motherhood" is what they call the conflicting issue. What trite terms. What tightly fitting labels. The women of my family. Women. Souls and spirits that could not and would not fit into manmade—and womanmade—constructions and labels. Did my mother choose motherhood or careerdom? My answer would be neither. She chose life, learning, thinking. She chose to explore human existence and challenge it with her entire being. And she brought her kids along for the ride. An adventure, she would call it, of home and travel, of work and play, of love and hurt, of happiness and sorrow, of stability and unpredictability. It has most certainly been a bumpy ride—but Pierre and I are damn glad we got to tag along.

PART TEN

How It Could Be: Strategies and Models for Change

Silent Parenting in the Academy

Constance Coiner

Tillie Olsen's *Tell Me a Riddle* and *Silences* are virtually unique in American literature for their uncompromising look at the anguish of women who must choose between having children and the need to carry on other serious work. In the 1970s, when many feminists forewent or delayed childbearing, *Silences* dared to raise the issue of responsibility for children. By broaching it, Olsen entered what in *Silences* she termed "an almost taboo area; the last refuge of sexism" (202). Today, two decades since the publication of *Silences*, responsibility for children remains the last refuge of sexism, the Achilles heel of the women's movement. Even the women the movement has most helped to advance, its educated professionals, have with a sense of déjà vu felt that old shock of sudden recognition, that familiar "click": equal opportunity vanishes around the issue of who will take care of the kids.

Attempting to parent within the academy, I have experienced such "clicks," as the following anecdotes show. When I was a graduate student and my daughter, Ana, a newborn, I received a note from Tillie Olsen on one of those scraps of paper that are her trademark. "Thieve all the time you can for Ana" was all it said, but I have hung on to that scrap of permission to love my child while working my way into a profession that is often incompatible with the needs of children and parents.

When I completed my Ph.D. and went on the job market in 1987, the professor responsible for shepherding candidates through the job

---

Before her death Constance Coiner was an associate professor of English at the State University of New York at Binghamton.

search advised me to replace the message on my answering machine that included Ana's cheery four-year-old voice. "And I wouldn't let her answer the phone 'til this shootin' match is over," he added ominously. With misgivings I complied with his instructions. But Ana, who was proud of her newly acquired phone answering skills, was not to be silenced. Unexpectedly, at 8:00 one Saturday morning, the phone rang. Forgetting about the time difference between the East and West Coasts, I relented and allowed her to answer, believing that only my mother would call at such an early hour. Ana put down the phone receiver and screeched, "Mommy, Mommy, it's the University of Transylvania!" In the seconds before I spoke to the chair of the University of Pennsylvania's search committee, I saw my fledgling career as a minefield.

I took a job as an assistant professor at SUNY–Binghamton in part because I was assured that my daughter would have access to its highly regarded campus preschool/kindergarten. I was thinking short- and long-run: in a pleasant setting near her parents' offices my child would enjoy a smooth transition into our new life, and the preschool/kindergarten, which enrolls children from the age of two on, would later provide care for a possible second child. As it turned out, the preschool/kindergarten had overenrolled, anticipating atrophy that didn't occur, and my daughter wasn't admitted. I immediately went to the public elementary school, where the principal told me that the kindergarten Ana would attend ended at 10:30. Having had my expectations affected by sixteen years in what *Sixty Minutes* dubbed the People's Republic of Santa Monica, California, I asked, "And what provisions are made for children after 10:30?" "Oh, their mothers come and pick them up," he offered with a shrug. "What about *parents* who work outside the home?" I said, emphasizing "parents" through gritted teeth. "Oh, they get baby-sitters," he replied ("family day-care providers" had not yet found its way into his lexicon). "Maybe you could run an ad for a baby-sitter in the *Pennysaver*," he added, referring to the local throwaway newspaper.

A final anecdote has to do with preparing a talk that my university's women's center asked me to give about combining parenting with my profession. The request came during my first semester at the university, when I was developing two courses for the first time and writing three papers to be presented at professional conventions. During that semester I confessed my exhaustion to a colleague's wife, who with good intentions tried to reassure me that my experience was not unusual: "Oh, how well I remember George [not his real name] when he was at your stage in his career. He worked round-the-clock. The boys and I never saw him."

I brainstormed at the computer the night before the event, managing at least to come up with what I considered a clever title (a quotation from Rosa Luxemburg), but some family obligation—I don't remember what—interrupted my work and, out of necessity, I ended up speaking extemporaneously. All that I produced in that thwarted brainstorming session was the following:

Title: "Ach, I Know of No Formula to Write You for Being Human"

Can you combine parenting with professoring? Yes. Well, maybe.

If you get a job at a research institution, you'll have to live three-and-a-half lives:

Mother Life = one life

Teaching Life = one life

Publishing = one life

Maintaining a Home (hopefully sharing that responsibility equally with another adult) = half-a-life

If you get a job at a "teaching institution," you'll have to live only two-and-a-half lives—unless you're employed by a school that is increasing publication requirements while maintaining heavy teaching loads:

Mother Life = one life

Teaching Life = one life

Maintaining a Home = half-a-life

I would try to . . .

The material circumstances of a mother's life—one that is, as Olsen has put it, "instantly interruptible"—prevented my getting any farther (18).

Prior to the contemporary women's movement, many male professors produced while their wives enabled them to do so without distractions. A professorship was often a two-person operation, with two people, in different ways, supporting one career. Olsen contributed valuably to the unmasking of the hidden labor that often supports intellectual production. *Silences* foregrounded domestic labor and especially child care, which may be the most invisible, the most "naturalized" labor of all. One of many memorable passages from *Silences* describes what Edmund Wilson's second wife, Elena, provided him daily: "tea on a tray for his 'elevenses'; absolute silence in his working hours, and good meals at appropriate intervals" (221). Although some of us have moved beyond the world of the Wilsons, the academic profession, in its structure and expectations, does not reflect the reality of our post-housewife era. The academy assumes a freedom from responsibility for maintaining a home and family that, for many academic women (and for some of our male allies), simply does not exist. The profession is still defined by the assumption that we have at our disposal what *Silences* terms "the essential angel," someone responsible "for daily living, for the maintenance of life" (34). And because few in positions of power acknowledge that assumption, probably because most of them have been insulated from family responsibilities, it is all the more insidious, all the more difficult to confront.

Moreover, though the academic profession is no longer the province primarily of a gentlemanly leisured class, we daily experience remnants of that empire, including a polite code of silence about certain topics. One of the unspoken requirements for tenure is that junior faculty appear to be coping well with their myriad responsibilities. At faculty meetings and social gatherings it behooves us to look relaxed and on top of things rather than frenzied, fatigued, malcontent. We have to prove that we're "one of them." It's a catch-22: the people in the profession most likely to need parental leave and child care are often the same people expected to be on their best behavior. Most of the untenured faculty I know believe that they would jeopardize tenure by making demands or simply by admitting the truth about the quality of their lives. It's time for people to be honest about the tremendous emotional cost of women's—and men's—professional advances. Unless we radically change the structure of the academic career and what Arlie Hochschild terms "its imperial relation to the family," it will be difficult for mothers "to move up in careers and for men to move into the family" (48). Both women and men will live less than full lives.

Before proceeding I must enter a three-part caveat: first, the spirit of *Silences* would have me underscore that nonacademic parents employed at universities experience pressures also. Many departments depend heavily on administrative assistants and staff members—mostly women, many of them parents—who, as much as their academic counterparts, deserve parental leave, on-campus child care, and flextime. We must organize within the academy, building alliances and unions with other university employees, such as clerical, maintenance, and food service workers. As Carl Freedman argues, "a great many reified myths will be dissolved or eroded when teachers, whose labor is predominantly mental, bargain and picket alongside those who sweep classroom floors and serve food in university cafeterias. To think of ourselves as workers at all is, indeed, in itself a powerful demystification of the ideology of professionalism" (81). Second, in this essay "family" refers to nontraditional as well as traditional configurations, including partners of the same or opposite sex in living arrangements approximating marital partnerships. Third, I want to acknowledge that feminist agendas in the early seventies addressed a number of the points I raise; some of these have not been resolved and are still urgent.

I begin by surveying attempts by the Modern Language Association (MLA) and the American Studies Association (ASA) to address feminist concerns that bear on parenting. While I refer often to efforts by people within these organizations, I recognize that members of other organizations have also addressed them and I intend my discussion and recommendations to apply to the academy as a whole.

At the business meeting of the 1969 MLA convention, Florence Howe, chair of the newly established Commission on the Status of Women in the Profession,[1] which had been charged to "investigate 'discriminatory practices' in order to assure 'equitable standards,'" issued the commission's preliminary report ("The 1969 Business Meeting" 645). The commission made a series of recommendations, including some pertaining to parenting (e.g., the establishment of university-supported, parent-controlled day-care centers). Ellen Cantarow also urged the MLA Resolutions Committee to bring several resolutions to the same meeting. In the March 1970 *MLA Newsletter* these resolutions—with accompanying explanations written by Cantarow, Lillian Robinson, and Jacqueline Tunberg—were sent, along with other resolutions, to the members (31,607 in that year) for a vote. Each resolution received over 4,000 votes, which, when compared to returns on MLA mail ballots in other years, represents a very good response.

One resolution, approved by a close vote of 2,246 to 2,149, urged the establishment of day-care centers on college and university campuses. "These centers," the explanation read, "should be institutionally-funded, parent controlled, staffed by both men and women, and open to children from the age of six weeks on, whose parents are students, teachers, employees, or neighbors of the institution" ("The 1969 Business Meeting" 651). Another critically important resolution—for paid maternity and parental leave for both men and women—failed in a close vote (2,026 to 2,321).

In addition, by overwhelmingly positive votes, members urged universities to overturn antinepotism rules (3,526 to 754); to allow flexibility in faculty appointments, facilitating transitions between part- and full-time positions (3,368 to 821); and to provide women employees with benefits such as health and retirement equal to those of men (3,900 to 178). In another overwhelmingly favorable vote members requested that *PMLA* and the *MLA Newsletter* provide space for women's professional concerns (3,268 to 922).

Members also passed a resolution exhorting universities to call for the repeal of all state laws regulating contraception, abortion, and voluntary sterilization and to press university medical centers to offer free birth control information and devices (2,304 to 2,057). And they passed a resolution urging that "the position of women, the conventions of love, courtship, and marriage, and the stereotypes involving women be made the subjects of courses and scholarship in the humanities" (2,866 to 1270; "The 1969 Business Meeting" 651). A resolution to give preference to women, including women of color, in hiring, promotion, and tenure was defeated (1,639 to 2,767).

In summary, of the nine resolutions related to women and to family care issues, seven were passed and two rejected. Thus, in 1970, a majority of voting MLA members supported significant institutional reform. But as readers of this essay know only too well, some of these reforms—such as the establishing of campus day-care centers—have not yet been widely implemented.

In 1984–85 Tey Diana Rebolledo, a member of the MLA Commission on the Status of Women, reviewed parenting leave policies for some fifty academic institutions as well as the then-current literature on parental leave policies within the academy and private industry in the hope of assisting universities in developing codified parental leave policies. Her report is one indication that the 1970 MLA resolutions had not made sufficient impact on university administrations. According to Rebolledo, many universities lacked formal policies, relying instead on administrators' discretion. As she pointed out, these ad hoc policies allow administrators to be lenient in some cases and not in others. Many institutions had only "sick" leave for mothers, with no paternal leave. While some institutions provided full pay and benefits for up to three months, others allowed only a leave of absence without pay. Rebolledo finished her term on the commission not long after completing the report and, unfortunately, the MLA neither published it nor pursued the project until 1993. Through the efforts of Sarah Webster Goodwin, with help from Naomi Miller and myself, the MLA Committee on the Status of Women in the Profession established a subcommittee on family care issues chaired by Goodwin. It published a call for information about universities' family leave policies in the spring 1993 *MLA Newsletter* and organized a session on family care for the 1993 MLA convention. It investigated differences in cost between the current dates for the convention, December 27–30, and the first week in January, a more convenient time for those with family responsibilities. It also prepared a memorandum urging the Committee on Careers, in its preconvention workshops, to alert candidates searching for jobs to be vigilant about family care issues. At MLA conferences after 1993, the work of the subcommittee has continued, and we are making slow but genuine progress.

In 1972 an eighteen-month-old ad hoc committee, the Women's Committee of the American Studies Association, became permanent and began to address issues pertaining to the lives of women and families within the academy. In her afterword to a report compiled in 1988, Linda Kerber discussed the 1972 resolutions. They centered on "structural and ethical" issues concerning equal treatment of women and men within the academy, in the ASA, and on the editorial board of the *American Quarterly,* the association's journal (29). The resolutions dealt with child care, pregnancy leave, parental leave (for men as well as women), and options in the pace of career advancement. They opposed nepotism policies and encouraged universities to include women's studies courses in their curricula. Moreover, they called for equity in faculty recruitment, hiring, salary, and promotion; in graduate student admissions; and in the awarding of grants and fellowships. The concerns of the ASA Women's Committee were those of the MLA Commission on the Status of Women; thus there was a consistent effort to promote reform by the women's organizations of two major academic associations.

Kerber describes the results of the 1972 ASA push for reforms (which resemble the results of earlier MLA attempts):

> Here we are nearly twenty years later, and on the face of it, much of this agenda is apparently accomplished. Anti-nepotism policies have indeed fallen; sex-biased questions have been removed from the hiring process; women's studies courses are widely available; women have for several years composed a majority of the ASA Council and serve in official capacities throughout the Association; three of the last four Gabriel Dissertation Prize recipients have been women. The academy is a considerably more decent, more open, more ethical institution. (30)

In a foreword to the report Lois Banner noted, "By the mid 1980s issues raised by the [ASA] women's committee in earlier years seemed to have been addressed to the point that the question was raised of whether or not the organization needed a women's committee" (i). It would seem, then, that attention to "structural and ethical" issues had produced some satisfying results.

The value of these reforms should not be underestimated. Yet, as Kerber noted, "academic women continue to find themselves uncomfortable in the academy" (30). Undoubtedly some of that discomfort reflects the fact that "structural and ethical" reforms, while broadly successful, have not been equally realized in all institutions. However, for some women the discomfort stems significantly from work-family conflict, as the report reveals. The committee comments on the importance of the unexpected questions that emerged at the end of one 1985 convention session at which Lois Banner and Annette Kolodny presented papers: "a number of younger women remained in the room. They had very pointed questions for the participants regarding their careers: when they rested, how they avoided 'burn out,' what they did about competing responsibilities in their professional and personal lives" (Banner et al. 1).

To explore these and related questions, Banner, Kolodny, Eileen Boris, Mary Kelley, Lillian Schlissel, and Cecelia Tichi constructed a questionnaire that was mailed in 1986 to 1,100 women in the ASA and to 1,831 women in the Organization of American Historians. The questionnaire was also sent to a random group of 200 male members of the ASA. Women in the ASA returned 23 percent, or 238 questionnaires; women in the OAH returned 13 percent, or 199; ASA men returned 30 percent, or 67. The survey results were published in the 1988 ASA Women's Committee report. Respondents talked about stress they and their families experienced, burnout and anxiety, and problems of survival in the professional marketplace. In her afterword to the report Kerber describes what the committee received, on paper and in crowded sessions at both the ASA and OAH conventions: "outpourings of anxiety, frustration, and despair that are not unlike what we heard 20 years ago, in those early attempts to articulate an agenda for political change" (30).

I attended the emotionally charged ASA convention session in which the questionnaire responses were discussed, and Kerber's word *outpourings* is apt. People couldn't wait to speak; some exploded. As Banner insists in her foreword to the report, "this is not just a document produced by numbers of discontented women: it speaks truths about the *nature of modern professionalism*" (emphasis added). "We all decry the rigors of the academic life," Banner continues, "but few of us do much to change the contours of a system rooted in capitalist competition and male hierarchy. . . . Both men and women need to recreate the academic workplace so that it becomes a humane alternative to corporate America, not merely a replica of its negative features" (i–ii). The issue of parenting within the academy, then, is only one element—albeit a crucial one—in a more general dialogue about our profession that ought to take place, as Banner rightly insists, "in open convention forums and in public department colloquia, not just fugitively over beers late at night or privately in the security of individual offices" (ii).

The following is my mushrooming list of recommendations for changing the academy's practices to acknowledge broadly defined parenting needs.[2]

1. Establish a national clearinghouse for collecting and disseminating information about colleges' and universities' profamily policies (or lack thereof). This information would then be available to all institutions wanting to model their policies on peer institutions, to all major professional organizations, and to all job candidates.

2. Fund adequate paid maternity leave.

3. Fund adequate paid parental leave.

4. Offer family-related services and benefits to nontraditional families, including partners of the same or opposite sex in living arrangements approximating marital partnerships.

5. Provide adequate, subsidized child care on or close to campus that will accommodate all preschool children, including infants as well as children with disabilities or special needs.

6. Establish child-care training programs and referral services to put university families in touch with community homeday-care providers.

7. Establish reimbursement account plans that allow employees to pay dependent-care expenses using pretax earnings.

8. Expand work-study programs (programs in which university students are employed by their university) to contribute to child care.

9. Involve the community's elderly in campus child care on a voluntary or paid basis.

10. Allow faculty members with primary responsibility for a young child to stop the tenure clock temporarily.

11. Create half-time and three-quarter-time tenure-track positions.

12. Permit tenure-track job-sharing. This arrangement should be allowable for a "team" of two parents from separate families as well as a couple who have had a child together.

13. Permit early sabbaticals for infant care, as proposed by Andrew Cherlin, a sociology professor at Johns Hopkins. As Cherlin recognizes, "the biological clock and the tenure clock tick away in unison." He suggests that the sabbatical be offered to male and female parents on the usual terms of full pay for one semester or half pay for two. "In effect, the first sabbatical would be borrowed and used a few years early," Cherlin reasons. "The only significant cost—one semester's pay—would be incurred when someone who had taken an advance sabbatical was later denied tenure" (B2). I would add the suggestion that these early sabbaticals not be used as a substitute for paid maternity/parental leave.

14. Formally recognize that faculty members with primary responsibility for child care may have slower career tracks. Lotte Bailyn recommends two different career ladders, the familiar one and one that "defines a different career curve, one that rises more slowly but eventually may end up at the same point, though at a later stage in life" (55). While I worry that the slower track might become "the mommy track," with real power residing with those who take the traditional route, we should nevertheless explore alternatives in career pace.

15. Schedule meetings and colloquia when parents can attend. Meetings that can't be scheduled for the noon hour should be scheduled to end by 4:30, when possible.

16. Schedule major conventions at times that don't conflict with family holidays (for example, the MLA convention falls between Christmas and New Year's; the ASA convention usually takes place in late October or early November and may coincide with Halloween).

17. Become leading public advocates for federally sponsored child care and parental leave.

18. In the interest of parents and nonparents alike, be creative about dual-career recruitment and hiring among university employees to eliminate long commutes and, in some cases, the expense and stress of maintaining two households. Commuter relationships can be especially difficult for parents of young children and can subvert efforts to share child care equitably. Universities can also help partners of university employees find employment in the community.

19. Academic associations should modify preconvention workshops on job searchs to include some reference to parenting-related issues—e.g., caution candidates who have or hope to have children to be vigilant about various universities' policies regarding parenting and child care.

20. Career guides should be revised to reflect the reality that an increasing number of candidates for academic positions—female and male—are or hope to be significantly involved parents. They further

should be augmented to advise candidates to inquire about programs such as parental leave, on-campus child care, stop-the-tenure-clock policies and to advise search committees to provide such information routinely.

21. Unless a national clearinghouse is established, academic associations should annually survey universities about their profamily policies and publish that information.

22. Each academic association should publish a collection of the various equity studies it has sponsored in the last twenty years. Such a collection would reveal what has been called for in the past, would allow us to measure past recommendations against present realities, and would suggest areas for future efforts.

Enacting these recommendations requires mobilizing according to a slogan Olsen has often repeated to me: "Educate, organize, agitate." Such mobilizing is generally more familiar to political activists than to most academics. But, to return to Carl Freedman's terms, we must demystify the ideology of professionalism, recognizing ourselves as workers even though our labor is primarily intellectual. If these recommendations seem a mere "wish list," we should recall that many reforms we now take for granted, such as the eight-hour day and the vote for women, once seemed fanciful, too.

Action on the twenty-two recommendations above and others like them is especially important for academic parents who do not have the financial means to employ household maintenance and extensive child-care services. In contrast, professions such as medicine and law, while at least as demanding as the academic profession, are usually remunerative enough to fund services that ease the difficulties of maintaining a home and family.

If solutions to problems of parenting in the profession are available only to those with access to funds in addition to their incomes, the careers of mothers belonging, by birth or marriage, to an elite class are far more likely to flourish than those of women of lesser means. Gender inequality in the academy will have been countered, then, partly by a reliance on class privilege.[3] While the hidden injuries and cushions of class are not about to disappear from the academy, paid maternity and parental leaves, subsidized child care, and other profamily policies would help to democratize the profession.

Many of my female students love the line from Alice Walker's *In Search of Our Mothers' Gardens* that describes our mothers and grandmothers as "moving to music not yet written" (232). That phrase seems to capture for them the quality of their lives. But it is time we composed the music—not just privately, individually, and improvisationally, as many of us have been doing for years, but formally, publicly, institutionally. We owe it to ourselves, to our children, to the friendships we let die because we are insanely overworked. We owe it to our female students who are lowering their aspirations partly because they look at their role models and see horror shows, not because we aren't happy but because we're killing ourselves in the process of keeping all parts of ourselves alive. We owe it to our male students, who also stand to benefit if their careers allow them to be more involved in family life. And finally, we owe it to "mothers" such as Tillie Olsen, a pioneer in raising the issue of silent parenting.

NOTES

An earlier version of this essay appears in *Concerns* 24.3 (Fall 1994): 37–49. A longer version of this essay appears in *Listening to Silences: New Essays in Feminist Criticism*, ed. Elaine Hedges and Shelley Fisher Fishkin (New York: Oxford University Press, 1994). The essay and book originated in a 1988 Modern Language Association session observing the tenth anniversary of the publication of Olsen's *Silences*, which explains the essay's several references to Olsen's work.

1. The Commission became the Committee on the Status of Women in the Profession around 1990.

2. In *Listening to Silences* I provide examples of significant pro-family innovations within a few universities.

3. I share Ruth Sidel's concern that immigrant women, as nannies and housekeepers, often sacrifice caring for their own children while making it possible for "our new" professionals to "have it all" (199).

WORKS CITED

Bailyn, Lotte. "The Apprenticeship Model of Organizational Careers: A Response to Changes in the Relation between Work and Family." *Women in the Workplace*. Ed. Phyllis Wallace. Boston: Auburn, 1982.

Banner, Lois. "Foreword." *Personal Lives and Professional Careers: The Uneasy Balance*. Lois Banner, Eileen Boris, Mary Kelley, Annette Kolodny, Cecelia Tichi, and Lillian Schlissel. Report of the Women's Committee of the American Studies Association, 1988. i–ii.

Banner, Lois, Eileen Boris, Mary Kelley, Annette Kolodny, Cecelia Tichi, and Lillian Schlissel. *Personal Lives and Professional Careers: The Uneasy Balance*. Report of the Women's Committee of the American Studies Association, 1988.

Cherlin, Andrew. "Needed: Early Sabbaticals for Pregnancy and Infant Care." *Chronicle of Higher Education* Nov. 22, 1989: B2.

Freedman, Carl. "Marxist Theory, Radical Pedagogy, and the Reification of Thought." *College English* 49.1 (1987): 70–82.

Hochschild, Arlie. "Inside the Clockwork of Male Careers." *Women and the Power to Change.* Ed. Florence Howe. New York: McGraw-Hill, 1975. 47–80.

Kerber, Linda. "Afterword." *Personal Lives and Professional Careers: The Uneasy Balance.* Lois Banner, Eileen Boris, Mary Kelley, Annette Kolodny, Cecelia Tichi, and Lillian Schlissel. Report of the Women's Committee of the American Studies Association, 1988. 29–31.

"The 1969 Business Meeting: Actions and a Summary of Discussion." *PMLA* 85.3 (1970): 644–54.

Olsen, Tillie. *Silences.* New York: Dell, 1978.

Rebolledo, Tey Diana. "Parenting Leave: Law, Policy, and Practice." Unpublished report of the MLA Commission on the Status of Women in the Profession, 1985.

Sidel, Ruth. *On Her Own: Growing Up in the Shadow of the American Dream.* New York: Penguin, 1990.

Walker, Alice. *In Search of Our Mothers' Gardens.* New York: Harcourt, 1983.

Family Care in the Profession

Sarah Webster Goodwin

Remember Zoe Baird? During her confirmation hearings for attorney general in 1993 the focus rested on her child-care choices, not her legal views. She seems like ancient history now but I wanted to remind people about her because at the time of the hearings lots of people didn't "get it." They didn't understand that Zoe Baird's problem was the symptom of a much larger social problem that affects every stratum and every subculture in our society. They still don't get it. This is the problem, succinctly put: our policies and services have not caught up with the needs created when women moved into the paid work force outside the home. (Never mind that for many occupations and groups that movement happened generations ago. We still haven't caught up.) We are still basically expecting every woman to reinvent the wheel for herself: to find on her own the support and services she needs to keep the household functioning.

The needs of the family and of intimate relationships often create pressures, even to the point of breaking down that brick wall between workplace and home. When that happens, there's a shock. I take what happened to Zoe Baird to be an instance of such a breakdown. In the wake of that particular shock some people asked, Why don't they ask male candidates for the cabinet whether they have any foreign domestic workers in their home? They do now. But however much we may recognize that men, too, have families, and that men have family care issues, the fact remains that this is still largely a woman's concern.

That brick wall that the professional woman is expected to erect and maintain is just an illusion, a magic trick. Sometimes maintaining

Sarah Webster Goodwin is a professor of English at Skidmore.

it requires acts of desperation. How many mothers among us have been up all night with a sick child only to stagger into class and teach as though nothing had happened? How many have chosen not to have children because the money for child care and household help simply wasn't there? How many have mentally banked on a baby-sitter's flexibility while we sat trapped in a meeting that would not end?—maybe even fretting for the baby-sitter's *own* family as we did so? How many, after the Zoe Baird incident, had to do some soul searching about the status of our domestic workers? How many have skipped faculty meetings to visit a critically ill parent in another town? How many have cared for an ill partner without so much as knowing that she was officially recognized as family by the institution?

Each of us is subject to pressures from family relationships that at times become so intense as to threaten disruptions, not just of our personal lives, but also of our effectiveness at the workplace. Perhaps more important, many among us suffer intensely and alone, without a clear sense of resources or support available. Aren't there practical, affordable practices our employers could adopt that would ease some of the pressure? For example:

1. Parental leave policies for childbirth and infant care. I envision a staggered menu of possibilities, ranging from a brief paid leave to a longer unpaid leave with job security.

2. Postponed tenure decisions on application for parents of infants and young children.

3. Extension of parental leave and family emergency benefits to domestic partners on application.

4. On-campus quality child-care centers with calendars and hours appropriate for campus employees.

5. Institutionally subsidized sick child care for employees' children with short-term illnesses.

6. Family emergency leave policies for those who must take time off to care for a critically ill family member.

7. Adequate workplace replacement for employees whose children or other family members have short-term illnesses. This means both adequate temporary help for support staff and—why not?—a pool of available substitutes for lower-level courses.

These practical answers to address the global and rather nebulous body of problems called family care issues sound rather utopian, but almost all are already in effect at some institutions.

As long as we're bringing in the body here, I want to get personal for a minute. One of my first thoughts after I got tenure was: "Good. There's work to be done; now I can do it." Women have had too tenuous a hold on the treasure chest of academe—its tenured positions—to risk much by agitating for maternity leave, health insurance for domestic partners, and a chance to nurse their parents and partners. And yet family care not only needs to be done but also is supremely important. It is not work that can always be done on a strict schedule or in one's leisure time. Most academics cannot afford first-rate domestic help, even when it can be found. *There is no system yet in place to handle anything beyond the healthy family.* We need to recognize that it is *normal,* not unusual, for children to get sick; that our parents or partners will not schedule their incapacitating illnesses conveniently from May to September; that we will *all* benefit from a saner workplace if consistent policies and benefits are in place.

When I was on the MLA Committee on the Status of Women, I had to miss one of its precious few meetings. It was during a semester that seemed like one long nightmare. My husband was commuting to a job two hundred miles away; our three children came down with the chicken pox—first one, then the other two—right at the time that our much-loved housekeeper was hospitalized with heart failure. It was late March, and the end of the semester was heating up. I was immobilized. I couldn't find child care; I was up most of the night comforting one or another miserable child, until I was almost hallucinating with fatigue; and then one day in class—somehow I did manage to get to class—a student complained that I wasn't getting their papers graded fast enough. So I broke down and told them why. (My brick wall went down.) They were not very understanding. I could hear echoes of my mother's voice when I said, "Someday you'll understand." And I thought: maybe they shouldn't have to. Maybe we can work our way out of these Dark Ages and make another world possible.

It will involve hard work, something most of us don't have time for. But I think it's hitting home close enough, to enough people, that more and more are going to "get it." Family care is not just a domestic issue, it's also a workplace issue and a social issue, and we need to address it. We can start here.

APPENDIX: RECIPE FOR SUMMER CHILD CARE

In the fall of 1993, a committee met at Skidmore for the first time to discuss setting up a summer camp to provide child care for the school-aged children of employees and the community. The college has an eight-year-old child-care center that is flourishing, despite the perpetual problem of balancing its budget, and we had become accustomed to having on-campus care for our children. But the outlook was not promising. Some disgruntled faculty still feel that on-site child care is a preferential (unfair) benefit, despite the fact that the center is under constant pressure to be self-supporting. The summer camp came up not only as a way to provide child care but also as a fundraiser for the child-care center.

So when Camp Northwoods at Skidmore opened its doors in July, some of us were ready to pop champagne corks. We felt that we'd made a discovery: This solution to a problem can make life easier for a good many people. Without—amazingly—making enemies. Our kids loved it, the campus setting proved ideal for it, and the camp better than broke even, despite hefty start-up costs, and despite a significant bill from the college for office expenses.

Here's the recipe.

1. *Assemble an effective committee.* Ours was small—about four people—but committed. It included two faculty members, one graphic artist on the staff, and the chair of the Child Care Center Advisory Board. All were parents of potential campers.

2. *Enlist the appropriate advisors.* We had a group of official advisors who couldn't really make it to the meetings but whose good will was crucial: the director of the Center for Child Study, the associate dean of student affairs, the assistant director of Special Programs (the office that oversees all summer events on campus).

3. *Establish the need.* We began by surveying the entire Skidmore community to ascertain whether such a summer camp was needed and how much people would be willing and able to pay. The response was strong: from these numbers, we could expect to fill a modest-sized camp (about forty campers). This gave us our first ammunition.

4. *Find a site.* This is probably the most difficult step. Like most campuses, Skidmore has a chronic shortage of space, even in summer. But a group of forty children, broken into two or three smaller groups, really does not need a whole lot of room. It can be found. All that's necessary is a home base. Much of the activity can take place elsewhere on campus—at the pool, athletic facilities, museums, studios, libraries, computer centers, and labs. Our camp wound up in a student-owned pavilion in the woods that is underused in the summer. It did need—and still needs—some adjustments to make it a safe and appropriate set-up for children.

5. *Make a wild-guess budget.* Ours wound up having little to do with the eventual real budget: all they had in common was the rosy bottom line. The camp both spent more and took in more than we projected. But it did give us a starting point to assess economic feasibility.

6. *Identify other success stories.* We found a camp not too far away, run by a child-care center at a hospital, that claimed to be pulling in $15,000 a year. We don't see quite how they do it, but at least we believe they're not costing their institution anything, and they're providing a needed service. It was astonishing how many minds were changed by that figure. One success story, it seems, engenders another.

7. *Present your case.* With a site, an established need, and a wild-guess budget, it's time to go to the appropriate office. You will have been talking casual-

ly with them all along, identifying the parents in the group and dropping up-beat hints about how well it's all going. In our case, the crucial office was Special Programs; once they said yes, it was smooth sailing: we had a budget line and an office staff. It also helped enormously that one particularly energetic member of their support staff has two young children and an indefatigable commitment to our cause.

8. *Get it underway.* We advertised for a director and hired two co-directors with complementary experience in March. They immediately set out to hire counselors. From among a surprisingly large pile of applications—it seems the education majors got wind of this and all wanted in—they assembled a superb staff of counselors. Even before they started, our committee had issued camp registration forms within the Skidmore community, and after a decent period we opened it up to the public at a higher fee schedule. The camp filled rapidly and remained filled throughout the seven weeks. We also solicited parental involvement in planning the campers' activities. Faculty parents volunteered to take groups of kids into the labs, the studios, and the woods for a rich variety of activities. The directors arranged for daily swimming, tennis lessons, ceramics lessons twice a week, and visitors and field trips.

9. *Watch it happen.* For committee members, the first summer still involved a fair amount of work. We met regularly with the directors to address any problems or concerns. We also conducted an official evaluation of the camp, including providing evaluation forms for campers and parents, a staff evaluation, and on-site observation, and wrote up a detailed report with the recommendation that the camp be continued.

Our children were happy. They were reunited with old friends from the child-care center, they were busy having fun, and they were nearby. We are still hoping that the camp can provide a way for the college to forge a link with the community of Saratoga, both by bringing in paying campers and by subsidizing some children who might not have such opportunities. In our case, this may not be just a pipe dream.

One senior faculty member stopped me in the hall in August to thank me profusely for overseeing the launching of the camp. She was having her first productive summer in years. I'm looking forward to more of those—and to watching the campers troop by my office window, singing the camp song on their way to the pool.

It's one local solution. One tiny, necessary building block in the ant-work of solutions, this enormous project of making the arduous balancing act work better.

Of Parents Born: Changing the Family Care System in Academe

Naomi J. Miller

Over the past several years as an assistant and an associate professor, I quite often have found myself engaged in discussions with graduate students about how to balance work and family as they prepare to enter the profession. Usually these conversations arise informally—during the break in a graduate seminar, in the hallway outside the department office—but they are marked by an intensity that signals the pressing and unresolved nature of the problem. Some of my graduate students have young children, some have grown children and care for elderly parents. The challenges they confront are familiar to academics across the country: men and women, full-time and part-time teachers, biological and adoptive parents, adults with aging relatives, two-career couples, single parents—practically all of us, and across the entire spectrum of academic disciplines. Although many of us may have felt isolated in our struggles, unwilling to break the decorum of professional silence regarding personal concerns, we are in fact a "body" and need to start acting like one to effect change.

My work on these issues arises from my experiences as a parent, as well as a scholar and teacher, working within the academic system to bring about action on family care issues. Spurring me on in a very real sense are not only my discussions with friends and colleagues around the country as we work to address these concerns but also my conversations with my graduate students, who I hope will be entering a pro-

Naomi J. Miller is an associate professor of English and women's studies at the University of Arizona.

fession in which it is possible not only to talk about but also to act upon our concerns—and even to see results. And, of course, I am speaking my own story as well. Although one of the graduate students I talked with expressed impatience with the "feminist genre" of including personal narratives in discussions of political action, our individual histories impel our action and our sharing of them enables us to act in concert.

I am a mother of four and an associate professor of English literature and women's studies at the University of Arizona. I have chaired my university's Childcare Steering Committee; I have chaired the Association of Women Faculty Family Care Issues Committee; and I have been a member of the university's Commission on the Status of Women Ad Hoc Committee on Family Support/Child Care. On a national level, I have chaired the Modern Language Association Committee on the Status of Women in the Profession and am currently vice president of the Women's Caucus for the Modern Languages. While committee work is not faculty members' most favorite activity—certainly not mine—I have nevertheless found that committees involved with family care issues have been among the most challenging and most effective of any I have served on, because of the dedication and intensely shared concerns of their members.

During my tenure on the Association for Women Faculty Parental Leave Committee, we surveyed the parental leave policies of a number of peer institutions, compiled written interviews with a range of women faculty at our university, and produced a lengthy report analyzing the issues and precedents associated with parental leave, which prompted the university to decide to offer a one-year stoppage of the tenure clock to new parents. On the Association for Women Faculty Family Care Issues Committee, as well as on the university's Commission on the Status of Women, we are supporting the establishment of an on-site child-care center, while continuing to encourage the development of paid parental leave and other family-friendly university policies, such as options for part-time tenure-track positions and pretenure or tenured job sharing.

As for my own history: I had my first child while I was finishing my dissertation and my second while teaching part-time and working to publish some articles. I was actually pregnant with my second child when I applied for my first full-time position as an assistant professor and discovered that my visibly pregnant state at an on-campus interview suddenly seemed to transform me from a serious candidate to a visual embodiment of maternity, whose commitment to the profession could somehow be regarded as suspect. I subsequently learned, when an acquaintance without a finished dissertation or published articles but also without any visible "disabilities" such as pregnancy was offered the position I had been interviewed for, that her questions about parental leave policies and child-care options were met with the spontaneously dismayed question, "You're not pregnant, are you?" followed by apparent relief when the answer was no.

By the time I was pregnant with my third child I was also chairing a special session at the 1991 MLA convention entitled "This Self Which Is Not One: Childbearing, Childrearing, and the Profession," which addressed the concerns experienced by academics attempting to balance the often conflicting demands of family and profession, from graduate school to deanship, from job interview to tenure decision and beyond. I earned tenure and promotion to associate professor fourteen months after the birth of my fourth child.

Media articles and presentations have called attention to the existence and quality of European legislation guaranteeing maternity leave (fourteen weeks minimum of job-protected leave at full pay in some countries and up to twenty-eight weeks at 90 percent pay in others) and supporting child care. In the United States, the Family and Medical Leave Act (FMLA) went into effect for the first time in 1993, guaranteeing *unpaid* leave for the birth or adoption of a child or to care for an immediate family member with a serious health condition, if one's employment meets certain specified conditions. In the American business community, some corporations already offer more progressive child-care benefits, ranging from eight weeks of paid maternity leave followed by up to three years of unpaid leave (IBM) to one-year family leaves with full benefits, adoption benefits, and on-site child care (Johnson and Johnson). Within the academic profession, however, family policies have lagged far behind. For teaching faculty in particular, many of whom are on ten-month appointments and unable to earn "vacation leave" and "compensatory time" on the basis of "hours worked," the Family and Medical Leave Act does not address many practical difficulties.

In a paper presented at the 1990 International Conference for Women in Higher Education analyzing maternity, sick, and family leave policies at a number of major research universities, Patricia Laughlin and Mary Jane Trout Barretta observed that many universities are only "belatedly attempting to come to grips with a policy problem which already affects many women already in the tenure pipeline . . . and has profound implications for both male and female faculty" (2–3). Many of the universities surveyed—including the University of California at Berkeley, Ohio State, Pennsylvania State University, Stanford, Northwestern, and Yale—rely heavily on "the discretion of the department chair or dean" while task forces study the issues and debate the form new or revised "family concern" policies should take. In their conclusion, as in the conclusions of similar studies conducted over the past decade, Laughlin and Barretta point out that the provisions of current policies, whether for providing leave, stopping the tenure clock, or supporting child care, "lag behind the needs of junior faculty—both men and women" (14). They also note, significantly, that "the child-bearing years coincide with the years in which the greatest productivity in scholarship and research is expected" (16).

In the July 1993 issue of *Women in Higher Education*, Gayle Kimball underscores that "although colleges and universities are think tanks for future advances," they are far behind "corporations and government agencies in creating a supportive work environment for employees" (1). The costs to women in particular emerge not only in the documented attrition rate of women versus men making it through the tenure pipeline all the way to full professorship but also in the statistic, cited by Kimball, that only 17 percent of female full professors are parents, compared with 82 percent of their male counterparts. Urging investigation of a wide range of options, Kimball observes that "family-friendly options are limited only by the creativity of those seeking solutions" (1).

Following the birth of my third and fourth children, unlike many of my colleagues across the country, I was fortunate to be granted a paid semester without teaching responsibilities, which was the direct result of Dean Annette Kolodny's progressive and proactive stance on family care matters in the University of Arizona's College of Humanities. I also chose to take the one year stoppage of the tenure clock that the efforts of the Parental Leave Committee had helped make available.

My narrative, however, is flanked by the far less rosy experiences of many other faculty at my institution. As chair of the Association for Women Faculty Family Care Issues Committee, I have frequently been contacted by female junior faculty members seeking to learn their options, in the face of active discouragement from their departments. In the course of these informal consultations, I have been appalled to discover that even the tenure-clock stoppage, now officially "on the books" in the university handbook, is routinely not mentioned or incorrectly associated with extra conditions (such as unpaid leave) by the department heads and deans they question. These discrepancies within a single institution clearly bear out Laughlin and Barretta's warning that "a good number of 'unwritten' policies are in effect at many institutions—all of them hinging on the orientation of the department chair, dean, or provost and how they use their discretionary powers" (16). Working to address precisely that inequity, the Family Care Issues Committee at the University of Arizona helped to develop a formal policy supporting one semester of "modified duties" for any employee upon the birth or adoption of a new child, which was passed in 1997 by the faculty senate.

I have come to realize that although those of us with young children, or elderly parents as the case may be, may find that we have no extra time to devote to "political" action above and beyond our "professional" responsibilities, no one else will do it for us, because no one else feels the need quite so pressingly. All we can do, then, is to keep moving ahead, one step at a time, although there are no guarantees about the outcome of our trek. Recently I saw a notice on one of the bulletin boards of my financially beleaguered state university announcing, "Due to budget cuts, the light at the end of the tunnel has been turned off." Sometimes it may feel as if that is what some administrators are trying to tell those of us working on family care issues. But then again, students, faculty, and administrators at all levels are increasingly beginning to recognize that it is time to stop tunneling "underground" and break through to the surface instead.

To that end, my university established the Childcare Steering Committee with the support of the provost and vice-provost for academic affairs and appointed a coordinator of child care initiatives to address many of the family care needs on campus. Issues still to be addressed by many universities and colleges across the country range from paid parental leave and job-sharing options on the tenure track to dependent care assistance.

No matter how far we have lagged behind the European community, the American business community, or any other community until now, it is time for the university community to institute progressive family policies for the twenty-first century. Let's keep talking to each other and, always, keep moving ahead, one step at a time, knowing that we are not alone and that together we have the possibility of effecting change—not only "underground" or "behind the scenes" but out in the open.

NOTE

An earlier version of this essay appears in *Concerns* 24.3 (Fall 1994): 13–19.

WORKS CITED

Kimball, Gayle. "No Money for a Family-Friendly Campus? No Problem!" *Women in Higher Education* (July 1993): 1–2.

Laughlin, Patricia, and Mary Jane Trout Barretta. "An Analysis of Maternity, Sick, and Family Leave Policies at Sixteen Major Research Universities." Paper presented at the International Conference for Women in Higher Education, El Paso, Tex., Jan. 8, 1990.

Domestic Partnership Benefits at the University of Minnesota

Greta Gaard

In the fall of 1993, employees at the University of Minnesota received domestic partnership benefits that purportedly extended to gays and lesbians the same rights and privileges enjoyed by heterosexual married couples. By February 1994 problems had already begun to surface. If they are not fully addressed, a lawsuit in the name of gay and lesbian employees may be filed against the state of Minnesota. To understand the problems, however, one must look at the context and the history of gay and lesbian rights in Minnesota.

Minnesota: Land of Ten Thousand Progressives

Variously attributed to either the severe winters or the Scandinavian diet of lefse and lutefisk, Minnesota has a history rich with political activism and progressive thinking. In that tradition, and particularly since 1970, the Twin Cities has been the site of increasing visibility for gays and lesbians, inspiring similar activism in outlying cities such as St. Cloud and Duluth. In 1973, legislation made it legal to be gay or lesbian in the Twin Cities, and although the city of St. Paul (the state's capitol, considered less progressive than Minneapolis) attempted to revoke that legislation in 1978 and again in 1991, it was upheld.

The movement for gay and lesbian rights gained strength when a gay man and a lesbian joined forces in the state senate. Since the mid-seventies a professor of history at the University of Minnesota, Allen

Greta Gaard is an associate professor of humanities at Fairhaven College, Western Washington University.

Spear, has served in the state senate and is currently its vice president. Since the early eighties Karen Clark has served in the state house of representatives. Their efforts for gays and lesbians received additional support in the late eighties when Brian Coyle, an openly gay city councilman, became vice president of the Minneapolis city council. Their united efforts, coupled with popular support, brought about domestic partnership registration for Minneapolis residents in the fall of 1990 and health benefits for city employees in August 1993. The following month, the Minneapolis school board extended full health care coverage to same-sex and opposite-sex domestic partners.

These 1993 rulings were made possible as a result of statewide human rights legislation. On April 1, 1993, Governor Arne Carlson signed into law a bill to include sexual orientation as a protected class in the Minnesota Human Rights Act, making Minnesota the eighth state in the United States to offer such rights (along with Wisconsin, Massachusetts, Vermont, New Hampshire, California, Hawaii, and New Jersey). And later that same month, graduate students at the University of Minnesota hosted the third annual national queer studies conference.

In addition to this cultural context, the University of Minnesota also functions in an academic context that transcends state boundaries. The examples of the University of Massachusetts at Amherst, Stanford, the University of Michigan, and others inspired faculty at the University of Minnesota to move toward claiming rights for ourselves. Initially a select committee on gay, lesbian, and bisexual concerns was appointed by the president, Nils Hasselmo, in October 1990, and worked for two years to gather statements from students, civil service employees, and faculty about the campus climate for gays and lesbians. In November 1993, just a few months after gays and lesbians in Minnesota were guaranteed full human rights by state law, the committee issued *Breaking the Silence: Final Report of the Select Committee on Lesbian, Gay, and Bisexual Concerns,* containing five recommendations proposed and passed at the University of Minnesota:

1. Establish a Gay, Lesbian, Bisexual, and Transgender (GLBT) Programs Office.
2. Provide a full benefits and privileges package for the families and children of gay and lesbian employees.
3. Establish a Gay and Lesbian Studies Program.
4. Develop educational training programming on gay, lesbian, bisexual, and transgender issues and concerns.
5. Update all printed publications and materials to reflect diversity in sexual orientation.

By 1996, the year before I left the university as an associate professor, four out of five of these recommendations had been fully or partially implemented, though the development of a GLBT Studies Program lagged behind. While these recommendations are being enacted universitywide, implementation focuses primarily on the Twin Cities campus. Employees at the coordinate campuses of Crookston, Duluth, and Morris may enjoy the same employee benefits and will eventually receive updated university publications, but their campus climates are more in tune with the small towns where they are located and less receptive to change.[1]

Domestic Partnership Benefits In/Action

The University of Minnesota seems genuine in its concern for the rights of gay and lesbian employees; however, it has not been entirely effective in delivering them. The responsibility lies not only with the university but also with the state and with the health care providers, whose policies seldom include same-sex partners and their dependent children. Delivering truly equal employee benefits to gays and lesbians at the University of Minnesota will require changes in state legislation and state tax laws. Meanwhile, the university has attempted to enact its own benefits policy with varying levels of success.

On October 6, 1993, gay and lesbian employees received a notice from the employee benefits program inviting our applications to register our domestic partners by signing and returning an affidavit. Upon its receipt, we would be sent information about reimbursements for health care benefits for the fall quarter.

Signing the affidavit meant that the domestic partners declared themselves "domestic partners, *as established by the following criteria*" (emphasis mine). What followed was a list of criteria that my partner Shawn and I read with increasing trepidation. I had assumed the list would read like heterosexual couples' marriage vows and was surprised by its length and detail. Shawn and I were satisfied with our partnership; would our private agreement satisfy the University of Minnesota? We read the list anxiously:

1. We are engaged in a long term committed relationship and intend to remain together indefinitely.

2. We are not married and neither of us has any other domestic partners.

3. We are the same sex and for this reason are unable to marry each other under Minnesota law.

4. We are at least 18 years of age and have the capacity to enter into a contract.

What a relief—so far, we were thoroughly qualified to be involved with each other. Imagine our dismay at the next criterion:

5. We share a residence.

Certainly this criterion was our dream. Two years of commuting 150 miles each way between Minneapolis and Duluth was exhausting and financially draining for both of us. The year before I had been able to arrange a single quarter research leave that allowed us to live together for six wonderful months. However, neither of us had been able to find jobs in the other's city and we were just beginning to accept the probability of having to relocate. Heterosexual couples face this two-career commuting as well—but their relationship is seen as valid nonetheless.

After discussing how to satisfy the "residence" criterion, we decided to leave two of my bookcases and a dresser at Shawn's house when I returned to Duluth, and I would continue to pay a portion of her mortgage. We thought the university would be pleased and read on:

6. We are jointly responsible to each other for the necessities of life. If asked, we could document at least three of the following items as evidence of our joint responsibility:
   a. a joint mortgage or joint tenancy on a residential lease;
   b. a joint bank account;
   c. joint liabilities such as credit cards or car loans;
   d. joint ownership of significant property;
   e. durable property or health care powers of attorney;
   f. naming each other as primary beneficiary in wills, life insurance policies, or retirement annuities;
   g. written agreements or contracts regarding our relationship showing mutual support obligations or joint ownership of assets acquired during the relationship.

More financial criteria—was ours a relationship or a business? While we had already named each other in our wills and in life insurance, this criterion prompted us to complete forms giving each other durable powers of attorney for health care and for finances. There still remained the problem of "ownership" and "liabilities," both of which have been out of the question, given our situation as commuters. After more debate, we decided to buy a couch together on our credit cards and hoped that this qualified as *significant property.* We were relieved to find that the last two criteria posed no formidable challenge:

7. We are not related by blood closer than permitted under Minnesota marriage laws.
8. The children identified above qualify as dependents under IRS regulations.

We had come to the end of the list. We were qualified to be involved with each other. What was missing, we wondered? Surprisingly, there was nothing on the list about "love"—or, barring that, "homosexual activity," supposedly the real reason we had to register as domestic partners instead of simply taking out a marriage license. All in all, it was a curious experience. We replied and, three weeks later, Shawn received a Domestic Partner Identification Card. Fortunately it didn't list her as "Mrs. Gaard."

On November 3, with the ID card, we received a memo instructing us how to file for fall quarter health care reimbursement. We were dismayed to learn that this procedure would be repeated each term and that reimbursement would be mailed in March, six months after we had paid the insurance premium. Seeking some answers, I stopped in the employee benefits office and was told that the details and timing of reimbursement had yet to be worked out. Given that this was a new policy, I was satisfied with the explanation. I was not satisfied, however, with the office worker's informing me that I was lucky to be receiving these benefits at all. For some reason I had assumed that the people handling domestic partner benefits had undergone some kind of "unlearning homophobia" training. I realized I had been mistaken.

The Problems

In January 1994—just three months after *Breaking the Silence* was published and its recommendations were passed—64 people had registered with the university's Employee Benefits office as domestic partners. Of these, 19 had registered for dental coverage and 16 for medical reimbursement. Between 1994 and 1997, 163 employees had registered their domestic partnerships, with 141 registered as of October 1997 (64 faculty and 77 civil service employees). Of these, only 21 registered for medical reimbursement and 36 for dental insurance.[2] The disparity between those who register their domestic partnerships and those who actually file for benefits attests to the important social and psychological benefits derived from institutional recognition and visibility—benefits that cost the university virtually nothing. But those of us who do file for benefits continue to encounter the following problems:

1. We have to pay for health care insurance up front and then wait for reimbursement. Not everyone can comfortably come up with three hundred dollars, which is what Shawn and I have had to pay for her quarterly health care coverage.

2. The reimbursement from the university counts as taxable income.

3. Employees cannot put money into a health care reimbursement account, where it would be considered pretax dollars.

4. Since the university is forced to offer us reimbursement rather than actual coverage, we have to buy health insurance as individuals rather than get a less expensive group rate. Moreover, individuals with preexisting conditions may not be able to obtain coverage or the coverage costs may be prohibitively high.

5. A heterosexual couple with stepchildren can resolve insurance problems by having the stepparent adopt them, but same-sex couples cannot adopt their partner's children without invalidating their partner's legal parental rights. Under current university health care policy, only the employee's domestic partner can be insured, not her or his children.

In each of these cases, the coverage offered to same-sex couples is not equivalent to that offered heterosexual couples. Changing these circumstances goes beyond the power of the university and will require new statewide legislation. Gays and lesbians at the University of Minnesota are generally encouraged by these attempts at equality. Therefore, if a lawsuit is filed, it will not be aimed at the university but rather at the state, where the next level of change needs to take place.

NOTES

An earlier version of this essays appears in *Concerns* 24.3 (Fall 1994): 25–30.

1. Beth Zemsky, "GLBT Program Offices: A Room of Our Own," *The New Lesbian Studies,* ed. Bonnie Zimmerman and Toni A. H. McNaron (New York: Feminist Press, 1996), 209.

2. These statistics are from Beth Zemsky, personal communications, Feb. 4, 1994, and Oct. 7, 1997.

WORK CITED

Select Committee on Lesbian, Gay, and Bisexual Concerns. *Breaking the Silence: Final Report of the Select Committee on Lesbian, Gay, and Bisexual Concerns.* 1993.

Teaching, Research, Service: The Impact of Adoption

Penny Schine Gold

Part of the acculturation to professional life that we undergo in graduate school and, perhaps most intensely, in the early years of teaching is to make a separation between personal life and professional persona. To be "professional" is to be calm, collected, distant, serious, and always working. The women's movement has long challenged the supposed separation of the "personal" and the "political"; I will examine the fruits—in one person's life—of also breaking boundaries between the "personal" and the "professional."

By the end of my first year in graduate school, a year marked by the deep disruption of the invasion of Cambodia, I decided that I could fit into the graduate school regime only if I shaped the subject of my research according to my new and intense interest in feminism. The resulting focus on the history of medieval women was, for me, a long-successful strategy for integrating personal concerns with professional life—in my research, teaching, and collegial networks. But fifteen years after that initial decision, the experience of adopting and rearing a child prompted a new kind of intrusion of personal experience into the professional domain.

The adoption was sudden and a surprise. After eight years on a waiting list for an older child, my husband and I had put aside the hope for children and gone on with life. But then came a phone call telling us we could pick up our three-week-old infant in four days. We brought Jeremy home on December 23, 1985, leaving me nine days to

Penny Schine Gold is a professor of history at Knox College.

experience, uninterruptedly, the profound delight of a new life added to mine. It didn't occur to me to ask for a leave of absence or a reduction in teaching load. We couldn't do without my salary (my husband was in graduate school), and there were no paid leaves. And I hadn't given birth to this new child, so had no physical disability that might give me time off from work. In fact, no female faculty member had gone on maternity leave in the ten years that I had been at Knox.[1] So I plunged into the term. I feel sorry, in retrospect, for the students in my courses that term, as they certainly could not compete with the enchantment of the baby. After that first term (ten weeks), I found myself ready to pay attention to my students again, and my life began to take on its new shape as teacher-and-parent. And I became determined to help shape a parental leave policy for Knox that would give all new parents—fathers and adoptive mothers as well as birth-giving mothers—paid leave. In the wake of my experience, even while relatively easy—I became a parent after tenure, after my first book was published, and at a time when my husband had a flexible schedule and could share parenting equally with me—the structure that made me try to "do it all" seemed unfeeling, cruel.[2] I wanted to contribute to the construction of a community in which parents would automatically be offered leaves—where leaves would be seen as a good thing for all involved, for the college community as well as for the parents and children.

I collected sample policies from other colleges and passed them along to members of the college's Executive Committee, who were also concerned to have a policy in place. Although a commitment was made orally by the dean (who chairs this committee), nothing was put in writing and the availability of leave for fathers was not clear. When I was later elected to the Executive Committee, I put the issue back on the agenda and kept pushing. The faculty on the committee were all in favor of such a policy, though it was not a priority item to all. The dean was sympathetic to a policy, but was reluctant to write it down.[3] Although it took two years, the committee and the dean finally worked out a policy for the faculty handbook in 1990 and the committee issued guidelines for its implementation (see the appendix for both documents). I felt like a broken record whenever I asked us to turn our attention again to the issue of parental leave, but I stuck with it because my experience convinced me of its urgency. I also felt free to risk the antagonism my persistence sometimes caused because I was tenured and because, not planning another adoption, I was not acting in self-interest.

The policy has since been used for numerous leaves. On our six-courses-over-three-terms teaching load, fathers and adoptive mothers get one course off; birth-giving mothers get two, taken either as one full term off or two terms teaching only one course per term. The dean has been generous in the timing of these leaves, giving fall term off, for example, to a woman who gave birth in June. While the burgeoning birth rate has meant more replacement costs than the dean had anticipated and the policy has not provided the edge in recruiting new faculty that he had hoped for, the college remains committed to the policy. It gives a clear sign that the college cares about the family life of its faculty, both male and female. There is no going back.

My efforts on behalf of this policy is one example of how my personal experience influenced my professional activity, here the "service" aspect of my work. It has also influenced my teaching and my research.

As an instant parent (and as an older parent, whose friends had teenagers, not babies) I relied heavily on advice books. While Penelope Leach, Eda Le Shan, Adele Faber, and Elaine Mazlich (my personal favorites) all write about raising children, the more experience I had with a child, the more obvious it was to me that similar strategies could be applied to students. No one teaches us in graduate school how to motivate students or how to enlist their cooperation. But learning about a two year old's need for at least limited autonomy taught me much about college students' parallel need. I prescribe much less now in my courses and structure in choices. To my child I say, "Do you want apple juice or orange juice?" (instead of "Drink your juice"); to my students I say, "Do you want to write two book reviews or one longer research paper?" In this and many other ways, I think I am a better teacher because of my struggles as a parent.

Parenting has also contributed to my research program. Not in the amount that is done—that has decreased—but in the choice of research subjects. As my book on medieval women was in press, I found my interests shifting to modern Jewish history. The early years of parenting coincided with years in which I was building a base of knowledge in an entirely new field. When I was ready, some four years later, to define a specific research project, a connection to the personal realm of child rearing presented itself. As I became involved, as a parent and Sunday school teacher, in the religious education of children, I was disturbed by the disjunction between the message of biblical texts and my values. At home and religious school I handled this by deletion—cutting out Bible stories from bedtime and from the religious school classroom. But then I realized that my discomfort was a piece of the central phenomenon in Jewish history that had come to preoccupy me in my scholarly reading—the transformation of Judaism and Jewish life in response to changed conditions in the modern world. I was not alone, among moderns, in my discomfort with the ethical framework of the Bible. I realized I could once again join my personal—now, parental—concerns with my research program by investigating the ways in which modern Jewish educators used and transformed the Bible in an attempt to "modernize" it for American Jewish children. My goal now is to complete this book before my child is beyond religious school age.

I am a different teacher, scholar, and academic community member because of my experience as a parent. More: being a parent has enhanced my contribution to the profession. My hope for the future is that the boundaries between the personal and the professional will be permeable in both directions, and that the academic profession may, some day, make us better parents.

APPENDIX: CHILDBIRTH AND PARENTAL LEAVE
KNOX COLLEGE
GALESBURG, ILLINOIS

PARENTAL LEAVE (from the *Faculty Handbook*)

The College's health plan allows six weeks of sick leave with pay. In interpreting this policy as it affects academic obligations, the College recognizes the special nature of faculty obligations on the term system by granting a birth giving parent one term of leave with pay, or a two-course reduction in teaching responsibility. For fathers or non-birth giving parents the policy is a one course reduction in teaching responsibility.

CHILDBIRTH LEAVE AND PARENTAL LEAVE FOR FACULTY (Executive Committee document, April 2, 1990)

Childbirth leave: A childbirth leave is comparable to other medical or disability leaves, and is intended to provide a woman time to recuperate physically from childbirth. Given her particular health circumstances (vaginal birth versus caesarian, complications or not), she might need more or less time, as could be ascertained by her physician. Some women also need time off from work before the birth, again depending on particular circumstances. Any such time is directly related to the physical condition of pregnancy and childbirth, and so is comparable to any other kind of medical needs (some of which are gender specific, like prostate surgery). Current health insurance covers such medical leaves. Length of the childbirth leave will be *six weeks at full pay* for a "normal" childbirth; more time will be given when medically needed.

Parental leave: This leave is meant to provide a parent time to focus on the needs of a new child and to have some respite from work in order to rearrange life to accommodate both child and work. Such a leave is not contingent on physical disability from childbirth and so is available to *all* parents: that is, adoptive mothers and all fathers, as well as birth mothers. Length of the leave will be *five weeks at full pay.*

Ways in which parental leave may be taken:

1) As five weeks of full-time leave. Combined with six weeks of childbirth leave, this would result in one full term of leave.

2) As ten weeks of half-time leave, thus the teaching of one course instead of two.

3) As five weeks of full-time leave, with another five weeks taken without pay, resulting in one-term's effective leave.

Details of how a parental leave will be taken will be worked out between the parent, the department, and the Dean. In the case where both parents of a child work for the College, a five-week parental leave may be taken by both.

NOTES

1. The one faculty woman who bore a child during this time was a part-time language instructor. She had another faculty member cover her class for a couple of weeks, and was then back in the classroom.

2. The stress of "doing it all" is compounded by an expectation that family life will not intrude on one's professional life. I'd like a portable crib and an infant carrier delivered to the offices of new faculty parents; many mundane chores of academic life can be done in the company of an infant. We need more babies on campus even if they cry occasionally.

3. The dean's reluctance to publicize the policy in writing was based, I think, on a concern for flexibility, as well as a (justified) discomfort over the dissimilarity the policy created between faculty and staff benefits, an inequity still not addressed, though it is on the agenda.

On Learning Not to Love
the Oedipus Complex

David Leverenz

Several years ago, two male col-
leagues in different parts of the country, Dan Cottom and Gordon
Hutner, told me they had made an identical Freudian slip in the classroom. While they were teaching one of Foucault's most well-known
books, they each referred to it as "Discipline and Publish." The pressure to make it, and therefore to make it new, impinges on our minds
with a quiet relentlessness. "Being a feminist literary scholar," as Molly
Hite puts it, requires "keeping abreast of the current repudiations"
(125). A few years ago Stanley Fish was quoted in *Newsweek* with the
male version of Hite's formulation: "Now critics have to retool every
eighteen months" (Prescott 50).

When I received tenure at Rutgers University in 1975, I had published just one article, with another in press and two accepted. Rutgers
rewarded me for my ardent commitment to teaching at its newest
college and for my promise as a scholar.

By the early 1980s, Rutgers was already witnessing the fruits of the
buyer's market, in the arrival of the radical yuppies—a new generation
of extraordinarily smart and ambitious careerists, several of whom soon
zipped past me in professional reputation as well as productivity.

At the same time, I had made some life choices, particularly
parenting choices, which demanded a daily attentiveness at odds with
writing well and prolifically. When I married my wife in 1973, two years
Before Tenure, I became an instant stepfather of two girls, Allison and

---

David Leverenz is a professor of English at the University of Florida.

Elizabeth, then nine and seven years old. Shortly after tenure, I coaxed, cajoled, and finally convinced Anne to have two more children. Since Anne was about to change careers, from early childhood education to law school, she was reluctant. We finally agreed on a deal: for the first few years, tenured Daddy would put writing on a back burner to do the lion's share of the weekday child rearing. And so Trevor and Nell were born, in 1978 and 1981.

Was I a good male feminist, with children of my own and five hundred diapers a year? Not quite. Even as I consciously chose to postpone my career ambitions, my desire for "children of my own," as I thought of it, turned out to be a more intimate form of the competition I witnessed all around me, and in myself. To be a good stepfather to Allison and Elizabeth made me, in my own mind, "number three," after Anne and their father, Peter, who lived nearby. I wanted kids for whom I could be number one Dad.

I've had to realize how much I loved the Oedipus complex, in both its professional and its familial forms. In the first years of our marriage, I would occasionally explode in anger, particularly when Allison or Elizabeth had not stopped doing something I had gently, kindly, quietly, self-effacingly intimated I didn't like, and sometimes when I hadn't said anything at all but had been feeling irritated for a while.

It took me a good many conversations with Anne to realize that what I took for a real self was modeled on my father, an eminent corporate research scientist and workaholic who when he felt his dominance at stake, even in conversations at the dinner table, would tense up his whole body in fury. Dad's anger manifested and restored his power. It also blocked the voicing of family conflicts until I and my sisters had reached adulthood.

For thirty years I had always been a "good boy," while the hidden Oedipal boy-man bided his time. In my twenties, a child had drawn a picture of me and put a third ear where my mouth should have been. But marriage had given me a license not to be quite so good, all the time. I could be angry at last, and I wouldn't feel squashed or abandoned.

Fortunately for everyone, I had not inherited or assimilated my father's need for control. I thrive on mutuality, in the classroom and more intimately with the people I love. As I entered more fully into my new family's atmosphere of open talking, shared decisions, unstinting nurturing, and adventurous living, my need to erupt receded. In retrospect, the two older girls helped to train me for the much more stressful parenting that came with Trevor and Nell. Now, when we talk about all this, Allison and Elizabeth say they don't even remember my explosions. I do, vividly.

My parenting of Trevor and Nell—more than a traditional father, much less than a traditional mother—proved to be not only the second stage but also a fulcrum that reoriented my values. Parenting affected my reading of American literature and made me see the workings of manhood in me, my friends, and my daily life. Without that experience, I never would have written a book about manhood, since my deviation from the traditionally manly mode of workplace self-definition helped me to see how my competitiveness and my desire to be number one were not the "real me" but an accommodation to a script narrated by my culture and enacted by my parents. Helping to nurture Trevor and Nell taught me a down-home Lacanian truth: that one's most fundamental desires can be imposed narratives.

Being a parent of very young children has made me jettison much of Freud and Lacan, however, particularly their universalizing of the Oedipus complex. I've seen in myself the beginnings of that complex, from the father's side. Far from being an ahistorical human given, it's instituted by fathers who feel entitled to claim first priority for mother's attention, sexually and otherwise.

Anne and I let our children climb into bed with us at any hour of the night, whenever they wanted to, even when they were over ten years old. At times I resented this; I felt shunted aside. I also resented Anne's insistence on never locking our bedroom door. My sexual frustration was part of a more unacknowledged desire to be the most important person in her life—to be number one, in yet another manifestation of that desire—even as I acknowledged how sex and friendships as well as career had to be put on hold.

The locked door, the primal scene, and the Oedipus complex, those basic staples of the Freudian system that seduced me in graduate school for such obvious reasons, reflect the father's need, the father's will, and the father's presumption. Enforcing a scarcity economy of emotions, they validate a family pattern in which the woman tries to balance her two mothering roles, to her children and to her husband. For the traditional wife, this is a no-win situation, since, as Virginia Woolf memorably described that role in *A Room of One's Own,* she has to mirror her husband at twice life-size. For the traditional husband, he can win only through dominance, by turning the mother's daytime nurturing into nighttime scarcity. He wins at a price, by cauterizing the needs and emotions flowing between him and his children.

Trevor and Nell have never experienced the locked door, and they've encountered a dominating Daddy at very infrequent intervals. So far as I can tell, neither our son nor our daughter has Oedipal dynamics. Nell did suffer from mother's relative absence in the early years, when Anne worked late hours to establish herself as an attorney. Anne's need to reestablish intimate contact with our children at night exacerbated strains between us, as I wished for more of her undivided attention. And that helped to bring on my third stage, really ours, when we moved to Florida in 1985 to embark on what Anne called "our midlife adventure."

In effect we were downshifting, ten years before the phrase became fashionable. Both Anne and I felt in a perpetual state of burnout. By then she was a deputy attorney general and making as much as I was. We had money, but almost no time for each other, and she keenly missed being central to the children's formative years. We both felt the need for a less toxic environment, emotionally as well as physically. While Anne immediately fell in love with Gainesville's subtropical profusions, I experienced a more relaxed intellectual atmosphere, where I could think my thoughts at my own pace without feeling second-rate if I hadn't published an article in a year or so. I said aloud, "Maybe down here I could start to like myself."

They made me a full professor, four years before my second book. I felt suitably senior, at last. By moving a good many rungs down the status ladder of graduate English departments, I had found a balanced life in a health-giving place. I could continue to give abundant time and thought to our children, while Anne and I at last had time to rediscover each other.

Every weekday night Anne and I become a homework support service. As they sit at the kitchen counter, reading and writing, or bantering, raging, belching, squabbling, and giggling, I sometimes think how utterly different this is from my childhood, when each child worked in a separate room, alone. When Trevor or Nell calls me a jerk, I occasionally wonder what my father would have said, and how he would have said it. Then I remind myself of my permanent Oedipal triumph: I've been the father I never had.

So, what lessons from all this? First, a man who thinks of himself primarily as a workplace competitor needs two prompters: a strong spouse to help resocialize him and an unacknowledged part of himself that wants to break out of his scripted narrative. Even with both, it's still a struggle. Anne made the demands clear, early on: no work during evenings and on weekends—that's family time. We both occasionally violate the letter of that, but not its spirit. Second, equal partnering and parenting really do mean sacrificing ambition to some degree. Though the experience has probably enhanced the originality of what I've written, it has nipped five or ten essays and maybe a book in the bud. Camping through the Southwest or through Europe does not make for dazzling close readings and matrix-shifting arguments. Third, parenting brings rewards different in kind from the pleasures of cultural capital.

One of the upper circles of Hell has a ring reserved for those who give unsolicited advice; it's an intermediate form of pride. Nonetheless, I have several suggestions. For partners who are parenting young children: don't squeeze out more computer time in the early morning hours. Instead, make more time for each other than Anne and I managed. For partners considering having children: have two, not just one. After the hellish first four or five years, they start to take care of each other in wonderful ways. And for men who are anything like me: don't do it until you have tenure. On that ground, you can grow your own narratives.

WORKS CITED

Hite, Molly. "'Except Thou Ravish Mee': Penetrations into the Life of the (Feminine) Mind." *Changing Subjects: The Making of Feminist Literary Criticism.* Ed. Gayle Greene and Coppélia Kahn. New York: Routledge, 1993. 121–28.

Prescott, Peter S. "Learning to Love the PC Canon." *Newsweek* Dec. 24, 1990: 50.

Staying Whole

David Chin

I've been a parent for nine years under three sets of conditions: as a laboratory researcher for a pharmaceutical corporation, as a graduate student, and as a tenure-track assistant professor of English. Most men in the West are socialized to see work as the most important part of their lives, and during the past nine years I have had to reevaluate and consciously redirect my focus to my daughter while struggling with my personal growth and goals. My experience as a father has been shaped by this as well as by my experience as a child raised in a two-parent family during the fifties and sixties.

Since I was born in 1953, my formative years came before the resurgence of the women's movement in the late sixties. My parents were a racially mixed couple and led in many ways the typical life of their generation. My father was a machinist, toolmaker, and eventually assistant foreman for a company that manufactured machines that print the outside of beer cans and yogurt cups. He was hard-working, sober, monogamous, church-going, and, paradoxically, as loving as he was inarticulate about emotional matters. He was sensitive enough to communicate to me a suggestion of the depth of his character and the depth of his love for my siblings and me. Most often, though, he was either worn out at the end of the day or inarticulate in an affectionate kind of way. I have tried to express my sense of this loss in a poem:

David Chin is an assistant professor of English at Pennsylvania State University at Wilkes-Barre.

Sleeping Father

My father sits in his chair and snores.
Inhaling, he rasps like an anchor chain
rattling off a ship, dropping into the sea.
When he exhales, waves hiss on distant shores.

In his dream, he carries the kite
his uncle made for him and walks the village path
thinking of his father who sailed for America years ago.
I wonder if it has to be this way with fathers.

As he sleeps with his head tipped back,
his mouth half open, behind shut eyelids
the frailest of objects climbs the sky
and a string slides through his fingers.

My mother nurtured four children and managed the emotional well-being of the household. That my mother was white shifted the power dynamics of the household in ways that make it difficult for me to gain perspective. What role did cultural differences play amid gender role differences? Did my father rely on my mother to instill my siblings and myself with distinctly "American" social skills? Was my father's masculinity assimilated or ancestral? Internalized racism and media stereotypes of Asian men as slightly effeminate relative to a white male norm coupled with my own hybrid status complicated my relationship with my father. At the same time I never doubted my father's complete and self-sacrificing devotion to our family. I still wonder how he was able to make himself available, albeit in a limited way, to his children. Although ambitious for us, especially concerning education, he was never overbearing. In some ways I was freer to create my own masculine identity than my peers, whose fathers pushed them into little league or football. What saved my father for me, I think, was that my father was sensitive enough before I was born to have a nervous breakdown and recover; he was capable of experiencing the power of his emotions. Somehow this was conveyed to me. In many ways, as a parent, I am my father.

After an undergraduate degree in biology, two years in the machine shop with my father, a year as a laboratory technician, and an M.F.A. in creative writing, I married Lorna (also a laboratory technician) and we continued to work for pharmaceutical corporations for the next few years until a childhood injury to Lorna's back suddenly worsened, leaving her virtually bedridden for six months. We delayed having our daughter, Rachel, until we were financially established and Lorna's health had improved. After Rachel was born, Lorna remained mostly at home as primary caregiver.

I often worked late in the lab—long hours in the interests of research projects is the way salaried employees are expected to demonstrate their commitment to the corporation. Those evenings I was home, I worked on biweekly research progress reports, helped with the endless round of housework and child care, and adjusted to a more secondary role in Lorna's world. Rachel's fussy time began when I got home from work and lasted until about one in the morning. She was soothed only by being continuously held or nursed.

Holding Rachel, I felt a quiet awe and sense of responsibility— whole new vulnerabilities. I thought: we have to get these first crucial years right. I wanted to be the "good family man" my father was, but felt unprepared and also squeezed by the demands of my work. My father's blue-collar job often required that he work overtime and left him physically drained, but at the end of the day he could put the job down. My work followed me. Although my mother had occasionally involved me in the care of my younger brother and sister and I read the same new-parent books as Lorna (an only child), I nevertheless deferred to Lorna's judgment on the best way to parent.

Although I was dutiful and involved, I never felt fully prepared or confident as a father during Rachel's early years. Lorna always seemed better attuned to Rachel's needs and desires. At times, I felt both relieved and guilty to let Lorna carry the larger burden for Rachel's emotional and physical care. I understood Lorna's greater sensitivity as the product of gendered differences in our respective socialization. At other times, I felt I was making the best of it. Despite an awareness that Lorna and I had fallen into fairly traditional roles, we saw no easy means to escape.

When Rachel was two, I began to experience the beginnings of a midlife crisis that precipitated a career change. I had fulfilled most of my father's working-class requirements for masculine success: a good career, a good marriage, a home, and a start on a family. But I'd reached a career plateau in science; I felt stifled, unfulfilled, and condemned to a future that would be a stale repetition of the past. I'd bought the stereotype that Asian Americans belong in the sciences, even though I wanted to write poetry and teach. I recognized that the person I was— depressed and resentful—carried over into my fathering. Although it would be wrong to say I changed careers for any reason other than my need for a more fulfilling life, I nevertheless hoped that changing careers would make me a better parent.

When I left my lab job I couldn't sleep for two days; I stayed up pacing, processing grief, fear, and an incredible sense of failure—a sense that, acting on a self-indulgent narcissistic fantasy, I had failed in my responsibilities to my family. From a working-class perspective, I risked throwing everything away. Lorna, however, was incredibly supportive of my decision, and I developed a whole new level of respect for her.

I believe I am a better parent for changing careers. If I hadn't depended on Lorna to economically support our family, given up the ego investment in an established career to start another, and learned how patience and attunement are needed in the classroom, I don't think I would be as capable as I am of warmth and tenderness in my interactions with Rachel. In terms of lost income and benefits my five-year return to graduate school probably cost a quarter of a million dollars, but I like who I am now. This counts for something.

Further, teaching literature and composition engages me in parenting issues through my interactions with students, literary texts, my own poetry, and criticism because they force me to work on my moral and emotional growth. Teaching fulfills my need for generativity; it legitimizes the need to nurture the intellectual growth and career aspirations of young people.

As a creative writer, I am interested in the psychology of creative impulse if only to try to make sense of the challenges brought on by the decisions Lorna and I made. Poetry is a space where feelings that make me and other men uncomfortable as we gradually learn to relax our capacity for repression—a fear of failure, narcissistic rage, aggressive sexual fantasies, infantile longings, midlife grief—can be explored and shaped. Male socialization compresses the spring of hoarded repressed pain, rage, and grief. Unless these emotions are allowed to uncoil, the flip side of all this repression—a capacity for empathy, genuine warmth, the pleasure of nurturing, connectedness, dependency needs, generativity—all the emotions many men have never learned to fully articulate or value—are lost.

The acceptance and admiration men are trained to expect within the dyadic mother-son relationship as the reward for a warrior/breadwinner's accomplishment sets us up for disappointment. When we discover that we are at emotional arm's length from the world our wives and children share (not to mention our own emotions), nothing will fill that void. No consumer consolation prizes—houses, cars, boats, hobbies—and no career accomplishment—salary attainments, promotions, books, awards—will replace what was lost. Our early socialization often leaves us inadequately prepared to provide much of what our wives and children really long for, emotional availability. Marriages and families crack under this strain.

I think that psychically we relive our own childhood as our children experience theirs. Fathers are caught between the unfinished business we have with our childhood socialization and the simultaneous necessity of learning how to parent. Unless you are totally incapacitated by mourning or the incapacity to mourn that accompanies the resurfacing of your childhood, your relationship to your child is enriched as you become more emotionally available. The intellectual is easy; the gut transformations are slow. Despite my belief that there is nothing more individual and personal than my relationship with Rachel, I also believe more is required. Overcoming the limitations of male socialization requires emotional work motivated by an ethics of equality between the sexes in order to provide children with a wider (and less gender bound) range of role models. It also means finding ways to break out of the gendered division of labor within marriage.

The shift in psychological thinking from sexual drive theories to an ego psychology that emphasizes individuation, separation, and autonomy as crucial to childhood developmental processes has had a powerful impact on how I think about parenting. Chodorow's description of the pattern for the reproduction of fathering in *The Reproduction of Mothering* is instructive. Is a father's role limited to the disrupter of the dyadic mother-daughter relationship and bringer of symmetry to a daughter's Oedipal project? Does a traditional father's inconsistent or sporadic emotional availability socialize his daughter to accept emotionally distant men as partners later in life? What constitutes good-enough fathering?

It is real work for men to continually refocus on the importance of family and children—the real work of learning to become attuned to the emotional world of a child. Rachel's world as I perceive it is not the same world as Lorna perceives it. I continually have to do the work of reality testing—the work of relationship building, of learning what is important to Rachel's world. Here again, I'm caught between career demands and the reality that Rachel cannot be picked up and put down between career projects, on weekends, over semester breaks; she requires an ongoing relationship.

I work at communicating what I'm feeling in simple ways with her, though her favorite play activity with me is roughhousing. Rachel's playtimes with Lorna, however, involve elaborate playtalk where she brings unconsciously those emotional concerns she doesn't feel quite comfortable sharing with me. Rachel says, "It's between me, Mom, and the back fence, Dad." I feel I'm missing the opportunity for the emotional attunement this affords. But Lorna tells me I've always been good at the unconditional loving part of parenting—accepting without rushing in to fix a problem, avoiding the overly intrusive quick fix. As Rachel wrestles with taking on more responsibility for her actions and with our expectation that she find her own terms for defining a problem, I'm getting called upon to provide reassurance and support in ways and areas that are more exclusively our own. I also find myself saying—more often than Lorna—things like, "If Rachel doesn't learn to obey these rules now, develop self-discipline, she will have one rough time in the 'real world.'" Instead of concentrating on present needs, men bound by traditional gender roles focus on preparing a child for a future career.

As a father in what looks like a traditional two-parent heterosexual family system, I know I inhabit a mythic structure in which men have enjoyed real economic and social privilege at a tremendous moral and psychic cost. I also know I am far less at risk than academic colleagues who are mothers on the tenure track. It is too often assumed that women who have children before tenure are making a "career mistake." Administrators want junior faculty members (like our corporate counterparts) relentless in the pursuit of research or creative excellence to win fame and visibility for the institutions we serve. The cultural premium put on the ability to manipulate abstractions over parenting will continue to reproduce itself in the current climate.

Wanting to reject patriarchy and the gendered division of labor force men dissatisfied with the status quo to join women at the margins. I suspect that for many men this calls for living beyond their emotional means. I know I feel squeezed by this phenomenon. When I think of my male mentors in graduate school, I have a sense of their unspoken deep regret as well as, on occasion, their knowing and unspoken support for my struggle to keep career, marriage, and family intact; however, there really isn't much of a context within which to think about this as a man—men are socialized to tough it out, not seek support, and continually reinvent the wheel. As a father I need something more than exhortations to "open up."

So what has to change? At the very least academics need better and more fully available day care as well as greater flexibility within the tenure system. In part because we don't have such systems, Lorna and I decided not to have more children. When I ask myself whether the life choices we made were the best, I wonder whether they were both our choices. Did they cut off options Lorna might have pursued? Since our move to Pennsylvania Lorna has reentered the job market, but at its lower rungs. Our long-term commitment affords the chance of understanding and working to balance inequities over the long haul, but there are no easy answers.

In my own career, in contrast, I have been astonishingly fortunate. I have a more flexible schedule, the chance to explore work and family issues in my writing, more work at home where I can be a presence for Rachel, and more rewarding interactions with students and colleagues. Some of the same stupidities and injustices I've seen in the corporate world are present in the academy, but academics have the skills to articulate problems and a tenure system to protect them when they voice what they see. Unfortunately, junior faculty with children, especially women, are less likely to make it into those tenured ranks.

The currently overcrowded job market, budget cutbacks and retrenchments, multi-tiered systems of teaching assistants, part-time adjunct positions, fixed-term faculty, tenure-track and tenured faculty, increased course loads and class sizes, shrinking enrollments, and the shift to a more corporate style of university administration make for interesting times. The worsening climate will make it more difficult for parents in the academy, especially those on the lowest rungs of the hierarchy, to simultaneously advance a career and provide for the emotional and financial well-being of their children. Although I believe I'm working for more equity in my relationship with Lorna and Rachel, and I'm sensitive to the contradictions and injustices of the gendered division of labor and career advancement in and out of the academy, I'm still left counting the number of times I've said to Rachel, "I just can't right now" and the number of times I've reminded myself the chance won't come again, crossed my fingers, and took the time.

Creating the Family-Friendly Campus

Annette Kolodny

*The goals of the feminist movement
have not been achieved, and those who
claim we're living in a post-feminist era
are either sadly mistaken or tired of
thinking about the whole subject.*
—Margaret Atwood, Second Words

In August 1988, as a new dean with an emphatic mandate from the central administration to diversify the faculty by increasing the numbers of women and individuals from underrepresented groups in the tenure ranks, I needed incentives to attract the best and the brightest. In my view, I especially needed incentives to attract those younger assistant professors who would hear the tenure clock tick alongside their own (or a partner's) biological clock. When I made inquiries in the university's Human Resources Office, I was assured by a staff member that a recent campuswide survey indicated no immediate need for any additional child-care services. That office's distribution of information about private providers in the area met the current demand. Still, I remained concerned. In my own office, there was evidence of a range of child-care needs.

Even after we adjusted individual schedules and offered flextime options, on certain occasions—generally the state's grade school holidays or teacher in-service training days—our office looked like an elementary school, with a five year old cutting recycled paper into notepads, while a seven year old tried to change the color images on his mother's computer screen. Whether as single mothers or as the wives

Annette Kolodny is a professor of comparative cultural and literary studies at the University of Arizona.

of men with full-time jobs, several secretaries could not afford the loss in pay or the deduction of precious vacation time that would result from their staying home on scheduled school closings. And because university wage scales are chronically low, private day care was beyond their means. When their children were sick, however, these women had no choice but to lose a day's pay (or give up a paid vacation day) and stay home. No one else was available for caretaking.

I had also become aware of the little girl who spent her nights in the basement ladies' room of the student union. One evening, when my administrative assistant and I had worked late in that building, we encountered her, sprawled on the linoleum floor of the ladies' room entry, silently drawing with crayons on a large pad of white paper. She looked up and smiled when we addressed her—first in English, then in Spanish—but she responded to none of our questions. From members of the custodial staff, we learned that the girl, seven years old, slightly retarded and slow of speech, was the daughter of one of the women on the night crew cleaning team. The entire crew, along with the child's mother, took turns checking on her regularly. Together, the crew members had identified the bathroom as the safest place for her because, if left anywhere else, the child might wander off in search of water or toilet facilities and get lost. In about an hour, we were told, the girl would fall asleep, and her mother would cover her with a blanket. The mother was single and without any family in the area, one custodian volunteered, and the night shift job was the best she had been able to secure. Without it, she would be forced back on welfare. Finally, to quiet our obvious unease, the same custodian suggested that, if things went well, the mother might be reassigned to the day shift, and then a neighbor could be asked to take care of the child after school.

It was a chilling encounter, but it opened my eyes. I began to notice how often junior faculty women brought their infants or small children to class, and I watched young student parents—men and women alike—perched on the sills of open windows in ground-floor classrooms, trying to attend to the lecture within while also keeping their eye on a small child playing just outside. Seeking to understand how a campuswide child-care survey could generate data that so starkly contradicted my own observations, I learned that the questionnaire had been sent to a randomly selected group of faculty from the tenured and tenure-eligible ranks only. No staff or students had been included. Once I understood how the data had been compiled, it was no surprise to me that over 80 percent of the respondents expressed no urgency on the subject. The professoriat at the University of Arizona, like the professoriat nationwide, was still overwhelmingly white, male, and over fifty. Not only did the recipients of the questionnaire represent the demographics of the past but, in addition, the vast majority of those who responded were men who had never been primarily responsible for any child's daily care.

Campus sentiments on the subject of child care slowly changed during the years of my deanship, however. Organized faculty women's groups, staff women, student government leaders, and a few well-placed women administrators became increasingly vocal on the issue. And, with a transition in the president's and provost's offices, a new administration found itself pressured to look at the question anew. This time, "600 University of Arizona employees who currently use child care services" were surveyed (Hartmann 1). According to the front page story in the February 11, 1994, *Daily Wildcat,* "about half of the employees reported having problems with child care affecting their work responsibilities, while 57% reported having their work affected by someone else's child care problems" (Hartmann 1). The report accompanying the survey recommended an on-campus child-care facility "open for extended hours on weekdays and open on weekends to accommodate working parents and students" (Hartmann 4). Independent surveys by the university's Commission on the Status of Women estimated 2,203 child-care users in the employee population and "between 2,500 and 3,500 parents who are . . . students," all with different requirements, including needs for summer care, sick-child, and drop-in care facilities (Leibold 3).[1]

To be fair, the University of Arizona was not alone in its earlier inability to ask the right questions or to target the right audience for those questions. Like most of the nation's higher educational institutions, until quite recently Arizona's policymakers were rarely those who shouldered significant responsibility for family care—whether the care of children or the care of an aging parent—and a workplace constructed around a male wage earner with a supportive wife at home remained for them both familiar and comfortable. As a result, long after that model was no longer feasible, in everything from department meeting schedules to timetables for intellectual achievement, Arizona—like the rest of the academy—continued to operate on outdated assumptions of childless female workers and males with wives as primary caretakers for the family. Few senior administrators nationwide viewed family care issues as a pressing priority, even though predictions of two major demographic shifts should have caught their notice.

Those shifts are now upon us, and no workplace—certainly not academe—can turn away from the projection of the National Commission of Working Women that "by the year 2000, 80 percent of women in their prime childbearing years (between 25 and 44) will be in the labor force" (Coiner 213). Nor can any employer afford to ignore that, by the year 2025, a full 20 percent of the United States population will be 65 or older, and "nearly half of those will be 75 or older" (Park A40).

But while radically shifting demographics and the collective voices of women (and a few men) may finally be focusing campus administrators on a spectrum of family needs, the question of how to respond to those needs is being framed in an atmosphere of sliced budgets and demoralizing scarcity. Endless task forces and countless committees puzzle over how to finance benefits packages for domestic partners, how to pay for child-care centers, or, at state-supported campuses, how to subsidize on-site child care in the face of local laws that prohibit public entities from competing with the private sector. And because most central administrations have been unprepared for the rising demand for campus-based family services, they find themselves forced to respond before assessing what precisely is wanted or before determining how to ensure quality in the delivery of such services. Lacking sufficient hard data and without an adequate conceptual framework to guide them, discussions in deans' councils and presidents' cabinets thus degenerate into predictable debates over money and competing campus priorities while what is really at issue never surfaces. In other words, rather than face up to a complex set of challenges relating to the changing structures of the American family, the institutional focus remains fixed, almost exclusively, on dealing piecemeal with one or another manageable (and hopefully affordable) component—like maternity leave, child care, or domestic partner benefits.

The purpose of this essay is to add my voice to the voices of many others who now seek to enlarge the dialogue surrounding the evolving reshapings of family structures and the consequent redefinitions of family needs. Drawing primarily from my experience as an administrator at the University of Arizona, but drawing also from my acquaintance with activities on other campuses, I will try to offer some practical suggestions for the ways in which academic institutions can begin to address at least some of those needs. Having served on the statewide Commission on the Status of Women, created in the fall of 1989 by the Arizona Board of Regents to improve "the conditions of employment for women at the state's three public universities" (Arizona Board of Regents' Commission 4), I am convinced that the will exists to make the required accommodations. During the commission's two and a half years of fact-finding, it became clear to me that colleges and universities everywhere—large and small, residential and commuter—were responding to the same demographic shifts and were experimenting with a variety of strategies. That said, this essay makes no pretense to comprehensiveness. On the contrary, my highly selective recommendations are intended to add to, complement, or even highlight many efforts across the country. Above all else, however, this essay is aimed at renewing a creative activism in the face of complicated issues. As we race into the twenty-first century, our old ways of running a campus will no longer serve.

Mine is an improbable voice in these matters, I admit. Although happily married for over a quarter century, my husband and I have no children. And although I sometimes conferred with her doctors regarding her prescriptions and medical tests, I was never responsible, in any extended way, for caring for my mother. Even so, as I begin to look back upon a full, generally satisfying, and often frenzied life in academe, I find myself questioning which of these circumstances was really freely chosen and which the unacknowledged by-product of a career path that always demanded too much. Other women academics, I know, have broken under the strain of trying to do it all.

The urgency in this essay does not derive from personal experience, therefore, but it is certainly personally felt. Over the years, I have had too many conversations with bleary-eyed junior colleagues who tried, at the same time, to raise their children and to finish a book manuscript before tenure review. Nowadays, I regularly receive letters from women colleagues my own age—in their fifties—who tell me they eagerly contemplate early retirement because they are just too exhausted to go on.

That women in academe were in crisis became brutally apparent to me in 1986 when Lois Banner, Eileen Boris, Mary Kelley, Cecelia Tichi, Lillian Schlissel, and I designed a questionnaire to assess "the uneasy balance" between the "personal lives and [the] professional careers" of women who were members of the American Studies Association and the Organization of American Historians (Banner et al.). In answer to the question, "How do you find time to rest? to exercise? to maintain social contacts?" 25 percent "of the respondents indicated some degree of difficulty in finding time for one or more of these" (Banner et al. 6). As I wrote at the time, "typical responses to the question about rest were 'rarely,' to the one about exercise 'sporadically,' and to maintaining social contacts, 'marginally.'" The difficulties were acute for women with children, "whether they were single parents or part of a two parenting household" (Banner et al. 6). Sobered by what Joyce Antler called an "often disturbing picture of how women in the academy view their lives and careers" (25), I made the move into academic administration two years later, determined to work with students, staff, faculty, and other administrators in a shared effort to find institution-based solutions.

Women simply cannot be persons within the present system of work and family, and they can only rise to liberated personhood by the most radical and fundamental reshaping of the entire human environment in a way that redefines the very nature of work, family and the institutional expressions of social relations.
    —*Rosemary Radford Ruether,*
    Liberation Theology

To conceptualize what I am calling the "family-friendly campus" means *re*conceptualizing what we include in the term *family*. An urban single mother with a part-time job in the campus cafeteria, for example, may well find herself sharing child-care and food purchases with a nearby relative in similar circumstances. As the anthropologist Carol B. Stack observes, theirs may not be a traditional "co-residential" single family unit, but "the two households" clearly function "as a single domestic unit of cooperation" (552). In another nontraditional family configuration on my campus, a professor of classics has just taken into her home the critically ill mother of her former husband. Although the professor and her husband are long divorced and never had any children, still she maintains a loving relationship and wishes to care for the older woman in her last years. Consider also the department secretary, a single mother who has designated a close, gay, male friend and colleague as the legal father of her adopted child. As instances like these make clear, the family of the twenty-first century will no longer be identified solely by blood ties, by legalized affiliations, by cohabitation, or by heterosexual arrangements. As a result, benefits packages and family care policies narrowly designed around the model of the heterosexual nuclear family (or even the heterosexual extended family) invite legal challenges on the grounds of discrimination, and they increasingly prove themselves hopelessly anachronistic.

Ironically, anachronisms surface even when schools pursue such laudable programs as child care, tenure-clock delays, flextime, half-time tenure-track appointments, and family care leaves, because, too often, policy statements revert to a vocabulary that assumes rigidly gender-inflected family roles. By adopting the language of the so-called "special needs of women," or by designating only a single "primary caregiver" as eligible for benefits, college and university administrators (even if unintentionally) reinforce outdated family patterns and all but ignore the responsibilities of men in child rearing and family care. Indeed, *every* senior administrator of my acquaintance, male or female, unhesitatingly admits that the primary caregiver envisioned as eligible for leave to look after a sick child or an incapacitated family member is always *female*. In this regard, higher education administrators differ very little from their counterparts in the corporate workplace where "many CEOs still see careers as inherently masculine and parenting as inherently feminine" (Jones 56).

To be sure, some special provisions for women—like paid medical maternity leaves for childbirth and early infant care—must remain in place and be expanded. But all other family-sensitive policies, including provisions for infant care in cases of birth, adoption, or foster care placement or leaves to attend a sick family member, should be developed within the guidelines of Title VII of the 1964 Civil Rights Act and Title IX of the 1972 Education Amendments to that act, both of which declare unequivocally that campus workplace privileges must be accorded to women and to men equally. Legality, however, is not the only issue. With women coming into the academic work force at all levels in increasing numbers, it becomes a practical necessity to ensure those women's effective performance by tenaciously rejecting the notion that it is always and only women who bear the major responsibility for caretaking in the family.

Such notions are ubiquitous, of course. A 1987 study of corporate employees indicated that while there were no statistically significant differences in the hours that men and women devoted to the workplace, there were "major differences . . . in the amount of time spent on home chores and child care. Married female parents spent 40 hours at work, and an additional 45 hours in home chores and child care." Married male parents with full-time working partners, by contrast, spent an average of 44 hours at work, but only "14 hours in child care, and 11 hours in household chores" (Jones 56–57). The 1986 survey conducted jointly by the American Studies Association and the Organization of American Historians documented a similar situation in academe. Amid uniformly "poignant" remarks about child care and in answers crowded with anecdotes about physical exhaustion and career setbacks, women respondents revealed that "nearly forty percent of [them] . . . took on between seventy and one hundred percent of the responsibility for the care of their children" (Banner et al. 4). Younger, beginning graduate students noted that among their older, married peers, it was always the women "in the marriage who sacrifice" (Banner et al. 6).

Without question, these gender-based inequities must be countered by policies that allow—and more importantly *invite*—men to share in family care responsibilities. In defining those responsibilities, however, we dare not focus exclusively on infant and child care lest we ignore another major demographic shift: our society is aging. "By 2030," according to Denise Park, director of the Center for Applied Cognitive Aging Research at the University of Georgia, "the United States will actually have more older adults than children" (A40). While these statistics will surely force schools to develop enhanced life-long learning programs and perhaps even specialized degree programs for the elderly adult population, the statistics also predict that families of the twenty-first century will become increasingly responsible for the care of aging and infirm members. In anticipation of these changes, colleges and universities would be wise to look ahead and review benefits packages accordingly, while prudent financial planning is still possible. University medical centers and colleges of nursing might be brought in as prospective partners in eldercare benefits, another move that requires advance planning. At the same time, the position of child-care coordinator or an on-campus office of child-care initiatives—like the one funded in 1994 at the University of Arizona[2]—should be expanded to embrace a larger definition of multigenerational family care requirements. Indeed, as the numbers of children dwindle and the numbers of those over sixty-five increase, eldercare services may be even more in demand than child care.

If conceptualizing the family-friendly campus means reconceptualizing our understanding of "family" and family roles, it also entails recognizing the student body we now serve and refining our concept of "campus" with that student body in mind. While a relatively small group of elite private institutions will continue to attract a predominantly upper-middle-class undergraduate student body in the 18–22 age range, and while these schools will continue to graduate full-time students in four years, those conditions are no longer typical. "Since the 1970's," as Barbara Jacoby reminded us in 1994 in the *Chronicle of Higher Education,* "college populations have changed dramatically; 85 percent of today's undergraduates commute to campus, nearly half are 25 years old or older, and more than half attend part time. In addition, two-thirds are employed, some working full-time or at more than one job to pay their college expenses" (B2).

Significant within this changed population are the increasing numbers of students who would welcome access to off-campus or distance learning sites that offer degree programs. Such students would include those with chronic illnesses or disabilities that make on-campus life difficult, those in rural areas whose family or job responsibilities make it impossible for them to travel any distance to campus, and those juggling work and family responsibilities who need convenient part-time educational options. With the rapid development of satellite, CD-ROM, and computer technology, high quality interactive distance learning services for these students are not only possible, they are also increasingly cost-effective. For reasonable fees, "extended campus" sites can be located in public schools, on military bases, in properly equipped public libraries, or even in private workplaces. And while the initial start-up costs for this technology are still relatively high, the costs can be amortized over several years and paid off through student fees, revenue bonds, or private sector support. Once the technology is in place, moreover, schools can pool resources and create new degree programs by combining courses already taught on various campuses, delivering these courses electronically both to distance learning sites and to on-campus classrooms at the same time.[3]

The overwhelming majority of students to take advantage of the extended campus, not surprisingly, will be women, all of them part-timers, many of them parents. Of course, part-time enrollments for both men and women have been growing steadily since 1970—"128 percent, compared with 38 percent growth among full-time students, according to the National University Continuing Education Association" (Feemster 28). But what has swelled that growth is that "enrollments among women over 35 quadrupled between 1970 and 1991" (Feemster 28). We may expect those numbers to continue to rise, thus exerting even more pressure for services that offer working women and women with children both greater accessibility and more flexibility in scheduling.

The value of distance learning services notwithstanding, whether they attend school full-time or part-time, older students with families can also benefit from a variety of experiences on the more traditional campus. The geography of the campus, after all, generally provides instant access to a library, to quiet study areas, to personal conferences with instructors, and, perhaps most important, the campus represents that rare space that enables the open exchange of ideas and the excitement of shared explorations. Unfortunately, the working woman of thirty-five, with a child to raise on her own, seldom feels either comfortable or welcomed in the current environment of most four-year colleges and universities. As one such woman explained to the *New York Times*, "I didn't see myself in school" because "I wanted to be in a situation where I was taking classes with my peers, not with kids my daughter's age" (Feemster 28).

To accommodate the bulge of students in their late twenties and thirties who return to college after a break of some years or who first begin a degree program, and especially to accommodate those who must work and care for children at the same time, community colleges have been singularly innovative in developing highly specialized weekend and evening programs. Students at Oklahoma City Community College, for example, can enroll in "classes 24 hours a day," thus turning the campus into what its president terms "the college where learning never ends" (Shea A44). Even so, as the sheer numbers of older and part-time students continue to increase—as all indicators predict—and as many of these students seek education beyond the associate degree, liberal arts colleges and research universities also will have to expand, rethink, and revise their programs and schedules. At the moment, there is little incentive to do this, because federal aid and most local and private scholarship funding favor the younger full-time student. But it is precisely this unfair tilt that must be adjusted, with higher educational institutions lobbying actively in Washington and, where feasible, reviewing the aid distribution formulas of their own endowments and alumni organizations. Additionally, local employers might be approached for contributions to scholarship funds earmarked especially for the working student and, at the same time, schools can encourage employers to provide tuition vouchers for workers who upgrade their skills through a bachelor's degree program.

By generating an entirely new cohort of grateful "instant alumni" (Feemster 29), scholarships, scheduling, and programmatic redesign for the older student can prove of enormous financial benefit to colleges and universities. As the president of a small, private women's college that experimented successfully with specialized degree programs, Patricia McGuire told the *New York Times*, "It takes younger graduates years to become regular contributors. Some of the part-timers will write us a check [right after graduation] and write: 'If it weren't for Trinity, I couldn't write any checks like these today'" (Feemster 29).

Having made the case for distance learning services as well as on-site specialized programs to accommodate the older, part-time student, I also want to emphasize the wisdom of redesigning the residential campus to accommodate these same undergraduate students on a full-time basis—including those single parents with children. The most obvious benefit of full-time status, of course, is the relative speed with which the degree can be completed (followed, presumably, by immediate increased earning capacity). The intangible benefit may be total immersion in a learning environment and, with that, an enhanced *quality* in the learning experience—especially if that immersion can be shared with others in similar circumstances. The thirty-five-year-old single mother or father who resists returning to school because she or he fears the absence of supportive peers may be far more enthusiastic if the on-campus living site could provide those peers, along with cooperative living arrangements for the children. After all, why should the student with children be deprived of the late-night discussions of books and ideas, the dormitory gabfests about teachers and courses, and the varied out-of-class exchanges that are remembered later as the intellectual exhilaration of college life?

Since undergraduate dormitories are regularly renovated and new ones built in response to enrollment pressures, planning for future construction should begin now to include floors with communal spaces—shared kitchens, eating, play, and study areas—all serving one- and two-bedroom suites specifically designed for single parents and their children. In addition to the usual sources of funding—state appropriations, revenue bonding, or endowment income—schools might consider seeking eligibility for grants and low-cost loans from the Department of Housing and Urban Development, under HUD's provisions for low- and middle-income family housing supports. These new undergraduate facilities would then complement the low-cost housing units that many comprehensive universities already provide for married graduate students and their families.

All of the reconceptualizations and renovations recommended so far adhere to the common ideal of the campus as a haven of learning. It is harder to admit that, to be truly family-friendly, the campus must also become a refuge from violence. But officials at Michigan State, like college administrators across the country, every year "see evidence of domestic violence: Female students drop out or transfer to get away from abusive boyfriends on the campus. First-year students are stalked by the high-school sweethearts they left behind. Foreign women who came to campus when their husbands enrolled suffer beatings from their spouses rather than risk having to return to their home countries" (Leatherman A5). Prompted by the concerns of the president's wife, Joanne McPherson, Michigan State responded by "setting up education programs for abusers and their victims, and training volunteers who will work with both" (Leatherman A5). In an even bolder move, according to an article in the June 29, 1994, *Chronicle of Higher Education*, "the university opened a permanent shelter . . . to serve as a temporary refuge for battered women who are affiliated with Michigan State" (Leatherman A5). In the view of McPherson, the campus shelter was not simply a reaction to the fact that the women's shelter in nearby Lansing was always filled. For her, the shelter and its associated programs represented both a needed intervention to curtail the escalation of violence to "the point where a woman gets killed" and, just as important, a valuable educational enterprise "for students in counseling, nursing, medicine, and criminal justice" (Leatherman A5).

The sad truth, however, is that most college administrators would view Michigan's shelter as an unaffordable luxury and admit that, when they think of "violence," they think of the violence being done to their annual budgets. The unprecedented rise in the national debt during the twelve years of Ronald Reagan and George Bush presidencies effectively bankrupted the nation's ability to support needed social programs. And when Reagan ended the federal government's revenue-sharing with the states, few states could raise sufficient local revenues to make up the difference. As a result, public education began to suffer everywhere. Currently, even in the face of rising undergraduate enrollments, no state in the nation can afford to support public colleges and universities at the levels of fifteen years ago. "Downsizing" is thus the fashionable response.

One ironic outcome of the forced downsizing of academe is that schools are now more willing to experiment with family-friendly policies, not only because those policies respond to the real needs of otherwise restive faculty, staff, and students, but also because they are either revenue neutral or may even bring savings. The cost of establishing and staffing a shelter for battered women and children may seem prohibitive, but rescheduling department meetings to accommodate individuals with children in school or allowing for delays in the tenure clock are generally without economic consequence. Half-time or shared tenure-track appointments for faculty, combined with flextime, part-time, or flex-year schedules for staff, can represent significant savings in salary (and savings in benefits payments, as well). A 1994 headline in a University of Arizona campus newspaper, for example, boasted that the "Flex-Year Option Aids Budgets and Burnout" both, with the article itself explaining how staff employees benefitted from extra time with their families while departments welcomed the option as "the answer to budgetary woes" (Kayler 1).[4]

In this anxiety-laden financial climate, it would be risky for any administrator anywhere to advocate introducing paid family care leaves for faculty and staff. In Arizona, the problem is compounded by the fact that university personnel are governed by state policies for all state employees, and the state has no provisions for such leaves. Nonetheless, as dean, one of my highest priorities was to initiate a process that might eventually lead to enhanced leave policies on a statewide basis, and certainly for the three state universities. As demonstrated by the continuing disappointing national statistics for women in the initial promotion and tenure review,[5] I knew that the professoriat was still losing too many bright young women to the conflict between career imperatives and the desire for family. And staff women confided that they put off the completion of a degree or additional skills training because they actually *feared* the increased responsibility of a promotion, even when they desperately needed the money. The combination of job, home, and child rearing was already too demanding, they said. Happily, the majority of department heads and program directors in the College of Humanities were sensitive to these dilemmas and shared my eagerness to *do something*.

By the end of my first year, therefore, the department heads, program directors, and I agreed to experiment with granting any faculty member who was to become a parent (by birth or by adoption) up to a semester of "adjusted workload" at full salary. This generally meant a semester free of formal teaching assignments *in addition* to the university's paid maternity leave. Adjusted workloads of up to a semester were also to be extended to faculty with the primary responsibility for nursing an ailing family member. Faculty could request an unpaid leave either in lieu of this arrangement or in addition to it, of course. In most cases, the semester's release from classroom teaching coincided with delays in the tenure clock. Similar workload adjustments were to be developed for staff, and I urged supervisors to try to accommodate staff wherever family responsibilities were at issue. Even so, because state and university policies at the time made no provisions for such family-related workload adjustments, we were unable to articulate this as a general policy, and faculty reassignments were termed "research semesters" on personnel forms.

When I discussed this experiment with other administrators or with members of the Arizona Board of Regents, I generally began by pointing to parallel policies at peer institutions. The University of California at Berkeley, I noted, at the time offered six weeks of paid maternity leave with the additional option of a semester's "modified duties" at full salary, while Indiana University at Bloomington offered six weeks of paid maternity leave followed by modified duties at half salary for the remainder of the semester. Despite examples like these, I was always confronted with the same set of objections: Such a policy would be unduly costly because hordes of absent faculty would have to be replaced in the classroom. I was providing an incentive for staff and faculty to have more children (and, thereby, take off more time from work). And male faculty would cheat by staying home and writing their books, whereas women on adjusted workload assignments would "really" be caring for their infants. As it turned out, none of this proved true.

During my five years as dean, only four faculty women requested nonteaching semesters, while a few female staff members requested workload adjustments for limited periods only. Each of them also utilized the university's standard paid maternity leave. A woman caring for her critically ill mother was offered the opportunity for a teaching reduction, but she declined; and no other employee with a sick relative was brought to my attention. No men, faculty or staff, requested adjusted workloads related to family responsibilities (though male faculty were rarely shy about requesting teaching reductions when involved in a research project or completing a book before tenure review).

My anecdotal observations over those years led me to speculate that nursing a sick relative was still not regarded as a circumstance for which people deserved accommodation—in contrast with attitudes toward infant and child care. And I was aware that, as the second largest city in a major retirement state, Tucson provided a vast array of senior care services, for those who could afford them. I also concluded that very few employees in the College of Humanities were having three or more children and that, overall, this was a relatively low birthrate population. Taken as a whole, our more than three hundred employees were far from even reproducing their own numbers. At least in part, this explained why so few individuals were taking advantage of our experiment.

Of the four faculty women who requested nonteaching semesters, all were untenured assistant professors, two from the same large department of about seventy full-time tenure-eligible faculty; but the two took their workload adjustments in different years. Another faculty woman was from a medium-sized department of about twenty-five; and the fourth was from a small department of fewer than fifteen members. At no point did the dean's office provide the departments with additional funding to hire replacement faculty, nor did the departments have the funding to do this on their own. Instead, with some advance planning and the minimal rearrangement of course assignments and class sizes, we were able to sustain majors, graduate programs, and general education offerings alike, with no loss in student enrollment numbers. In other words, neither our students nor our FTEs (the "full-time equivalents" on which funding is determined) suffered from the cancellation of any faculty member's two or three courses for a single semester. Considering that, even during tight budget times, faculty routinely enjoy sabbatical or fellowship leaves without being replaced, this was hardly surprising. Even so, to compensate the departments for whatever hardship might have accrued, I asked department heads to come up with a formula, appropriate to their unit, by which faculty on family care adjusted workloads would either teach an additional course or take on some additional student advising duties within three years. Unfortunately, this was not pursued in any consistent manner and, in retrospect, I regret that we did not formalize such a procedure so that it would be applied to everyone fairly. After all, as family-sensitive policies are put in place, it is crucial to protect the rights and privileges of faculty and staff who will never utilize those policies. *Their* revised work schedules, *their* adjusted meeting times, and any additional work loads that they occasionally shoulder to accommodate a colleague must also be recognized and rewarded.

To the best of my knowledge, only two male assistant professors (and no male staff) became fathers during the years of my deanship. I have continued to wonder why neither requested the available semester's reassignment of duties. On the one hand, I suspect that their male department heads may not have been aggressive in making clear to these men what was possible, whereas women were informed more consistently. And the women themselves activated a network though which they informed one another. On the other hand, for both the department heads and the prospective fathers, the idea of a work adjustment that allowed *men* time for parenting may still have seemed unusual, inappropriate, and even demasculinizing. Such attitudes would echo those of men nationwide regarding the Family and Medical Leave Act signed into law by President Clinton. According to an item in the December 27, 1993, issue of *U.S. News and World Report,* only 7 percent of the men surveyed said they "would take all 12 weeks of unpaid leave allowed after the birth of a child," while 43 percent of women expressed their intention to take full advantage of the new act ("Baby Makes Three" 106). Clearly, *un*paid leaves will do little to change such entrenched asymmetries. But *paid* leaves, or at least adjusted work assignments, accompanied by assiduous encouragement to utilize them, certainly should make it easier for more men to take on the full partnership of parenting, if only for a while.

In fact, the argument could be made that schools soon will have little choice but to accommodate the increasing participation of men in all family care responsibilities. With the continued restructuring of the American family, changing social mores, and hard economic realities—and whether in heterosexual or homosexual relationships—men are more and more often finding themselves expected to perform as caregivers and co-parents. It is a shift that campuses would do well to encourage. And if a few men on paid family leaves or adjusted workloads cheat—so what? At least, we may hope, their partners will insist they be at home some of the time, writing their books with one hand while rocking the cradle with the other (as women academics have always done . . . while also teaching full-time and running the house).

That said, my commitment to beginning a process that could lead to instituting paid family care leaves stems only secondarily from my conviction that this is the best available means for involving men in an altered orientation toward family responsibilities. Even more important, in my view, is that gender equity on campus has progressed very unevenly—for women. As Alison Bernstein and Jacklyn Cock put it, "Life is improving for the most advantaged women on the campus, but the basic structure and the inequities of non-professional women's lives have barely changed in the last 20 years" (B3). The Family and Medical Leave Act is itself a case in point, extending its benefits only to the few who can afford them. On my campus, the overworked and poorly paid custodial worker who had no other option but the student union ladies' room as a shelter for her daughter could hardly take advantage of an unpaid leave if her daughter became seriously ill. Without salary, she could not pay the rent, and there would be no food on the table. And although the situation might not be quite so dire for a young assistant professor, if she were in the arts or humanities (where academic salaries remain comparatively low), a semester without salary could also prove an impossible hardship—especially if she were a single parent with no other source of income.

Admittedly, while providing paid family care leaves for faculty might have minimal impact on an institution's budget, providing such leaves for all regular employees *will* cost money. To maintain vital campus operations, at least some of these employees will have to be replaced during their absence; or other employees will have to be paid overtime. My brief experience with adjusting staff and faculty workloads at the University of Arizona, however, suggests that most predictions of just how costly such a policy would be are probably exaggerated. In a related situation at Stanford University, for example, the initial financial objections to providing "health benefits to gay and lesbian couples and unmarried heterosexual couples who are in committed, marriage-like relationships" proved groundless ("In Box" A19). Once the policy was instituted, only twenty-nine people (and not the projected sixty) actually "registered for medical coverage" ("In Box" A19). As one official of the College and University Personnel Association commented, "Contrary to what people might say, there won't be this ground swell of thousands and thousands of people signing up" ("In Box" A19).

Similarly, with regard to paid family care leaves, until colleges and universities begin monitored case studies—experimenting within a single unit for three years, for example—and gather hard data on how many leaves are anticipated during any fiscal period, objections based primarily on cost can have no weight. Only when realistic cost projections are in hand can campuses assess their resources, determine what kinds of paid leaves are feasible (three months instead of a semester, perhaps, or some other form of paid workload adjustment), and begin the campus dialogue over priorities. As part of that dialogue, administrators need to examine national studies showing that employees will regularly accept reduced salary increases or even a lower wage scale if the workplace is supportive in other ways. Indeed, it just might be the case that a family-friendly environment reaps higher quality work from all its employees and, in the end, proves tangibly and intangibly cost-effective.

I suspect that objections to my particular mapping of the family-friendly campus will not be exclusively financial, though. When I was dean, a few faculty complained that my emphasis on affirmative action hiring, my activism on behalf of child care, and the new workload adjustments for family care were all evidence that I was attempting to use the campus to correct the ills of society and practicing "social engineering" in the process. But the fact is, schools *do* carry a range of societal responsibilities, among them responsibilities for the health and well-being of students and employees. Even in a state as politically conservative as Arizona, the Board of Regents accepted the view of the Commission on the Status of Women that universities must acknowledge "the importance of home, family, and community in a balanced life. By promoting the value of a balanced life for both men and women, university policies and university human resource programs provide the opportunity and climate in which women, along with men, can succeed" (Arizona Board of Regents' Commission 11). Most of the commission members went even further, arguing that family-friendly innovations could significantly reduce the currently high dropout rates among minority students, shorten the time to completion of degrees, increase the retention of women faculty, reduce staff turnover, and generally initiate a new climate of cooperation and collegiality among students, staff, and faculty alike. As one of our members liked to point out, surprising new friendships were often formed at the child-care center.

We are the least child-oriented society in
the world—10 years behind every other
civilized country in backing up families.
Our kids are suffering in ways no one
wants to face. . . . We have got to change
our systems.
  —T. Berry Brazelton,
  quoted by Gwen Kinkead

Bernstein and Cock are correct when they say "it doesn't cost the colleges much financially to make decrees about sexual harassment and sexist speech. Changing a family-leave policy, however, can be expensive. . . . Child care costs money" (B3). As a result, in the present climate of diminishing budgets and rising costs within higher education, discussions of family-friendly initiatives easily become mired in competing agendas as child care is played off against salary increases and paid family care leaves compete with the renovation of undergraduate classrooms. In such a climate, there is always the temptation to dismiss family issues as catering *only* to some small "special interest group" and to continue with business-as-usual, renovating classrooms and raising faculty salaries. But business-as-usual will serve neither the newly emerging work force nor the anticipated student cohorts of the twenty-first century, and funding in academe is not necessarily a zero-sum game. Creative approaches to funding challenges are available.

At the University of Arizona, for example, we have established a permanent "child-care endowment" within the university's private fund-raising foundation. When I first proposed this to the council of academic deans in 1988, I argued that, unlike endowments to fund chaired professorships for a privileged few and unlike endowments to equip the laboratory of a single scientist, an endowment for child care was both comprehensible and necessary to large numbers of faculty, staff, and students alike. Thus, as the university moved into a new phase of its capital campaign, child care could represent an endowment category capable of attracting substantial and sustained on-campus support. I even tried to persuade my colleagues that a quality child-care center might garner not only considerable public good will for the institution but local private sector contributions as well. In subsequent meetings, as my colleague deans raised the thorny problem of utilizing a tax-supported institution's facilities for an activity that might compete with the private sector—which is against the law in Arizona—it became increasingly clear that some kind of partnership between the university and private child-care providers was inevitable. In that event, I suggested, why not approach the best of the licensed corporate day-care providers as potential contributors to our own endowment, especially where the university wants to develop a long-term partnership with one or more of these for both on-site and off-campus operations? After all, where local laws prohibit a school from developing an independent child-care center, and where schools cannot be granted a legal exemption by embedding child care within a college of education or a school of social work (or the like), there is no alternative but partnership with qualified private providers. Still, this need not be a problem. Cooperative agreements can be reached that assure parental oversight, parental involvement, and quality services. And, no less important, with the private providers anticipating years of future earnings, it is not unreasonable to ask them to enjoy a substantial tax break by contributing to the child-care endowment that subsidizes the campus community's ability to afford their services.

How such endowment earnings are utilized must be determined by local circumstances, of course. In the early years, while the endowment is still relatively small, its limited earnings might be used to help furnish the on-campus facility, with user fees covering the costs of staffing. But in later years—especially if a private provider is involved—larger endowment earnings could supply an ongoing source of income by which to subsidize the costs of child care for college and university students and employees. In this way, where a private provider is involved, that provider receives its full negotiated fee per child, but the actual cost of child care to the student or employee would be tied to a sliding scale based on ability to pay. Where no private provider is involved, the school simply devises its own sliding fee scale and dips into endowment earnings to make up any shortfall. In either case, the full professor, presumably, would pay more than the groundskeeper or student—but all would receive the same high quality care for their children.

Eldercare offers still other opportunities for innovative funding. As the population ages and more healthy and vital people find themselves in retirement, educational programs for this population will be in great demand. As it is, Elderhostels—four- and six-week educational residence programs for seniors—have proved enormously successful and generally profitable for the schools that have hosted them. But while Elderhostel programs can certainly be expanded, other equally attractive educational options for retired seniors must also be developed. Good management and the use of facilities not otherwise employed (like empty dormitories and classrooms during the summers or midyear breaks) can turn such programs into what schools like to call "revenue centers," or profit makers, even when the program fees are modest. There may even be ways to combine educational opportunities for seniors with specialized eldercare "wellness" programs, especially at universities with nursing schools or medical centers. But the most intriguing possibility, to my mind, is the potential coordination of eldercare with child care. Here one can imagine a variation on the surrogate grandparent volunteer programs that many local communities have devised to pair retired seniors with lonely latchkey kids. The only essential difference is that the campus facility would bring both groups together in a safe and professionally supervised setting, all of it supported by fees, by associated educational programs, and by endowment earnings.

Clearly, none of the challenges posed by the changing structures of the American family need prove insurmountable. A fee-based eldercare "wellness" program or a child-care endowment seem relatively obvious—once they have been proposed, that is. Similarly, colleges and universities that already set aside monies for interest-free tuition loans for the children of faculty and staff might now consider converting at least some of those funds into vouchers for subsidized child care or for partial salary support during a family-care leave. Funding possibilities are thus limited only by the willingness of the campus community to pursue them.

By the first decade of the twenty-first century, colleges and universities should have had ample opportunity to gather the requisite data and to transform benefits and selected family services into a constellation of options that both cater to changing family configurations and also allow the institution to anticipate reasonable and stable funding levels for those benefits and services. One design that I particularly favor entails a virtual "menu" of variable options: Taking into account such factors as salary level, years of service, and full- or part-time status, schools would generate a formula for assigning annual "benefits credits" to all employees. After deducting required credits for mandatory minimal levels of health care and retirement contributions, employees would then enjoy the option of utilizing their remaining credits for benefits most useful to them at the time. A family with young children, for example, might utilize remaining credits to enhance their health care benefits and to subsidize child-care costs, while a childless family might invest those same optional credits in eldercare services for an aging parent or in additional retirement contributions. Still another family might trade their credits for course fees or tuition rebates. Individuals would have the opportunity to reassign their optional benefits credits at least once a year. In this way, as family needs change, so too do the benefits that respond to those needs. And from the point of view of the institution, overall costs remain relatively stable.

My point here is simple: Solutions and funding sources can be identified, but only when a school chooses to focus on the changing family and its multiple needs. The difficulties in creating a family-friendly campus do not derive entirely from a paucity of financial resources. Instead, the real problem is our long-term failure of commitment and imagination, a failure that we can no longer tolerate.

We must do the things we think we
cannot do.
    —*Eleanor Roosevelt*

In pursuing the initiatives I have outlined here, colleges and universities need not be alone. Socially responsible charitable organizations like the United Way are available for alliances in opening shelters for battered women and children. Government agencies, like Housing and Urban Development, can be approached as a partner in building innovative on-campus housing that responds to the needs of lower- and middle-income students with families. Private research foundations, like the Carnegie Corporation, which issued a report in April 1994 calling for paid leaves of up to six months for all wage-earning parents, can provide the necessary data to justify family-friendly policies (Kinkead 35). And sympathetic players in the nation's capital can be called upon as lobbyists. Attorney General Janet Reno, for one, has already "spoken out for a workday ending at 3 p.m. so that parents can be home when their kids return from school" (Kinkead 34).

Most important, as a group, college and university presidents and chancellors must stop closing their eyes to the impossible burdens facing the contemporary single-parent or two-wage-earner family. It is time for these senior administrators to risk (and perhaps thereby reinvigorate) their waning public prestige by confronting a government that does not provide adequate family supports and by challenging what the *New York Times* termed "a cultural ethos that has degraded" family roles, "rewarding only competition and wealth" (Kinkead 32). In other words, the leaders of institutions entrusted with the education and training of future generations must now insist that politicians forego the empty rhetoric of "traditional family values" and, in its place, return realistic family supports to the top of the national agenda. I would have these positions articulated not solely on the grounds of necessity or social justice, however, but on the firmer ground of *educational mission.* Let us be clear: Classrooms are not the only places in which learning occurs. We teach our students not simply by "professing" but, even more powerfully, by example.

As every educator knows, the structures and policies of institutions are themselves telling signifiers, teaching students (however silently and indirectly) what is and is not prized. And because neither students nor their teachers dissociate intellectual inquiry from the material conditions in which that inquiry is conducted, it *signifies* that, on some campuses, the business college is housed in the newest and best equipped building, centrally located, while the fine arts are taught in out-of-the-way, outdated facilities, much in need of repair. Similarly, it *signifies* that colleges and universities regularly grant paid research leaves to faculty. And these same institutions grant paid administrative leaves to faculty and senior administrators when they work on projects for local, state, or federal agencies. At the same time, it *signifies* sadly that those who care for young children or sick parents must take unpaid leaves or no leaves at all. In this society, where (for good or for ill) we pay for what we value, there is a terrible lesson in those facts.

Summary Checklist of Recommended Family-Friendly Initiatives and Programs

Begin campus dialogue that studies the diversity of family structures now emerging. Use this dialogue as the basis for reviewing all benefits policies so that they embrace care of both the young and the old and recognize nontraditional family arrangements, including (but not limited to) nonmarried domestic partners and cooperative domestic units.

Institute comprehensive data-gathering to assess current and future family-related needs and determine realistic cost projections for any anticipated new benefits or services.

Maintain a resource and referral service for all child and senior care needs and provide comprehensive information on services available both on and off campus.

Expand the current duties of an on-campus child-care coordinator to respond to multigenerational family needs.

Provide low-cost on- or near-campus housing for married students and their families and design campus dormitories to accommodate students who are single parents with young children.

Establish an on-campus shelter for battered women and children. The shelter should sponsor on-campus education and counseling programs for abusers and their victims; the shelter should work with other campus units—like a school of social work or a college of law—to educate the campus regarding the prevalence and prevention of domestic violence, battering, and abuse.

All female faculty and staff should be eligible for a minimum of twelve weeks paid leave for birth or infant adoption (i.e., maternity leave). Additionally, all faculty and staff—male and female alike—should be eligible for a designated period of paid family care leave at full salary for birth, adoption, or foster care placement as well as adjusted workload assignments at full or half salary for family emergencies. Men should be assiduously encouraged to take advantage of these benefits.

Faculty and staff should be offered flexible work options: Staff should be eligible for flextime, part-time, and flex-year schedules. Faculty should be eligible for tenure clock delays, as well as half-time and shared tenure-track appointments.

When scheduling department or committee meetings, the needs of those who must pick up a small child from school, be home to prepare dinner, or relieve a home health-care provider should be considered and respected.

Support a combination of on-campus and off-campus child-care facilities, staffed by qualified and well-trained personnel. Whether these facilities are operated solely by the school or operated in partnership with private providers, facilities should be available to students, staff, and faculty, with fees based on ability to pay, and parental oversight, supervision, and participation must be assured. Such child-care centers should be open for extended hours, on weekends, and during the summers, and they should be able to accommodate requests for occasional "drop-in" care.

In addition to child-care centers, schools should establish a subsidized sick child program, providing trained (and licensed) home health care professionals who will come to the home to care for a sick child when the parents (students or employees) must be on campus. Such services would cover occasional and minor illnesses only. The daily or hourly fee paid by the parent would be modest. In states where such services are not currently available for senior citizens, the school should expand the program to include occasional care for an ailing senior in a student, staff, or faculty household.

Enhance facilities and outreach programs for senior citizens. These might include fee-based life-long learning programs, expanded Elderhostel offerings, specialized degree programs, and "wellness" programs coordinated through a medical school or college of nursing.

Investigate opportunities for combining child-care and eldercare services in professionally supervised settings. Consider surrogate grandparent programs as one means for involving senior citizens in the care of young children within supervised facilities.

Review current financial arrangements that set aside monies for low-cost or no-interest college tuition loans for the children of faculty and staff. Consider converting some portion of those monies into flexible benefits options that may be used for other family needs, including child care, eldercare, or family-related medical emergencies.

Explore the development of a comprehensive benefits and subsidized family services program that offers a menu of variable options to employees; design the program so as to allow individuals to change their benefits/services options as circumstances demand.

Encourage local businesses and national corporations to support special scholarship funds earmarked for part-time working students and to grant tuition vouchers to employees seeking to upgrade their skills through a college or university degree program.

Review financial aid distribution formulas and work both locally and nationally to expand scholarship opportunities for older, part-time undergraduates.

Expand interactive distance learning services, especially with a view toward developing high quality off-campus degree programs.

Offer part-time students greater flexibility in course scheduling and develop on-campus specialized degree programs for working parents who can enroll only for weekend and evening classes.

Seek partnerships with the private business sector, government agencies, and private foundations for developing and funding appropriate family-friendly initiatives.

Establish private fund-raising endowments that can generate revenues to support family-friendly services like child care and eldercare centers.

As part of the national education agenda, senior administrators in academe must lobby the president and the Congress to forego the empty rhetoric of "traditional family values" and, in its place, develop realistic support programs for the changing American family.

Protect the rights and privileges of those who will never utilize family care benefits or policies and reward these individuals' cooperation in family-sensitive workplace activities.

NOTES

All references to persons at the University of Arizona have been substantially altered so as to protect the privacy of individuals.

Early drafts of this essay were reviewed by Charles Tatum, Debra Olson, Angie Moreno, Linda Stapleton, Elissa Gelfand, and Naomi Miller; each contributed helpful comments and valuable insights. The essay was prepared for publication by my graduate research assistant, Kate Ledger, who also offered keen advice on style and phrasing. My gratitude to each of them.

1. As of November 1994, according to a campus newspaper article entitled "Employees Can Obtain Child-Care Assistance," the University of Arizona provided students and employees with the Resource and Referral Service, designed to help people in "locating and selecting child-care arrangements" (8), and the Sick Child Program, "designed to support the working parent who has a mildly ill child unable to attend school or child care" (8). Under this program, "a trained provider will come to the employee's home and stay with the child while the employee is at work. . . . Parents are charged $1 an hour and the UA picks up the remaining charges" (8). Even with these services, however, as Mayhew makes clear in an *Arizona Daily Wildcat* article of September 2, 1994, an on-campus child care center still remained "on UA parents' wish list" (3).

2. According to Leibold (3), the new full-time child care coordinator will work closely with the established Child Care Steering Committee, made up of faculty, staff, and student members. Under the coordinator's direction, "the newly created Office of Child Care Initiatives" will develop goals and priorities for enhancing child care services and assess all related needs in this area.

3. For example, "the central administration office for the California State University system" was developing "a project intended to create a degree program in business administration by combining courses taught on various campuses and delivering them electronically" in 1994 (DeLoughry A36). Such a program could be delivered to any of the participating campuses and, as well, to appropriate off-campus sites to enable distance learning.

4. At the University of Arizona, according to Kayler, a flex-year arrangement requires the agreement of "the employee and his or her supervisor. . . . Eligible employees can take from one to four pay periods off each year, usually during the slowest time period for their department. Although this registers as unpaid-vacation time, the reduced annual compensation is distributed over the entire fiscal year so that employees still receive the normal number of paychecks during that time off" (1).

5. See Kolodny (especially 16–18); see also Noble (25) and Rohter (9).

WORKS CITED

Antler, Joyce. "Commentary." *Personal Lives and Professional Careers: The Uneasy Balance.* Lois Banner, Eileen Boris, Mary Kelley, Annette Kolodny, Cecelia Tichi, and Lillian Schlissel. Report of the Women's Committee of the American Studies Association, 1988. 25–28.

Arizona Board of Regents' Commission on the Status of Women. *Reaching the Vision: Women in Arizona's Universities in the Year 2000.* Summary report of the Arizona Board of Regents' Commission on the Status of Women, 1991.

Atwood, Margaret. *Second Words: Selected Critical Prose.* Boston: Beacon, 1984.

"Baby Makes Three." *U.S. News and World Report* Dec. 27, 1993–Jan. 3, 1994: 106.

Banner, Lois, Eileen Boris, Mary Kelley, Annette Kolodny, Cecelia Tichi, and Lillian Schlissel. *Personal Lives and Professional Careers: The Uneasy Balance.* Report of the Women's Committee of the American Studies Association, 1988.

Bernstein, Alison, and Jacklyn Cock. "A Troubling Picture of Gender Equality." *Chronicle of Higher Education* June 15, 1994: B1–B3.

Coiner, Constance. "Silent Parenting in the Academy." *Listening to Silences: New Essays in Feminist Criticism.* Ed. Elaine Hedges and Shelley Fisher Fishkin. New York: Oxford University Press, 1994. 197–224.

DeLoughry, Thomas J. "Pushing the Envelope: California State U. Seeks to Use Technology to Improve Teaching and Serve More Students." *Chronicle of Higher Education* Oct. 19, 1994: A36–A38.

"Employees Can Obtain Child-Care Assistance." *Lo Que Pasa* Nov. 7, 1994: 8.

Feemster, Ron. "College Goes to the Student." *New York Times* Aug. 7, 1994: sec. 4A, 28–29.

Hartmann, Adam. "UA Debating Child Care." *Arizona Daily Wildcat* Feb. 11, 1994: 1–4.

"In Box." *Chronicle of Higher Education* Sept. 21, 1994: A19.

Jacoby, Barbara. "Bringing Community Service into the Curriculum." *Chronicle of Higher Education* Aug. 17, 1994: B2.

Jones, Bonnie. "Redesigning the Ivory Tower: Opening the Drawbridge to Women with Multiple Roles." *Cracking the Wall: Women in Higher Education Administration*. Ed. Patricia Turner Mitchell. Washington, D.C.: College and University Personnel Association, 1993. 52–68.

Kayler, Kimberly. "Flex-Year Option Aids Budgets and Burnout." *Lo Que Pasa* Aug. 29, 1994: 1–4.

Kinkead, Gwen. "Spock, Brazelton, and Now . . . Penelope Leach." *New York Times Magazine* Apr. 10, 1994: 32–35.

Kolodny, Annette. "Raising Standards while Lowering Anxieties: Rethinking the Promotion and Tenure Process." *Concerns* 23.2 (1993): 16–33.

Leatherman, Courtney. "Michigan State Offers a Refuge for Battered Women." *Chronicle of Higher Education* June 29, 1994: A5.

Leibold, Janis. "Child Care Coordinator Takes Charge at UA." *Lo Que Pasa* Aug. 22, 1994: 3.

Mayhew, Sarah. "Child Care on UA Parents' Wish List." *Arizona Daily Wildcat* Sept. 2, 1994: 3.

Mitchell, Patricia Turner. "Introduction." *Cracking the Wall: Women in Higher Education Administration*. Ed. Patricia Turner Mitchell. Washington, D.C.: College and University Personnel Association, 1993. x–xi.

Noble, Barbara Presley. "Women Pay More for Success." *New York Times* July 4, 1993: 25.

Park, Denise C. "Research on Aging Deserves Top Priority." *Chronicle of Higher Education* July 27, 1994: A40.

Rohter, Larry. "Women Gain Degrees, but Not Tenure." *New York Times* Jan. 4, 1987: 9.

Ruether, Rosemary Radford. *Liberation Theology: Human Hope Confronts Christian History and American Power*. New York: Paulist Press, 1972.

Shea, Christopher. "Community College Will Schedule Its Classes Twenty-Four Hours a Day." *Chronicle of Higher Education* Oct. 26, 1994: A44.

Stack, Carol B. "The Kindred of Viola Jackson: Residence and Family Organization of an Urban Black American Family." *A Heritage of Her Own: Toward a New Social History of American Women*. Ed. Nancy F. Cott and Elizabeth H. Pleck. New York: Simon and Schuster, 1979. 542–54.